2-20-74

Inflation and the Structure
of Industrial Prices

Inflation and the Structure of Industrial Prices

Paul H. Earl
Georgetown University

Lexington Books
D.C. Heath and Company
Lexington, Massachusetts
Toronto   London

Library of Congress Cataloging in Publication Data

Earl, Paul H.
 Inflation and the structure of industrial prices.

 Bibliography: p.
 1. Prices. 2. Prices—Mathematical models. 3. Price policy. 4. Inflation
(Finance) I. Title.
 HB221.E23   338.5'21   73-6530
 ISBN 0-669-87056-0

Published simultaneously in Canada.

Printed in the United States of America.

International Standard Book Number: 0-669-87056-0

Library of Congress Catalog Card Number: 73-6530

To Dale

1793089

Contents

List of Tables

Preface

This book develops a comprehensive approach for analyzing the price behavior of industries engaged in manufacturing. Price models are specified, estimated, and simulated for a representative sample of United States industries. These results are further compared with those for several existing price models which are reestimated on the industries of this study. The simulations are designed to analyze the effectiveness of alternative policies in achieving the targets of the Economic Stabilization Program. Given the complex nature of the inflation which continues to grip this nation, it is hoped that this book will contribute to a better understanding of the structure of industrial prices.

The book evolved from my doctoral dissertation which was completed in August of 1972. I am particularly indebted to F. William McElroy, my thesis advisor, for his generous help and adept comments throughout my research. Sincere thanks go to Joel Popkin for concepts he originated which I have subsequently applied in this study. I also thank Joseph L. Tryon for his thoughtful comments.

The computations were performed at Georgetown University on an IBM 360-40 computer, and on a Burrough's 5700 time-sharing system through Data Resources, Inc. I am appreciative of the extensive data preparation performed by Ms. Madeleine Disario and her fellow workers in the Georgetown Economic Data Library. I am further grateful to Mrs. Kathleen Barker for her expert typing of the final manuscript.

I wish to thank my parents for their continuous support and interest throughout my education. Also, the financial assistance of the White Foundation is sincerely appreciated. Finally, the patience and understanding of my wife, Dale, along with her typing of all preliminary drafts and a majority of the final tables, is deeply valued.

Inflation and the Structure of Industrial Prices

1

Introductory Remarks

Recent Price Behavior and the
Intent of This Research

Analysis of price behavior has been the focus of many econometric studies over the past 20 years. The incidence of studies on pricing increased markedly in the 1960s, with much of the research concentrating on more disaggregate data (sectors or industries) than previously in an attempt to capture structural differences in pricing behavior from industry to industry. An outgrowth of this disaggregate analysis has been a movement away from reduced form price models and toward specifying structural models with prices, wages, profits, and other economic variables considered endogenous.

A brief comparison of certain key aspects of price movements in the decade immediately following World War II (period 1) with those since 1956 (period 2) will help clarify why there is this increasing interest in explaining price formation. These periods can be contrasted with regard to the spread between consumer (CPI) and wholesale (WPI) prices, the duration of inflations, and the average annual price change by the use of the data in Table 1-1. The earlier period is marked by two major inflations, one from 1946 to 1948 (following World War II) and the other from 1950 to 1952 (during the Korean War). The 1956-71 period also is characterized by two major inflations, the first of which occurred from 1956 to 1958 and was caused mainly by large wage settlements and rising price expectations. The second inflation, present since 1965, was stimulated initially in part by the Vietnam buildup and has been perpetuated by a wage-price spiral and sectoral demand pressures. Despite the 90-day wage-price freeze instituted on August 15, 1971, followed by Phases 2 and 3 of the Economic Stabilization Program, the rates of CPI and WPI increase through March 1973 have been rapid. The CPI increased 3.3 percent in 1972 while the WPI increased 4.5 percent. The increases for the first quarter of 1973 in the CPI and WPI were 6.2 and 16.4 percent respectively (annual rates).

With regard to the first point of contrast, the spread between the CPI and the WPI narrowed considerably during the post-World War II inflation and remained virtually constant for the remainder of period 1. Period 2 however has been marked by an increasing spread between the CPI and the WPI; since 1965, the CPI has increased 28.4 percent as compared with an 18.4 percent increase in the WPI (both on the base of 1967 = 100).

The inflations in period 1 are of shorter duration than those in period 2. This

1

Table 1-1

Movements in Consumer Prices (CPI) and Wholesale Prices (WPI), 1946-71

Date	CPI	CPI subperiod	CPI period	WPI	WPI subperiod	WPI period
1946	58.5	13.6% increase		62.3	20.5% increase	
1947	66.9			76.5		
1948	72.1			82.8		
1949	71.4			78.7		
1950	72.1	7.4% increase	21.7% increase	81.8	6.8% increase	25.5% increase
1951	77.8			91.1		
1952	79.5			88.6		
1953	80.1			87.4		
1954	80.5			87.6		
1955	80.2			87.8		
1956	81.4	5.2% increase		90.7	3.9% increase	
1957	84.3			93.3		
1958	86.6			94.6		
1959	87.3			94.8		
1960	88.7			94.9		
1961	89.6			94.5		
1962	90.6			94.8		
1963	91.7		41.1% increase	94.5		26.1% increase
1964	92.9			94.7		
1965	94.5			96.6		
1966	97.2			99.8		
1967	100.0	28.4% increase		100.0	18.4% increase	
1968	104.2			102.5		
1969	109.8			106.5		
1970	116.3			110.4		
1971	121.3			113.9		

observation, combined with information on average price change in the two periods, allows comment to be made on the price stability of period 1 relative to that of period 2. The average annual increase during period 1 is approximately 2.0 percent for both the *CPI* and the *WPI*. During period 2 the *CPI* has increased by about 2.5 percent annually whereas the *WPI* has increased by only 1.7 percent annually. However, since 1965 the *CPI* and the *WPI* have had average annual increases of 4.1 percent and 2.6 percent, respectively. Thus, the later period is characterized by both an absence of price stability and a widening of margins between consumer and wholesale prices. Such aggregate behavior has generated increased interest in the study of price formation at disaggregate levels in order to explain the underlying causes.

The studies have varied in their purposes, which have included the structural or reduced form explanation of price behavior, price prediction, ex post simulations, and policy simulations. The Economic Stabilization Program has spurred new interest in policy simulations regarding expected price movements, given different degrees of control. In general the results of these studies have been inconclusive regarding the specification of price equations that are generally effective in explaining price formation. Certain specifications of price equations accurately explain price behavior in selected sectors or industries of an economy but are highly unreliable in other sectors and industries; this result is reflective of the inherent structural differences from sector to sector and especially from industry to industry in an economy. Furthermore, even though most price equations have provided good fits over known sample periods, these same equations have not generally predicted future price behavior with a sufficient degree of accuracy.

The intent of the present research is to specify and estimate price models that explain the price behavior of 22 U.S. manufacturing industries over the 1958 to 1969 period. The industries analyzed are representative of a wide variety of industry characteristics. A comprehensive sample of past price models are also estimated on the same industries in order to provide a direct comparison of fit with the new models that are developed. The models to be reestimated include Klein and Ball, Liu, Nield, Fromm and Eckstein, Schultze and Tryon, Courchene, Laden, Eckstein and Wyss, Rushdy and Lund, McCallum, and Phipps. Certain industries are further analyzed by specifying structural stage of processing price models that include material and/or retail price equations where appropriate, in addition to the final industry price equation.[a] The additional price equations are estimated over the 1958-69 period; the entire models are simulated ex post over the 1965-69 period and, under hypothesized policy conditions, over the 1967-69 period. Ultimately, it would be necessary to study the behavior of the relevant cost and excess demand variables in each industry's price formation model in order both to study all simultaneous relationships between variables and to capture the total endogeneity of each industry.

An Overview of What Follows

To systematically satisfy the stated intent of this research, the organization of the study which is described in this section was adopted. Chapter 2 is concerned with the theoretical foundations of price behavior and the development of

---

[a]This idea originates from a paper presented by Joel Popkin before the Washington Chapter of the American Statistical Association in October 1969. I have assisted Dr. Popkin in further work on pricing by stage of process since July 1970 under a contract with his office at the Bureau of Labor Statistics. Dr. Popkin presented further results of this research in a paper before the American Statistical Association in Boulder, Colorado, in August 1971.

several hypotheses that represent generalized specifications of a majority of the price models that have been developed. A major problem in analysis of price behavior is identifying clear theoretical foundations of the various models that have been estimated. This is not surprising, since most price studies are of an aggregate nature (i.e., industry, sector, or economy) whereas the pricing hypotheses are based on microeconomic theories. In general these pricing hypotheses would not be expected to hold true for industry, sector, or economy price behavior, given the complex aggregation problems that exist.

Chapter 3 contains a general survey of the major price formation studies that have been conducted over the past 15 years. Because of the mixed theoretical basis of most of the models, the critique does not divide the studies into groups on the basis of price hypotheses. Instead, the studies are divided into three groups on the basis of the level of aggregation to which each is addressed. The general characteristics, data specifications, econometric model specification, and key contribution of each study are discussed.

Chapter 4 reexamines in detail each of the price studies whose models are selected for reestimation on the industries particular to the present research. These models are well representative of the research on price formation and provide a good standard of comparison for the new models that are developed.

Chapter 5 highlights the preanalysis aspects of the present research, including experimental design and data formation. The experimental design relates to the general sector and industry breakdown and the placement of the selected price models (of Chapter 4) within 10 price hypothesis categories. Data formation is concerned with both the data available and the variable transformations and modifications needed within those industries selected for the analysis. Comments on the organization of the analysis are made.

Chapter 6 discusses the results of reestimating the 18 selected models from previous studies on the industry data of this study. The results for the best-fitting industries in each of the 10 hypothesis categories are discussed first. Next, the optimum reestimated price equation for each industry (i.e., best-fitting and worst-fitting industries) is selected from among the 18 run on each, and tentative conclusions are drawn concerning the best hypothesis categories for explaining industrial price formation. Finally, the industries represented by these optimum equations are grouped according to several industry characteristics (e.g., concentration ratio and durability of product). These results are discussed so that tentative conclusions may be drawn regarding a variance in price behavior based on differences in industry characteristics.

Chapter 7 discusses the final industry price equations that are estimated. These equations represent such modifications of previous models as the specification of different lag structures, the normalization of material prices, the normalization of excess demand measures, and/or the specification of price equations that impart different combinations of price hypotheses. The results are discussed in a fashion parallel to that in Chapter 6 and are compared directly with the results discussed there, in terms of hypothesis categories represented, signs and values of coefficients, and overall fit of the equations. Conclusions specific to each industry's price behavior are presented.

In Chapter 8, stage of processing price models are developed for nine of the industries analyzed in this research. These industries are representative of both the cells in the experimental design (Chapter 5) and the results presented in Chapters 6 and 7. For each industry, the final industry equation of Chapter 7 is combined, where appropriate, with a material price equation and/or consumer price equation to form the stage of processing models. These models are then simulated ex post over the 1965-69 period so that industry comparisons may be made with respect to tracking ability and turning-point accuracy. Policy simulations are run over the 1967-69 period in order to measure and compare the effects of different policies on price change in each of the industries.

Chapter 9 sets forth the general conclusions that are drawn on the basis of the results given in Chapters 6 through 8, along with comments on extensions of the present analysis which should be made in future research.

Supplementary material is provided in six appendixes. Appendix A includes sources of data, variable construction, and time periods of availability of industry data. Appendix B explains the classification of industries by market categories, and Appendix C provides summary statistics on the price variables used in this research. Appendix D contains additional results for the final industry price equations of Chapter 7, including graphs of fitted versus actual price change over the period 1965:1 to 1969:2 (the first quarter of 1965 through the second quarter of 1969). Appendix E includes further material relating to the simulations of Chapter 8. Appendix F contains an alphabetical listing of the symbols of all variables referred to in this study, together with their definitions.

2

Theory and Hypothesis of Price Formation

Theoretical Basis of Pricing

A problem that has been supported as partially accounting for the lack of substantial progress in the econometric work on price formation is that the models developed in the studies lack a clear theoretical basis (i.e., the models are hybrids). Contributing factors to the problem, which will be brought out in this section, include those of aggregation, structural versus reduced form models, and micro versus macro theory. Nordhaus[180] comments in a recent study that most specifications of price equations have been advanced without a formal theoretical basis (i.e., a hodgepodge of variables are combined in order to provide maximum explanation of the behavior of a particular price). Kaplan[30] states that solid information is not available concerning the pricing process even though prices have been studied within both micro and macro theory for nearly a century. Both of these comments allude to the crux of the problem. There are two main microeconomic theories (which will be explained in limited detail in a following section): the competitive market theory and the oligopolistic market theory, each of which includes a specification of the pricing process. However, several testable hypotheses explaining price behavior can arise from each. Eckstein[80] notes that the oligopolistic theory of pricing melts into a competitive theory of pricing as prices become more sensitive to short-run fluctuations in demand. Furthermore, the specifications of these hypotheses are usually combined in formulating an explanation of price behavior, resulting in single-equation models that lack an explicit structural foundation and contain a mixed theoretical base.

A problem common to many price models regarding their theoretical basis involves determining the structural equations from which they were derived. Except for those price models which are part of a larger econometric model (e.g., OBE[107], Wharton[18], Klein and Ball[100], and Schultze and Tryon[185]), most price models are single-equation models, with all regressors implicitly treated as exogenous. Since the underlying structural model for these price equations is not easily determined, it is difficult to decide whether the authors of these models view them as reduced form or as structural equations. Some recent sectoral price studies (Laden,[171] Popkin and Earl[133]) have presented structural models. Halfter,[166] Eckstein,[80] and Schultze and Tryon[51] state a preference for a mixed theoretical base when analyzing actual industrial pricing decisions even though the two mechanisms may be polarized in theory.

7

There has been lively controversy over the past 20 years concerning the proper place of economic theory in the industrial pricing process. The major point of the argument is whether or not actual known cost and demand information (based on averages) is a proper proxy for the marginal data that are lacking. Furthermore, do businessmen actually think in marginal terms and do their pricing decisions reflect marginal concepts? Malchup[113] argues that marginal concepts are reflected in business pricing decisions, whereas Oliver[128], Vickery[143], and Gordon[86] dispute this contention. Gordon furthermore considers standard output as the proper basis for costs, and Vickery considers expectations as a key factor in the pricing process. Langholm[104] concludes that economic theory contributes virtually nothing toward industrial pricing rules and advocates the use of simulation techniques in the study of price behavior. A recent case study book by Hague[23] emphasizes the need for firms and companies to practice marginal cost pricing.

Both the competitive market and the oligopolistic market theories and the pricing hypotheses that are derived from each are based on the behavior of firms. However, since data on firms are not readily, if at all, available, it is the pricing behavior of an industry, sector, or economy that is ultimately analyzed. These larger data bodies are the aggregates that result from combining the data of many firms. Substantial differences in firms' behavior together with the nonlinearities present in aggregate data on firms can result in time series that do not necessarily closely resemble the behavior of any firm or group of firms included in them. Therefore, since the pricing hypotheses are based on firms' behavior, these hypotheses cannot be expected to accurately represent most aggregates. Therefore, a mixed theoretical basis (i.e., hybrid model) seems appropriate to the data.

These micro theories of pricing in turn underlie the macro theories of inflation. A survey by Bronfenbrenner and Holzman[9] thoroughly discusses the pure demand, supply (income), and mixed theories of inflation and their relationship to competitive and oligopolistic market behavior as well as to micro theories of wage-push, profit-push, and markup inflation.

The pure demand macro theories of pricing include the quantity theory and the Keynesian aggregate expenditure approach. Both of these theories are reflected in the regressors included in price models developed by Anderson and Carlson[63] and Fair.[84] Traditionally these theories were developed under the assumption of full employment. The demand variables in both studies have an adjustment for the unemployment that exists.

The supply (income) theory of inflation has as its basis the micro theories of wage-push, profit push, and markup. These micro theories depend on both market conditions (product and factor) and pressure groups and ultimately underlie the wage-profit-price spiral, which is macro in nature.

The mixed macro theories of inflation include Schultze's sectoral (demand shift) theory, Ackley's push-pull theory, and the flexible markup theory. All of these theories are based on behavior in individual markets where price is either adjusted on the basis of the gap between supply and demand or set according to one of the micro supply theories. The majority of the price models that have been specified reflect the characteristics of the supply and mixed theories of inflation.

The cost, excess demand, and hybrid hypotheses of price formation developed in the next section of this chapter are based on the microeconomic theories. These hypotheses cover the specifications of nearly all the price models that have been developed. A comprehensive list of the variables that appear in the various price models is given in Table 3-10. These variables are also included in Appendix F. Many of the variables assume varying lag distributions with price in the different studies. Many of these variables are endogenous in their behavior; however, with the exception of a few sector studies and econometric models, they are implicitly treated as exogenous when included as regressors in reduced form price models.

It will be apparent in Chapters 6 and 7 that a vast majority of industry models are hybrid in structure. It is not considered that this represents a lack of theoretical foundation, given both the complexity of the aggregation problem in going from firm to industry and the differences in behavior exhibited by firms in the same industry. Such a structure merely represents a combination of relevant aspects of different theories which results in theoretical specifications that best depict given industrial pricing situations.

Price Formation Hypotheses

The hypotheses of price formation developed in this section include in their specifications different sets of variables that reflect internal and/or external aspects of firm behavior. Each hypothesis is discussed in reference to its theoretical basis and the types of cost and/or excess demand variables it contains. Both short- and long-run cost hypotheses of pricing are discussed, based on either factor prices or unit factor costs. Target return pricing hypotheses also are discussed as well as excess demand pricing hypotheses. The final section serves to discuss certain combinations of selected cost and demand hypotheses (i.e., hybrid hypotheses) that reflect the most common price models. Note that all of the hypotheses discussed could contain the lagged price as a regressor. This modification introduces a lagged adjustment process into the explanation of price behavior.

All hypotheses are expressed in linear form. Each of the coefficients in these linear equations represents an add on to price resulting from a one-unit change in a regressor. Each add on, which is an absolute amount, remains fixed irrespective of the level of each variable even though the percentage markups in these linear equations differ as the levels of the variables change. Under special conditions, each coefficient will represent a fixed proportional markup on price irrespective of the level of each variable. Each hypothesis is also expressed in a loglinear form to allow interpretation to be made of each coefficient as a fixed percentage markup (i.e., elasticity) irrespective of the level of each variable. A residual is assumed to be present in each of the equations that follow.

Short-Run Cost Hypotheses

The short-run cost hypotheses are of two types and represent a cost function approach to explaining price behavior. The first is based on factor prices, with productivity effects in its most general form, and is represented in (2.1) and (2.2). The second type has as its basis unit costs instead of factor prices and is given in (2.3).

$$P = \alpha_0 + \alpha_1 AHE + \alpha_2 PM + \alpha_3 PP + \alpha_4 (M/Q) \qquad (2.1)$$

$$P = \alpha_0 + \alpha_1 AHE + \alpha_2 PM \qquad (2.2)$$

$$P = \beta_0 + \beta_1 ULC + \beta_2 UMC \qquad (2.3)$$

The variable factor prices included in (2.1) are average hourly earnings (AHE) and price of materials. (PM). In addition, labor productivity (PP) and the material-output ratio (M/Q) are present. This hypothesis considers a flexible relationship of price (P) with factor prices. In this case factor productivity and factor prices are both included explicitly. The coefficients of the factor price variables and α_4 have expected positive signs whereas α_3 has an expected negative sign.

The expected sign of the constant term is dependent on the form of data used. In level form, it is expected to be positive, since it is assumed that some positive price will exist even if all factors affecting that price have values of zero. In log form and change form, the constant may be negative. In the case of logs, a positive constant results when the exponential transformation from log to level is made. A negative constant in the case of change data may reflect the dampening influence of positive technological and productivity change on price change.

The influence of factor productivities is considered to change the relationship of product price with each factor price. Assuming that manufacturing wages are generally inflexible in a downward direction because of union influence, they will cause prices to increase. However, the increases will be less when there are productivity gains, since productivity effects are allowed to mitigate all or part of the effect of factor price increases. Even if factor price and factor productivity both change by the same amount, the product price will still change if $\alpha_1 \neq \alpha_2$ and $\alpha_2 \neq \alpha_3$. Therefore, the add on to price from each factor price will shrink in times of productivity gain and grow in times of productivity decline. Factor productivity is not explicitly introduced into price equations based on neoclassical theory; instead, it is assumed to grow smoothly over time and may be represented by a trend variable.

Assuming $\alpha_3 = \alpha_4 = 0$ reduces Equation (2.1) to the relationship given in (2.2). This hypothesis expresses price in relationship to only factor prices. This implies that the productivity of factors has an insignificant influence on price formation and that any movement in price with respect to either PP or (M/Q) approximates zero, which is consistent with short-run neoclassical theory. This formulation reflects rule-of-thumb pricing where the decision to change price is made with respect only to change in factor prices. The relationship of P to the price of each input does not vary significantly because of productivity or technological change; any slight influence of productivities on price is embodied in the constant term.

A tax variable could be introduced along with the factor costs in an equation similar to (2.1) or (2.2). It has been considered as a regressor only in studies by Klein and Ball[100], the Dutch[11], and Moffat.[118] The hypothesis being tested by its inclusion is the short-run shifting of the corporate income tax or sales tax (excise tax) to consumers through price increases at both the manufacturing and retail levels. In most market structures a sharing of the tax burden is possible. Realistically, the bulk of the tax is passed on to the purchaser through higher prices if demand is relatively inelastic. Furthermore, tax increases in most business situations can be considered as affecting, and most likely reducing, the normal rate of return and wages of management if not compensated for by a price increase (see Moffat). The above hypothesis views the pricing process as a series of simple add ons to variable costs, which does not necessarily yield a price in the short run consistent with profit maximization.

The second short-run cost hypothesis has as a basis unit costs instead of factor prices. Still no consideration is given to fixed costs such as capital costs. The costs included as a basis for product price are the same as those in the short-run factor price hypothesis, namely, labor and material. However, they are now expressed in relation to the output produced; that is, as unit costs as expressed in (2.3). The a priori signs for β_1 and β_2 are positive. The sum of unit labor cost (ULC) and unit material cost (UMC) approximates average variable cost in the classical sense. The apparent flatness of short-run cost curves, as evidenced by several cost studies (e.g., see Dean[74] and Johnston[96]), implies that marginal and average variable cost are equal to one another. There is no shift variable present in (2.3) which will allow the add on between price and each unit cost to fluctuate.

A unit tax variable could be introduced into (2.3), as in studies by Fromm and Taubman[21] and Moffat. The classical theory assumes that the short-run profit-maximizing price is the same both before and after the income tax and increases by the amount of the excise tax. However, several arguments have been advanced regarding the shifting of taxes (corporate income or sales) forward to the consumer through price increases. Viewing UT as a variable cost dependent on both the tax rate and the level of output allows tax to enter in the same manner as other unit variable costs; the resultant price is still consistent with long-run profit-maximizing behavior if the total UT is shifted forward.

Equation (2.1) expressed in loglinear form (i.e., derived from a nonlinear price equation of the Cobb-Douglas variety) may be converted to a loglinear version of short-run unit cost hypothesis (2.3) by making three assumptions and combining terms. First assume in (2.1') below that the effects on price with respect to each input's cost and productivity are equal in magnitude but opposite in direction. Therefore,

$$|\alpha_1| = |\alpha_3| \text{ and } |\alpha_2| = |\alpha_4|, \text{ so that}$$

$$lnP = ln\alpha_0 + \alpha_1 lnAHE - \alpha_1 lnPP + \alpha_2 lnPM - \alpha_2 ln(M/Q) \qquad (2.1')$$

Therefore,

$$lnP = ln\alpha_0 + \alpha_1 ln\left(\frac{AHE}{PP}\right) + \alpha_2 ln\left(PM \cdot \frac{M}{Q}\right)$$

By definition,

$$ULC = \frac{N \cdot AWH \cdot AHE}{Q} = \frac{AHE}{(Q/N \cdot AWH)} = \frac{AHE}{PP}$$

with AWH = average weekly hours and likewise for UMC.

(2.1'') may now be rewritten as follows.

$$lnP = l\alpha_0 + \alpha_1 lnULC + \alpha_2 lnUMC \qquad (2.1'')$$

Therefore, a direct conversion between the loglinear versions of the short-run factor price and short-run unit cost hypotheses may be made. Note, however, that the same conversion cannot be made between linear hypotheses (2.1) and (2.3). The coefficients in these loglinear equations represent percentage markups on the indicated short-run unit costs.

Long-Run Cost Hypotheses

These hypotheses are set apart from the short-run cost hypotheses because of the introduction of both capital costs and normalized productivities (based on standard levels of output). Therefore, fixed costs are included as a determinant in the pricing process while at the same time short-run productivity movements are netted out. Three types of hypotheses are included under the long-run cost category. The first, expressed with productivity effects in Equation (2.4) and without productivity effects in (2.5), is based on factor prices and includes those for labor, materials, and capital. The second type, (2.6), is based on unit costs whereas the third type, the target return hypothesis, is expressed in its strict form in (2.7) and in two modified forms in (2.8) and (2.9).

$$P = \gamma_0 + \gamma_1 AHE + \gamma_2 PM + \gamma_3 PK + \gamma_4 r + \gamma_5 PPN \qquad (2.4)$$
$$+ \gamma_6 (M/QN) + \gamma_7 (K/QN)$$
$$P = \gamma_0 + \gamma_1 AHE + \gamma_2 PM + \gamma_3 PK + \gamma_4 r \qquad (2.5)$$
$$P = \delta_0 + \delta_1 ULCN + \delta_2 UMCN + \delta_3 UKC \qquad (2.6)$$
$$P - ULCN - UMCN = \delta_0 + \delta_3 (K/QN) \qquad (2.7)$$
$$P = \delta_0 + \delta_1 ULCN + \delta_2 UMCN + \delta_3 (K/QN) \qquad (2.8)$$
$$P = \delta_0 + \delta_1 ULCN + \delta_2 UMCN \qquad (2.9)$$

The general specification for long-run factor price hypotheses, given in (2.4), has the add ons γ_1, γ_2, γ_3, γ_4, γ_6, and γ_7, all with expected positive signs, whereas γ_5 has an expected negative sign. In addition to factor prices AHE and PM, (2.4) includes both interest rate r, representing the cost of inventory investment and the cost of capital, and capital price PK, representing the cost of capital expansion of plant and equipment. The long-run productivity terms for labor (PPN), materials (M/QN), and capital (K/QN) reflect both technological change and capital improvements. A loglinear version of (2.4) can be formed in a manner analogous to the formation of (2.1'). The coefficients then represent percentage markups on price associated with each regressor.

PP equals Q/H where H is total hours worked. PPN is most commonly formed by taking a T term moving average of both Q and H, with the former divided by the latter as follows:

$$PPN = \frac{\sum_{t=1}^{T} Q_t}{\sum_{t=1}^{T} H_t}$$

Normalized M/Q is formed in an analogous fashion.

Setting $\gamma_5 = \gamma_6 = \gamma_7 = 0$ in (2.4) yields the hypothesis given in (2.5), which includes only cost terms. The add ons to the different costs in (2.5) are rigid, since long-run productivity considerations have been netted out. The inclusion explicitly of both PK and r will depend on the importance of both types of investment in a given situation. This formulation is made consistent with the neoclassical long-run competitive equilibrium by introducing a time trend for productivity.

The hypothesis expressed in (2.6) is analogous to the short-run unit factor cost hypothesis in that costs per unit of output are the relevant costs. However, standard (normal) output is the relevant output measure and unit capital costs (UKC) are now included. The normalized unit labor costs ($ULCN$), normalized unit material costs ($UMCN$), and UKC terms are all based on QN instead of Q. The short-run variable costs ULC and UMC may be transformed to normal long-run levels by netting out any short-term output changes.

$$ULCN \;=\; AHE/PPN \text{ with } PPN \text{ derived above}$$

$$UMCN \;=\; PM/(QN/M) \text{ where } QN \;=\; \sum_{i=1}^{T} Q_i/T$$

When long-run productivity measures are used, it has been implicitly assumed that the effects of wage and productivity changes on price changes are equal in absolute value, so that $ULCN$ and $UMCN$ are the only variables considered, along with the capital term.

The UKC term has been constructed as the ratio of depreciation (capital consumption allowance) to normal output (see Schultze and Tryon), the depreciation series being a proxy for the physical price of capital. It also has been expressed as the long-term interest rate, representing the cost of debt financing (see Eckstein and Wyss[159]). A better theoretical formulation in this case would be the total interest cost per unit of output. However, this variable is difficult to form empirically. The add ons δ_1, δ_2, and δ_3 all have expected positive signs.

From a loglinear version of (2.4) and assumptions similar to those made previously, one may directly convert from the loglinear version of the long-run factor price hypothesis to the loglinear version of the long-run unit factor cost hypothesis. This same conversion cannot be made between the linear versions of the hypotheses, (2.4) and (2.6).

A variation of the long-run cost hypotheses is the target return pricing hypothesis. Target return pricing theory has grown out of oligopolistic market situations where interdependence among firms in the setting of key decision variables, including the price level, is present. The theory expresses price as being based on normal variable costs (i.e., unit factor costs at the standard volume of output) and set so as to cover these costs plus earn a target return on capital at the standard level of output. Short-run changes in productivity and demand are absorbed in quantity changes and not in price changes. Therefore, prices change only on the basis of factor cost changes or technological advances. The following identity is used to define price in this theory.

$$P = ULCN + UMCN + r^*(\frac{K}{QN})$$

The target rate of return (r^*) is itself a function of many factors concerning market structure and long-run industrial conditions. Rearranging terms in this equation yields the following expression for the desired rate of return on capital at normal output levels.

$$QN(P - ULCN - UMCN) = r^*(K)$$

The target return theory is discussed in more detail by Eckstein, Fromm and Eckstein[81], Fromm[165], Moffat, Laden[103], and Schultze[137].

The target return pricing hypothesis implies that price is an add on to standard unit costs, the add on being a target return on the capital-standard output ratio. Whether or not the target (desired) rate of return on capital is introduced explicitly or implicitly into the price equation leads to one of three forms of the target return hypothesis. The strict specification of this hypothesis includes the target return explicitly as the only regressor, as given in (2.7). The gap between price and normalized unit variable costs is strictly a function of the target rate of return on capital at normal output levels. The target rate of return on capital is θ_3, and its value along with that of the constant term determines the spread between price and normal unit factor costs. If K/QN fluctuates only slightly around a constant, θ_3 is absorbed in the constant term and the relationship of price to normalized variable costs is in fact reflected by the constant term. Estimating the same price equation over different periods of time may result in differing values of θ_3, indicating a shift in the target rate of return. The target rate of return may vary for several reasons. Fromm and Eckstein[81] state that it is a function of barriers to entry, concentration, product differentiation, international trade barriers, equity and debt valuations in the capital markets, risk in operations, quantity and quality of management, and the long-run demand elasticities. All of these factors are related to market structure and long-run industrial conditions mentioned above.

One modified version of the target return hypothesis, given in (2.8), also includes normalized unit labor and unit material costs as regressors. The a priori signs of θ_1, θ_2, and θ_3 are all positive. The add on per unit change in the standard capital-output ratio is θ_3, which is estimated in this equation. Note that ULCN, UMCN, and K/QN each have an add on factor that affects price. Equation (2.8) is equivalent to the identity of $P = UTC$ given above, in the discussion of target return pricing theory, if $\theta_0 = 0$, $\theta_1 = \theta_2 = 1$, and $\theta_3 = r^*$, with r^* being the target rate of return. A change in unit cost of any of the factors influencing price leads to an equivalent change in price. The relationship of price to normal unit costs varies according to the value of r^* embodied in the $r^*(K/QN)$ term.

The other modified version, given in Equation (2.9), incorporates the target rate of return implicitly in the relationship of price to normalized variable costs by letting $\theta_3 = 0$ in (2.8). The consideration of a target rate of return is embodied in θ_0, θ_1, and θ_2, since the long-run costs form the basis for price formation. Price is set above these costs by an amount that allows for the desired rate of return on investment. It is assumed in both the above hypotheses that the target rate of return on capital is set in such a way as to at least cover the cost of capital.

In loglinear form (2.8) may be expressed as follows.

$$lnP = ln\theta_0 + \theta_1 lnULCN + \theta_2 lnUMCN + \theta_3 ln(K/QN) \qquad (2.8')$$

From the loglinear version of (2.6), (2.8') can be obtained by substituting the term $ln(K/QN)$ for $lnUKC$. This assumes that the physical cost of capital is not changing so that K/QN is equivalent to UKC. Therefore, since the loglinear (2.6) was derived directly from the loglinear (2.4), all three long-run cost hypotheses can be derived from one another when in loglinear form but not when in linear form. However, the assumption of a constant PK is difficult to support empirically.

Excess Demand Hypotheses

The competitive market theory of pricing is the basis for the hypotheses advanced concerning the relationships between price change and excess demand. Excess demand (ED), which is defined as the difference between the demand and supply of a product, has an expected positive effect on price. It is a proxy for the elasticities that exist in both demand and supply markets. Competitive market theory bases price behavior on the difference between supply and demand. Only in cases of infinitely fast price adjustment will equilibrium always be attained between supply and demand. In most cases, a gap between demand (D) and supply (S) exists as given in the following price adjustment equation, which in combination with a demand and supply function forms a model of competitive theory. The price hypothesis based on excess demand is as follows.

$$\Delta P = \lambda(D-S) = \lambda(ED) \qquad (2.10)$$

where λ = adjustment coefficient

Δ = change in a variable

This function was originally developed in the tatonnement hypothesis by Walras (see Nordhaus). Instead of measuring D and S directly, most studies utilize measures of excess demand which indicate the relative movements in the supply-demand situation (for an exception to this approach, see Laden[103]).

Two hypotheses may be derived from (2.10), depending on whether direct or indirect measures are used to represent ED. Both of these hypotheses are formulated under the assumption that the influences of costs and productivity are zero or are reflected in the excess demand variables included in the price equation.

The first market hypothesis states that price is a function of excess demand represented by direct excess demand measures (DED). These direct excess demand measures are those which represent economic behavior in the final product market. The capacity utilization index (CUI), industrial production index (Q), and sales-inventory ratio (S/INV) are broad measures that effectively represent the relative movements of supply and demand. The inventory change ($FDINV$) and change in unfilled orders ($FDUNF$) are quantity change indicators of the demand-supply gap, as posited in the competitive market pricing theory. To be consistent with theory, these measures are usually entered in constant dollar terms although in some cases they are entered in current dollar terms. A direct measure such as shipments (SHP) has an expected positive influence on price, whereas inventory (INV) terms in general have a negative sign. All of these variables are not usually included for DED, since they are often proxies for one another and all represent the same excess demand situation. A certain variable may be more appropriate than another depending on market conditions, a particular industry's structure, and the stage of processing at which it is operating.

Certain of the DED measures that represent quantity changes, such as Q and SHP, may actually be inversely related to price and therefore assume a negative sign in the price equation. There are two possible explanations for this result.

The first involves a cost interpretation relating to average cost pricers. In this case, the quantity variables may actually be reflecting movement along the declining portion of the average cost curve. Defining capacity output as the amount produced at minimum average cost, the firm is operating at less than full capacity. Thus, in highly capital intensive industries, an increase in SHP or Q in the short run may result in a substantial reduction in average fixed costs (AFC) and/or a sizeable increase in productivity. Depending on the degree of these effects, the fall in AFC (reflected by the SHP term) might counteract increases in other unit costs (ULC, UMC). Further, any increase in PP reflected through increased SHP may offset factor price increases in AHE or PM. Therefore, reasonable interpretations of the partial effects of different variables contained in certain hybrid formulations can be made. Laden[172] and Eckstein and Wyss contain further discussions of this matter.

The second relates to the degree of market power exerted by a firm (industry). Given a relatively inelastic product market, a firm that has a high degree of market power may be able to increase its price in a period of declining shipments and/or output. In this way it can maintain or increase its profit share by increasing the per unit profit margin.

In both of these cases, the quantity variables may not actually represent a *DED* influence and therefore should not be interpreted as such. Several of the estimated price equations in Chapters 6 and 7 include these quantity regressors with signs the opposite from those expected. A *DED* variable with an expected negative sign is *INV*, since a drawing down in inventories normally represents demand pressure and ultimately results in a price increase. However, the long-run form *INVN* could enter in a positive relationship with price for one of two reasons. If *INVN* is really a proxy for the cost of holding inventories, then increasing inventories will reflect increased warehousing and plant expansion costs. Secondly, persistent demand pressures over time may lead a firm to maintain higher inventories in order not to be caught short, and therefore to produce enough to satisfy increased demand and at the same time increase inventories.

The second market hypothesis has price as a function of excess demand represented by indirect product market measures (*IED*). Indirect excess demand measures are barometers of behavior in the labor market which in turn indicate conditions in the product market. The unemployment rate (*UR*) is inversely related to price change by Phillips curve theory, whereas the employment rate (*NR*) is merely one minus *UR*. The *IED* measures tend to lag behind the *DED* measures to which they are related and seem to reflect the strength of demand in present and future time periods.

Other measures representing *DED* and *IED* are used in certain studies (see Tables 3-3, 3-6, and 3-9). Furthermore, the *DED* and *IED* are consistent with one another with regard to a price change. For example, an increase in the capacity utilization index (a *DED*) will be accompanied by an increase in employment (an *IED*) if full employment of labor does not already exist. Therefore, the inclusion of either *CUI* or *NR* in this case indicates the same positive effect on price. The choice between using either the *DED* or the *IED* market hypothesis of price formation depends on both the available data and the characteristics of the industry being analyzed.

It is difficult to arbitrarily classify certain *DED* or *IED* as representing the demand or supply side of the market. For example, the level of *CUI* is considered by some to be a proxy for the strength of demand while at the same time a change in *CUI* changes the average costs of production and can affect supply of a product. For this reason, all *DED* and *IED* measures are referred to as excess demand measures in this study. Schultze, Zarnowitz[151], Courchene[73], Schultze and Tryon, and Perry[48], discuss this matter further.

Hybrid Hypotheses

In the preceding divisions of this section have been derived several short-run cost, long-run cost, and excess demand hypotheses of price formation, all of which are based on the competitive market and oligopolistic market theories of pricing. Although the hypotheses formed are either cost-based ((2.1) to (2.9)) or market-based (2.10), only a few studies depict price formation as either purely cost-dependent (the Dutch, Dow[79], Klein and Ball[35], Dicks-Mireaux[77], Klein and Skinkai[101], Vanderkamp[142], Nield[44], and Yance[147]) or purely market-dependent (Zarnwitz, Halfter, Anderson and Carlson, and McCallum[116]). Most studies have formulated price equations that contain variables representing various combinations of the hypotheses described.

The most common of these hybrid hypotheses contains the short-run factor cost hypothesis (2.2) and a *DED* measure for the excess demand hypothesis (2.10). (Liu[111], Kuh[170], Bodkin[7], Wharton[18], OBE[107], Perry, Solow[52], Laden[172], Courchene, Morkre[120], Hay[90], Klein and Goldberger[34], FED-MIT-PENN[158], deMenil[157], Wilson[187], Popkin and Earl, and Gordon[88]). Another common hybrid hypothesis includes the short-run unit cost hypothesis (2.3), long-run unit cost hypothesis (2.6), and a *DED* measure for the excess demand hypothesis (2.10). (Fromm and Eckstein, Schultze and Tryon, Fromm and Taubman[21], Moffat, Eckstein and Wyss, Rippe[135], Laden[103], and Eckstein and Brinner[161].) Some studies do include *IED* measures for excess demand in addition to the cost hypotheses of (2.2), (2.3), and/or (2.6). Rushdy and Lund[136], Gordon[87], Yordon[150], Phipps[182], Popkin and Earl, and DRI[186]). A variety of lagged relationships between the regressors and price are found in the studies. In addition, many of the equations that have been formulated include the lagged price itself as a regressor. (Liu, Vanderkamp, Anderson and Carlson, Nield, Wharton, Rushdy and Lund, McCallum, Yance, Zarnowitz, Rippe, Hay, Eckstein and Wyss, Solow, Popkin and Earl, Laden, DRI, and Fair.) Studies that have included both cost and excess demand variables have found the excess demand variables to be of secondary importance (exceptions are studies by Halfter, Zarnowitz, Courchene, Anderson and Carlson, McCallum, and Fair). However, it should be noted that the use of level data in many studies tends to overstate the price-cost relationships because of the strong underlying common trends in the data. This will be clarified by the discussion in Chapters 3 and 4.

3

General Survey of Price Formation Studies

The major price formation studies of the past 15 years are surveyed in this chapter. Each of the studies has been placed into one of three sections on the basis of the lowest level of data aggregation over which its equations have been fitted. The three levels of aggregation considered are economy, sector, and industry. Summary information is given in the tables of each section covering the general characteristics, data specification, and equation specification of each study. The equation specifications given in Tables 3-3, 3-6, and 3-9 contain the variables included in the final equations developed in each of the studies and do not contain all regressors that were considered. Definitions of the variables are given in Table 3-10.

The discussion within each section serves to highlight the similarities and differences of the studies both within and between levels of aggregation. The equation specification of each study is also viewed with respect to the pricing hypotheses developed in Chapter 2. Finally, additional comments are made pertaining to the key contributions of selected studies that were not chosen for reestimation. Chapter 4 contains a detailed discussion of the price equations developed in those studies which have been chosen for reestimation over the data bodies used in the present research.

General Critique of Economy Price Studies

The major economy level studies that include an endogenous treatment of prices are summarized in Tables 3-1 to 3-3. Six of the nine studies that actually estimate price equations are econometric models. These six models were all built for the purposes of forecasting (both ex post and ex ante) changes in key endogenous variables and performing policy simulations by hypothesizing the behavior of fiscal and monetary variables that are exogenous in the models. The other three studies (Dicks-Mireaux, Vanderkamp, and Fair) are aggregate analyses of the wage-price or price sector of an economy. The study by Dow contains no estimated price equations but instead is a theoretical study of price movements, using a price equation that is based on national income shares. Both stable and unstable behavior of prices over time are analyzed by changing the parameter values in the model of both the exogenous and endogenous factors.

All studies except those by Anderson and Carlson and by Fair include some or all of the variables from the short-run cost hypotheses (2.1) to (2.3). It is of

Table 3-1
Economy Studies: General Characteristics

Study and Year		Type of Study	Type of Model	Type of Analysis[a]	Key Contribution of Study
Dutch	1955	Econometric model	Single-equation	OLS	First noteworthy endogenous treatment of price in an econometric model.
Dow	1955	Theoretical price	Single-equation		Simulation and policy analysis by changing values of parameters in price equation. Sensitive to real wage-productivity behavior. Endogenous and exogenous shocks result in different final effects on price.
Klein and Ball	1959	Econometric model	Multi-equation	OLS LIML	First structural econometric model of price-wage sector. Examined dynamic properties using simulation techniques. ED effect on price is through the wage equation.
Dicks-Mireaux	1961	Wage and price	Multi-equation	OLS TSLS	Extensive treatment of price-wage lag structure. Alludes to standardized cost hypothesis. ED effect on price is through the wage equation.
Liu	1963	Econometric model	Multi-equation	OLS TSLS	Rigorous treatment of price-inventory nexus. Clear derivation of reduced form price equation from structural model.
Klein and Shinkai	1963	Econometric model	Single-equation	TSLS	Input productivity as well as input cost considerations. P is function of linear combination of labor share and import share.
Klein and Goldberger (revised)	1964	Econometric model	Single-equation	LIML	Price determined through labor share equation based on loglinear production function. Tax policy simulations and forecasts.
Vanderkamp	1966	Wage and price	Multi-equation	OLS TSLS FIML	Separate wage equations for organized and unorganized workers. ED effect on price is through the wage equations.
Anderson and Carlson	1970	Econometric model	Multi-equation	OLS	Emphasis on expectations (as indicated by past price changes). Simulations and forecasts based on different assumptions concerning money supply growth. ED effect on price is through the price anticipations equation.
Fair	1970	Price	Single-equation	Nonlinear, iterative technique	Modified Anderson-Carlson equation, including a demand pressure variable and no price anticipations term.

aOLS = ordinary least squares; FIML = full information, maximum likelihood; LIML = limited information, maximum likelihood; TSLS = two-stage least squares.

Table 3-2
Economy Studies: Data Specification

Study	Type of Data	Form of Data[a]	Time Period	Data Sets
Dutch	Annual	Level		Dutch economy
Dow				British economy
Klein and Ball	Quarterly	Level	1948-56	British economy
Dicks-Mireaux	Annual	PCH at ann. avg.	1946-59	British economy
Liu	Quarterly	PCH at ann. rate	1947:3-1959:4	U.S. economy
Klein and Shinkai	Annual	Level	1930-36, 1951-58	Japanese economy
Klein and Goldberger	Annual	FD	1927-64 (omit 1942-45)	U.S. economy
Vanderkamp	Quarterly	PCH	1947-62	Canadian economy
Anderson and Carlson	Quarterly	FD	1955-69	U.S. economy
Fair	Quarterly	PCH at ann. rate	1956:1-1970:2	U.S. economy

[a]FD = first difference; PCH = percentage change.

interest that those five studies which include a materials price index as a regressor all use an import price index as the relevant measure. This indicates the dependence of England, Canada, and Japan on imported materials in their manufacturing processes. None of the studies include any long-run cost variables or *IED* measures. The study by Anderson and Carlson incorporates only a *DED* measure and an anticipated price variable that is based on a series of past prices. Thus it may be classified as a form of the market hypothesis (2.10) that also includes a distribution of lagged prices. The Dutch and the United Kingdom (Klein and Ball) models both include a tax variable for indirect business taxes. The Klein and Goldberger and the Liu models both formulate a price equation containing short-run cost and *DED* variables. Four studies indirectly measure the labor market effect on prices by including an employment variable as a regressor in another equation, whose dependent variable in turn is a regressor in the price equation. The effect of the labor market on prices will therefore be apparent when systems estimation techniques are used and/or ex post dynamic simulations are performed. The studies containing this formulation are those by Klein and Ball, Dicks-Mireaux, Vanderkamp, and Anderson and Carlson. In the first three studies this labor market effect is contained in the wage equations, whereas in the Anderson and Carlson study it is expressed in the price anticipations equation.

Table 3-3
Economy Studies: Equation Specification

Study	Cost Variables		Excess Demand Variables		Lagged Price and Other Variables
	Short-run	Long-run	Direct	Indirect	
Dutch	AHE, PI, T				
Dow	W, X, PI, PR				
Klein and Ball	AWE, PI, T				
Dicks-Mireaux	W, X, PI				
Liu	AHE		INVD – INV		P(−1), P(−2)
Klein and Shinkai	ULC, UPI				
Klein and Goldberger	WB		Q		
Vanderkamp	WO, WU, PI				P(−1)
Anderson and Carlson		r	$\Delta Y - (Q - QCAP(-1))$		PA, MS
Fair			$1/[(Q - QCAP(-1)) - \Delta Y]$		

Several of the studies use two-stage least squares (*TSLS*), limited information maximum likelihood (*LIML*), and full information maximum likelihood (*FIML*) as the system methods of estimation in their analysis. This enables their parameter estimates to be consistent even when endogenous variables are present as regressors. All of the studies, except for that by Klein and Shinkai, which use system estimation methods are multiequation representations of price behavior. The earlier models were fitted over annual data in either level or first difference form. The limitation to annual data was caused mainly by availability problems regarding all of the time series needed. The use of annual series did minimize problems of lag structure specification and serial correlation. The use of level data increases the collinearity among variables because of the common trends that are present in the time series. A majority of the recent models use quarterly data. Although this increases the number of observations over which the relationships may be fitted, it also increases problems of seasonality and serial correlation and makes the proper specification of lag structures a more difficult task. Studies that use percentage change data (Dicks-Mireaux, Liu, Vanderkamp) are often motivated econometrically by a desire to reduce problems of both multicollinearity and autocorrelation (unless it is a result of misspecification because of excluded variables) and practically by a policy desire to study rates of inflation. The use of quarterly data in a difference or percentage change form becomes more common in the sector and industry studies reviewed below. Following are brief comments on the studies by Dicks-Mireaux, Klein and Shinkai, Vanderkamp, Anderson and Carlson, and Fair.

The Dicks-Mireaux study in 1956 concentrated on the relationships and feedbacks of prices and wages on one another in a wage-price sector. Several different lag structures were postulated and regressions run on the two-equation system that represented each one. No definite conclusions are drawn regarding the feedback relationships of price and wage on each other. Dicks-Mireaux used annual data which lead to lag specifications of questionable significance. This study is important, however, in that is is the first attempt to seriously consider lagged relationships among variables in the price formation process.

The Klein and Shinkai econometric model of Japan, developed in 1963, contains a price equation that is based on a linear combination of labor share and import share (which represents the material input for the Japanese economy), expressed as unit costs in the model. Therefore, the price-factor cost relationship may be modified by both labor productivity and the material-output ratio. This formulation differs from the Dutch and United Kingdom models where the material-output ratio was not considered. Both *ULC* and *UMC* are found significant.

The Vanderkamp study in 1966 of Canadian price and wage behavior differs from other studies in its treatment of wages. Separate wage equations are fitted for organized workers and unorganized workers, the distinction being made on the basis of the degree of unionization within each category. These separate wage variables are regressors in the price equation. The three-equation system is estimated simultaneously using *FIML*, and also by *TSLS*. Vanderkamp also tried the finished goods inventory rate as a *DED* measure in the price equation but it was found insignificant.

The studies by Anderson and Carlson and by Fair are the first contributions of the monetary school to the estimation of price equations. Both equations include a weighted demand pressure variable whereas the Anderson and Carlson equation includes a price anticipations term and tries both money supply and the interest rate as regressors. Both equations yield similar results regarding the explanation of price behavior, with Anderson and Carlson's model used primarily for ex post and Phillips curve simulations and Fair's model used for prediction. Nordhaus criticizes the Anderson and Carlson study regarding its theoretical foundation and the construction of the price anticipations term.

General Critique of Sector Price Studies

The studies summarized in Tables 3-4 to 3-6 are the major sectoral studies of price formation which have been advanced over the past 12 years. Note that four economy studies of price formation had been completed before the results of the first sectoral study were known. Furthermore, the vast majority of the sectoral studies have been concentrated in the last 6 years. Only five of the studies (Wharton, OBE, deMenil, FRB-MIT-PENN, and DRI) developed price equations as part of large-scale econometric models. In these studies as well as in that by Gordon the price models developed are used extensively both in sample period simulations and in forecasting future price behavior. The simulations and forecasts were all of the following types: (1) to test the stability of the model over a period; (2) to examine the effect on price behavior of changes in fiscal and monetary policy; and (3) to examine the relevance of Phillips curve theory in regard to the tradeoffs among prices and wages with unemployment.

The specifications of the price models developed all include cost and direct excess demand regressors except for the McCallum model, which explains price as a function of only its own lagged value and an *IED* measure. The cost of the labor input is treated in three ways. *AHE* is a regressor in half of the studies whereas *ULC* or *ULCN* enters the price equation in the other studies. The Fromm and Eckstein study includes both *ULCN* and *ULC − ULCN* in order to allow both short-run productivity change, as reflected in *ULC*, and long-run productivity change, as reflected in *ULCN*, to have an effect on price behavior. In only four studies (Kuh, deMenil, FRB-MIT-PENN, and Eckstein and Brinner) is productivity entered explicitly as a regressor. The cost of the material input is a regressor in nine of the studies; it always enters as a short-run cost (e.g., *PM*) and is never included in the form *UMC*. The variable most commonly used to represent *DED* is the capacity utilization index or some other representation of output in relation to capacity output. Five of the most recent studies (deMenil, Gordon[87], Gordon[88], Eckstein and Brinner, and FRB-MIT-PENN) use selected ratios combining unfilled orders, new orders, and shipments as the *DED* measure in their price equations. Rushdy and Lund include an *IED* measure as a regressor in their equation instead of a *DED* measure. Gordon[87] includes both *DED* and *IED* measures in his price equation. Solow uses a price expectations variable and a dummy variable for the wage-price guideposts. The deMenil price equation is a preliminary version of the FRB-MIT-PENN price equation. Both the Solow and the deMenil equations incorporate a time trend to measure the effect of neutral technological change on price behavior.

Structural multiequation models are developed in the studies by Bodkin, Perry, Laden, Gordon, FRB-MIT-PENN, and Popkin and Earl. However, in only the Perry and Laden studies is an estimation technique other than least squares (in each case, two-stage least squares) used to estimate the price equation, and in both of these cases the reduced form version of the price equation is estimated. The *TSLS* results do not prove to be significantly different from the *OLS* results. All of the studies except those by Bodkin and Laden use quarterly data. Furthermore, all of the sectoral studies with the exception of the first four studies (Kuh, Bodkin, Wharton, and OBE) use a form of data other than or in addition to level data which is more consistent with studying rates of change in prices. One study that includes lagged price as a regressor (Wharton) is run on level data. The presence of the lagged price variable results in biased coefficients. Furthermore, since the equations have high positive autocorrelation, the parameter estimates are also inconsistent. The Rushdy and Lund and the McCallum studies both include lagged price in their price equations, but these studies are performed on first difference data. If the residuals are generated according to a first-order Markov process and if $\rho = 1$, then autocorrelation is not present in the first difference data and the parameter estimates are consistent.

The key contributions (see Table 3-4) of certain sector price studies need to be further discussed. Kuh in his 1959 study has a descriptive discussion of the corporate markup, which he defines as the ratio of total receipts to the total wage bill. This markup varies most during periods of extremely rapid change, in the same direction for both price and demand. This result supports the incorporation of *DED* and *IED* measures in a price equation to account for the variability of the markup of price over costs. He also develops a "demand rachet" variable as a *DED* measure, which relates current output to past peak output adjusted for capacity change. This measure is tried by Phipps in his price equation.

Bodkin in 1963 introduced a time trend into the price equation to account for neutral technological change. This term has an a priori negative sign. Bodkin also tests for asymmetrical behavior of prices with respect to two different demand proxies that are both expressed as functions of capacity output. The price behavior is determined to be symmetrical with respect to the demand

Table 3-4
Sector Studies: General Characteristics

Study and Year		Type of Study	Type of Model	Type of Analysis	Key Contribution of Study
Kuh	1959	Price	Single-equation	OLS	Discusses markup of price over wage bill as an endogenous factor in the pricing process. Developed "demand ratchet" DED measure.
Bodkin	1963	Wage and price	Single-equation	OLS	Treatment of "peak" wage as determinant of P. Consideration of technological change and testing for asymmetrical demand effects in the pricing process.
Wharton	1965	Econometric model	Single-equation	TSLS	Extensive experimentation with linear and nonlinear relationships between CUI and price.
OBE	1966	Econometric model	Single-equation	TSLS	Introduction of nonlinear ED variable of change in sales adjusted for CUI level. Extension of Wharton price equation.
Perry	1966	Wage, price, and profit	Multi-equation	OLS TSLS	Consideration of both CUI and ΔCUI in the price equation as representing demand and supply pressures, respectively.
Rushdy and Lund	1967	Price	Single-equation	OLS	Extends Nield's analysis by incorporating a labor demand measure as a proxy for excess demand.
Fromm and Eckstein	1968	Price	Single-equation	OLS	Considers short- and long-run costs. Analyzed asymmetrical relationship of costs and price.
Solow	1968	Price	Single-equation	OLS	Considers price expectations as a regressor in the price equation.
Laden 1	1969	Price	Multi-equation	TSLS	Derivation of reduced form price equation from a demand equation, production function, and cost minimization conditions.
DeMenil	1970	Econometric model	Single-equation	OLS	Develops price equation based on theory of the firm. Concludes that price change can be dampened, given costs and excess demand, by increasing both rate of technological change and share of investment in total output.
Gordon 1	1970	Wage and price	Single-equation	OLS	Thorough policy simulation analysis using an applicable price equation. Incorporates both DED and IED measures.
FED-MIT-PENN	1970	Econometric model	Multi-equation	OLS	Oligopolistic markup price equation. Long-run simulations of Phillips curves.

McCallum	1970	Price	Single-equation	OLS	Linking indirect and direct ED measures. Pascal and Koyck distributed lags entered into price equation.
DRI	1970	Econometric model	Multi-equation	OLS	The ratio of price to normalized unit labor cost is incorporated as a regressor to indicate the effect of a short-run change in profit margin (i.e., markup) on price behavior.
Popkin and Earl	1971	Price	Multi-equation	OLS	Applied stage of processing format regarding prices within selected sectors. Differences in price behavior are noted across both sectors and processing stages.
Gordon 2	1971	Price and wage	Multi-equation	OLS	Emphasized formulation of a wage equation, wage-price simulations, and price-unemployment rate tradeoffs.
Laden 2	1971	Price, wage, and income	Multi-equation	OLS	Used stage of processing price format along with wage and personal income equations to perform various simulations.
Eckstein and Brimner	1972	Price and wage	Multi-equation	OLS	Emphasized wage equation specification and conducted wage-price simulations with reference to Phase II controls and Phillips curves.

Table 3-5
Sector Studies: Data Specification

Study	Type of Data	Form of Data[a]	Time Period	Data Sets
Kuh	Quarterly	Level	1950:1-1958:1	U.S. corporate sector
Bodkin	Annual	Level	1913-57	U.S. finished goods
Wharton	Quarterly	Level	1948-64	U.S. manufacturing (excluding food and farm products)
OBE	Quarterly	Level	1953-65	U.S. private output
Perry	Quarterly	PCH	1947-60	U.S. manufacturing
Rushdy and Lund	Quarterly	Level FD	1950-61 1953-61	British manufacturing (excluding food and tobacco)
Fromm and Eckstein	Quarterly	Level FD 4Q-PCH	1954-65	U.S. total manufacturing, durables manufacturing, and nondurables manufacturing
Solow	Quarterly	PCH	1947-66	U.S. private nonfarm
Laden 1	Quarterly	FD FDLN	1954-66	U.S. total manufacturing
DeMenil	Quarterly	FDLN	1954:3-1968:2	U.S. nonfarm private economy
Gordon 1	Quarterly	4Q-PCH	1951-69	U.S. nonfarm private economy
FED-MIT-PENN	Quarterly	FDLN	1954-68	U.S. nonfarm private economy
McCallum	Quarterly	FD	1950:1-1960:3	British manufacturing
DRI	Quarterly	Weighted PCH	1955:1-1970:2	Durable goods sectors, nondurable goods sectors, services, government, agriculture.

Popkin-Earl	Quarterly	PCH	1956:2-1969:4 1948:4-1969:4	Consumer durables, consumer nondurables less food; retail, final wholesale, and intermediate wholesale stages.
Gordon 2	Quarterly	PCH	1954:2-1970:4	U.S. private nonfarm
Laden 2	Monthly	LOG	1954-69	Consumer goods sector at retail; manufacturing sector at wholesale stages of processing.
Eckstein and Brinner	Quarterly	PCH	1955-70	U.S. private nonfarm sector

[a]4Q-PCH = 4 quarter percentage change; FDLN = first difference of the logs.

Table 3-6
Sector Studies: Equation Specification

Study	Cost Variables		Excess Demand Variables		Lagged Price and Other Variables
	Short-run	Long-run	Direct	Indirect	
Kuh	AHE, PP		DR, DR(−2)		
Bodkin	AHEP, ULCP ULC,PM		$\frac{Q - MA}{MA}$ or $\frac{Q - Q^*}{Q^*}$		P(−1), DUM1
Wharton	ULC		CUI		t
OBE	ULC		(Δ S)·CUI		
Perry	AHE, PM		CUI, ΔCUI		
Rushdy and Lund	PM, ULC			UI	P(−1)
Fromm and Eckstein	ULC − ULCN, PM	ULCN	CUI, $\Delta(\frac{UNF}{S})$		
Solow	ULC, PM		CUI		PE, DUM2
Laden 1	AHE, PM		K, Y		PG
deMenil	AHE,PP PM/AHE		UNF/Q^*		t, A
Gordon 1	ULC	ULCN	NOR/SHP	ER	
FED-MIT-PENN	PWM, PFM PP, AHE		UNFPD/EPD		t
McCallum	Wage	P/ULCN		UI(+1) UI	P(−1)
DRI	AHE, ULC, PM		D	WGHTD URI	P(−1), t
Popkin-Earl	TOT COMP/W		CUI	URI	P(−1), DUMMY
Gordon 2	AHE, PM		UNF/CAP, PP/PPN		
Laden 2		ULCN	PI		
Eckstein and Brinner	W − WCOMM PP − PPN	ULCN	$UNF/CAP -((UNF/CAP(-1)))$		P(−1), t

proxies constructed from values both above some average (+ proxy) and below some average (− proxy). A final contribution of Bodkin is his inclusion of a past peak wage variable as a regressor in the price equation. This variable is meant to measure the persistent influence of past peak wage levels on current prices; it is significant in most equations. However, Bodkin's is an annual study over the years 1913 to 1957 and includes periods of declining as well as increasing wages. Quarterly wages since 1956 have been continually increasing (in only 4 out of 60 quarters did the average manufacturing wage turn downward) so that this variable would be nearly equivalent to the actual wage series lagged one period and would not therefore be a significant addition to current price studies.

The treatment of the *DED* measure in the Wharton (1965) and OBE (1966) econometric models merits comment. In the Wharton model, much experimentation with nonlinear and other transformed forms of the *CUI* was performed to finally arrive at the linear *CUI*-price relationship. The OBE model on the other hand uses for its *DED* variable the two-quarter change in final sales adjusted for the level of the *CUI*. In this way, an increased sensitivity of prices as full capacity operation is approached may be shown. The *DED* measure in the Wharton model has a higher *t*-value than its counterpart in the OBE model, with the variable being significant in both cases.

The study by Perry includes both *CUI* and change in *CUI* (ΔCUI) as regressors in the price equation. The level of *CUI* represents demand pressure on price and assumes an a priori positive sign. On the other hand, ΔCUI represents the change in output per unit of labor input which results from firms not operating at normal capacity levels. As a firm approaches normal capacity, its output per unit of labor input increases and its average costs fall, leading to a decrease in prices. Therefore, ΔCUI is inversely related to price change. Perry's results indicate that *CUI* and ΔCUI are both significant, with ΔCUI having a substantially higher *t*-value and having a coefficient four times that of *CUI* in absolute magnitude. However, the effect of *CUI* still dominates, since the magnitude of the *CUI* series is so much greater.

Solow incorporates a price expectations variable (*PE*) into the price equation by taking a weighted sum of past inflation rates, with the weights geometrically declining as prices further in the past are considered. That is,

$$PE = \delta P(-1) + \sum_{i=2}^{T} \delta(1 - \delta)^i P(t-i)$$ where δ is the weight factor (0 < δ

< 1). Solow formed several *PE* time series, one for each hypothesized value of δ. A high δ makes the expectations most sensitive to recent observations. (When $\delta = 1$, $PE = P(-1)$ and a Koyck-type equation results.) Solow found the coefficients for all of the *PE* in a narrow range around 0.4, which indicates a considerable difference between *P* and *PE* and therefore points up the importance of excess demand factors in explaining price behavior and especially the gap between *P* and *PE*.

Both Gordon studies include extensive policy simulations regarding Phillips curve tradeoffs between price change, wage change, and the unemployment rate. A comparison of the simulation results indicates longer lag structures in the price and wage equations of Gordon[88], and therefore a lengthening of the period before rates of inflation along alternate paths of recovery converge to the same value. Gordon concludes from both studies that the inflation rate increases permanently when labor market tightness increases to a higher level.

The major differences in the price equation studies at the economy and sectoral levels of aggregation may now be noted. The inclusion of *DED* and/or *IED* measures in the price equation is found in all sectoral studies whereas excess demand indicators were included in only three of the economy studies. Furthermore, long-run labor costs are included as regressors in some of the sector studies whereas they are not considered in the economy studies. The combination of these two factors indicates a more balanced treatment of cost and excess demand variables in the sector price equations than is evident in the economy price equations. The frequency of the data used in the sector studies is higher than that used in the economy studies, being at least quarterly in all studies except Bodkin's. Also, there is less use of level data in the sector studies, which tends to lessen the effect of some of the econometric problems that were evident in the economy studies. A final comment concerns the types of models analyzed at the economy and sector levels. A greater number of multiequation models of price formation are solved by system estimation methods at the economy level than at the sector level. This indicates greater attention in the price studies at the economy level to the structural formation of prices and also points up the fact that more economy price equations are formed as part of large-scale econometric models. However, this result must be qualified, since the two-stage least squares results and ordinary least squares results on certain sectoral studies are not significantly different.

General Critique of Industry Price Studies

Summary information on the industry studies is given in Tables 3-7 to 3-9. Only two studies, those by Schultze and Tryon and by Fromm and Taubman, are part of an econometric model; both studies relate to the Brookings Quarterly Model of the United States. The studies by Courchene, Rippe, and Hay, besides analyzing price behavior, include in their models endogenous treatment of other variables including inventories, production, wages, and imports. The purpose of the models at the industry level of aggregation is almost exclusively to fit a model over a given sample period that best explains price behavior in a certain industry. Only the Fromm and Taubman study contains any policy simulations whereas only the Rippe and Nield studies attempt any short-term forecasting with the models developed. Excluded from this survey are the multitude of

1793089

business pricing studies such as those of Dean[74], Dean[75], Edwards[83], Pearce[129], Backman[2], Haynes[27], Lanzillotti et. al[106], Phillips and Williamson[50], Eiteman[16], Barback[5], Clark[14], and Fitzpatrick[19]. These studies relate to pricing practice at the company level within a given industry. The Rippe and Morkre studies described herein border on this approach to studying price behavior.

The price studies by Zarnowitz and Halfter both reflect hypothesis (2.10) in their formulation. Price change is strictly a function of DED variables. Each of the other industry studies forms a price equation that includes cost and DED regressors. All include in their price equations a labor cost variable, either AHE, ULC, or $ULCN$, reflecting short-run cost hypotheses (2.2) and (2.3) and long-run cost hypothesis (2.6). Productivity is not entered explicitly as a regressor in any of the price models developed. A further representation of those hypotheses is given in all but the Wilson, Morkre, and Hay equations by the inclusion of a material cost variable. Two recent studies, by Moffat and by Eckstein and Wyss, include variables that represent target rate of return pricing theory. All studies except those by Yance and Yordon include DED variables, reflecting hypothesis (2.10). Yance discusses demand measures but does not include them in his model whereas Yordon rejects DED measures in favor of an IED measure. Nield tried an IED measure but rejected it as insignificant and ended up with an equation that had no excess demand measure. Many of the DED measures incorporated in the equations have long-run, desired, and equilibrium values reflected in their forms. The deviation of actual inventory levels from desired or equilibrium inventories is included in Courchene's price equation. The equations developed by Wilson and Phipps both contain variables that reflect ratios of current to desired GNP or output. Desired and equilibrium capacity utilization indexes are included in Halfter's study whereas Moffat incorporates a variable that accounts for the deviation of the shipments-inventory ratio from its long-term moving average. The inclusion of these and similar variables in the price equation reflects consideration of long-term as well as short-term goals in making pricing decisions, which is discussed in the business pricing literature. This is not an unexpected result in the industry level price equations because the aggregation level of these studies is similar to that of many business studies.

All of the industry price studies specify single-equation price models, with the exception of the studies of Courchene, Morkre, Rippe, and Hay. Morkre builds a supply-demand pricing model whereas Hay builds a decision rule model with three decision variables (production, price, and inventories). However, in both of these studies a reduced form price equation is estimated by ordinary least squares. Courchene and Rippe both build structural models depicting economic behavior, including price behavior. However, the structural price equation is estimated by ordinary least squares in both cases. Ordinary least squares is the estimation technique used in all of the industry price studies. Rippe also uses a method of augmented OLS in order to arrive at consistent estimates from a

Table 3-7
Industry Studies: General Characteristics

Study and Year		Type of Study	Type of Model	Type of Analysis	Key Contribution of Study
Wilson	1959	Price	Single-equation	OLS	Demand-oriented price equation fitted to both a low-concentration industry (machinery) and a high-concentration industry (steel).
Yance	1960	Price	Single-equation	OLS	Stage of processing idea. Distributed lag analysis of P-cost relationship. Actual price adjusts to a normal price.
Yordon	1961	Price	Single-equation	OLS	Pricing behavior examined in concentrated and unconcentrated industries at both micro and macro levels.
Zarnowitz	1962	Price	Single-equation	OLS	Quantity adjustments as well as price adjustments. Distinction between production to stock and production to order industries is made.
Nield	1963	Price	Single-equation	OLS	Price equation built on polynomial and Koyck lag structures. Treatment of ULCN.
Schultze and Tryon	1965	Econometric model	Single-equation	OLS	Treatment of ED variables in an asymmetrical fashion around normal levels with respect to effect on price.
Halfter	1966	Price	Single-equation	OLS	International as well as domestic market situation is considered as affecting crude materials price.
Fromm and Taubman	1968	Econometric model	Single-equation	OLS	Simulations showing different excise tax effects on price depending on both the "pass on" assumptions adopted and the magnitude of the tax.
Courchene	1969	Price and inventory	Single-equation	OLS	Thorough treatment of price-inventory nexus and of various demand shifters in price equations. Extension of Liu's price equation to disaggregate data.
Morkre	1969	Price	Multi-equation	OLS	Tested importance of cost and ED on pricing in an oligopolistic industry. Compared results of price equation with BLS price versus transactions price.
Phipps	1969	Price	Single-equation	OLS	Comparison of demand effect on price depending on whether short- or long-run cost is important.

37

Author	Year	Variables	Equation	Method	Description
Rippe	1970	Wage, price, and import	Single-equation	OLS and Augmented OLS	Structural approach to a particular industry's behavior with respect to certain key decision variables.
Hay	1970	Production, price, and inventory	Multi-equation	OLS	Decision rule approach to pricing. Reduced form equation for price is systematically derived.
Moffat	1970	Price and tax	Single-equation	OLS	Theoretical and empirical treatment of various tax situations and relationships to pricing.
Eckstein and Wyss	1970	Price	Single-equation	OLS	Division of 2- and 3-digit industries into three approaches to pricing. Data are in a new form. Emphasizes industry-specific approach to pricing.

38

Table 3-8
Industry Studies: Data Specification

Study	Type of Data	Form of Data	Time Period	Data Sets
Wilson	Quarterly	FD	1953:3-1959:2	Machinery industry, steel
Yance	Monthly and two-monthly	FD	1947-56	Tanning, shoe industries
Yordon	Monthly and Quarterly	2-month FD	1947-58	Aggregate concentrated, aggregate unconcentrated; 14 4-digit industries, all industries.
Zarnowitz	Quarterly	FD	1948-58	Paper and allied products, textile mill products, fabricated metal products, nonelectrical machinery, primary metals, nonautomotive transportation equipment, others.
Nield	Quarterly	Level	1950-61 1953-61	British: manufacturing; chemicals; paper; manufacturing excluding food, tobacco, and beverages; textiles; timber; food.
Schultze and Tryon	Quarterly	Level	1948-60	Durable, nondurable manufacturing; wholesale, retail, total trade; regulated industries; construction; residual industries; private nonmanufacturing; 12 2-digit industries; 2- and 3-digit industries.
Halfter	Quarterly	PCH 4Q-PCH	1947-65	All materials; stable materials; unstable materials; 9 individual materials (e.g., iron, salt).
Fromm and Taubman	Quarterly	Level	1948-60	Same as Schultze and Tryon
Courchene	Quarterly	FD	1956-62	Canadian: Heavy transportation, heavy electrical equipment, iron and steel; textiles; leather; refrigerators; vacuum cleaners and appliances; total manufacturing.
Morke	Annual	FDLN	1955-65	Steel industry
Phipps	Semiannual	6-month OBS.	1957:4-1967:10	British: chemical, textile, paper, timber
Rippe	Quarterly	PCH	1953-68	Steel industry
Hay	Monthly	Level	1953:3-1966:8	Lumber and wood products; paper and allied products
Moffat	Annual	Level DERIVATIVE	1927-62	Rubber, textiles
Eckstein and Wyss	Quarterly	Weighted PCH	1954-69	12 2-digit and 4 3-digit industries

Table 3-9
Industry Studies: Equation Specification

Study	Cost Variables		Excess Demand Variables		Lagged Price and Other Variables
	Short-run	Long-run	Direct	Indirect	
Wilson	AHE		(NOR − S)/S, UNF/S, (GNP − GNP*)/GNP*		
Yance	AHE, PM				P(−1)
Yordon	ULC, +UMC, −UMC			AWH	
Zarnowitz			UNF, (UNF/SHP)		P(−1)
Nield	PM	ULCN			P(−1)
Schultze and Tryon	ULC, PM	ULCN, PMN	+CUI, −CUI, INV/Q		
Halfter			INVMAT, SHP, CUID, CUIE, (UNF/SHP)MAT		
Fromm and Taubman	ULC, PM	ULCN, PMN	+CUI, −CUI, INV/Q		
Courchene	AHE, PM, PUS		INVE − INV		
Morkre	WS		CS, YS, Q		
Phipps	ULC, PM		UI		
Rippe	WS, PM	PMN	(UNF/SHP), CUI		P(−1)
Hay	AHE		Q, INV, UNF		P(−1)
Moffat	ULCPR, ULCO, UMC	UK, UMCN	(SHP/INV) − MA		tx
Eckstein and Wyss	AHE, PM	r, PREQ	CUI, SHP		P(−1)

Koyck-type lag price equation. Only Morkre and Moffat use annual data; all other studies use data of a higher frequency. The Brookings studies and the Hay study use only level data. All other studies use at least one change form of the data.

The key contributions of certain studies will now be discussed. Yance (1960) developed a price model in which price adjusts to its normal level, which is unobservable but is a function of material and labor costs. By substituting the expression explaining normal price in the price change equation, price change is made a function of wage, material price, and lagged price. This equation is solved by *OLS*, with the results being used to compute the normal price series. Normal price and actual price may then be compared in order to analyze the process of adjustment of actual price to its normal levels. Yance did the same analysis at two stages of processing (final and intermediate) within the leather industry. He found the adjustment to normal prices about four times as fast at the intermediate level as at the final level. This may reflect a less important role for demand in explaining price formation at the lower stages of processing.

The Yordon study (1961) is testing the hypothesis that inflationary pressures are transmitted through concentrated and unconcentrated industries at the same rate. He concludes that cost behavior explains 98 percent of price behavior regardless of the concentration of an industry. The effect of demand on price change in both types of industries is negligible. Differences in degree of industrial concentration do not appear on the basis of this study to result in difference in price behavior. However, the more recent studies by Moffat and by Eckstein and Wyss conclude that there is a noticeable difference in the price behavior of an industry depending on its degree of concentration. The conflict in the results of these studies could be attributed partly to the use of *DED* measures in the latter studies whereas Yordon used an *IED* measure. The *DED* measures may be better indicators of a difference between unconcentrated and concentrated industries in the demand-price relationship if in fact a difference exists.

The studies by Morkre (1969) and Rippe (1970) both analyze price behavior in the steel industry. Morkre uses as his price variable gross margin (total receipts minus average variable costs), arguing that it is this variable that will be responsive to changes in demand. He solves a reduced form price equation using the gross margin and the Bureau of Labor Statistics (BLS) price as alternative forms of the dependent variable. He finds that the gross margin price variable is highly responsive to demand change whereas the BLS quoted prices are responsive only to cost changes. The conclusion is drawn that steel prices do behave similarly to prices in a competitive industry when data reflecting the actual market transactions are used. (There has been much discussion of the responsiveness of BLS prices to demand changes as compared with their responsiveness to cost changes, since BLS prices are based on manufacturer's quotes and not on market transactions. The discussion is exemplified by

Heflebower,[91], Kindahl[97], Wood[145], Moss[121], Backman and Gainsbrugh[153], and Stigler and Kindahl[55].) Rippe hypothesizes that there is a structural shift in steel price behavior in 1959 because of increased government influence on wage settlements and the increased importance of expectations. He supports this contention through the use of a Chow test and then develops separate models for the two periods. The equation for the later period includes the lagged price as a regressor.

In the price study by Hay (1970) a structural model containing revenue and cost functions is developed, from which is derived a Lagrangian expression based on the maximization of discounted future profits subject to constraints regarding inventory change and unfilled order change. Through differentiation of this function, three linear decision rules are derived. These are reduced form equations for price, production, and inventory decisions. Hay specifies various parameter values a priori in the structural equations in order to deduce the sensitivity of the reduced form coefficients to structural parameter changes and the ultimate effect of these changes on the values of the decision variables. From both this sensitivity analysis and the regression analysis, Hay concludes that price changes assume a very small role in absorbing increases in demand and that most adjustments occur in quantity produced.

Moffat (1970) regards the industry analyzed as a monopolistic firm and develops price models for it both with and without the inclusion of the corporate income tax as a regressor. He forms models based on assumptions of profit maximization, sales maximization, target return, and percentage markup. He concludes that taxes, along with unit labor cost and normalized unit material cost, are the most important factors in explaining price behavior. However, the weight assumed by the tax variable in the price equation is very small. He uses the corporation income tax-profits ratio as the tax variable. It varies sufficiently, since annual data over a 35-year period are used in the study.

Several differences between price equation studies at the industry level and those at the sector and economy levels are evident. First, the purposes of the studies are noticeably different. Simulation and prediction are common uses of the models at the sector and economy levels whereas hypothesis testing is the major use of the models at the industry level. Second, most industry studies develop single-equation models and estimate them by ordinary least squares whereas many sector and economy studies contain multiequation, structural models and estimate them by system estimation techniques. A multiequation approach to analyzing price formation is not as prevalent at the industry level. Thus, the level of aggregation of price studies closest to the microeconomic level is the weakest in regard to the theoretical structural explanation of the complete price formation process. Third, the industry price equations generally take a form that combines cost and *DED* hypotheses, which is also true of the price equations developed in the sector studies. However, there are some refinements at the industry level. There is explicit treatment of *UKC* variables in the price

Table 3-10
Variable Definitions

Symbol	Definition
AHE	average hourly earnings
PI	import price index
T	ratio of indirect taxes, less subsidies, to consumer expenditures
W	wage per person
X	output per person
PR	profit per unit of output
PP	productivity index (output per man-hour)
AWE	weekly earnings index
INVD – INV	desired inventories less actual inventories
ULC	unit labor costs
UPI	unit price of imported materials
WB	total wage bill
Q	output
WO	wage per person in organized labor force
r	long-term rate of interest (Moody's AAA bond rate)
$\Delta Y - (Q - QCAP(-1))$	change in spending minus deviation of output from capacity output
PA	price anticipations
MS	money supply
DR	Kuh demand rachet $(Q)/(QP)(.0375)^{t-p}$ where QP = previous peak output, p = peak period, t = time periods
AHEP	peak average hourly earnings
ULCP	peak unit labor cost
PM	material price index
(Q – MA)/MA	relative deviation of manufacturing output from moving average of output
(Q – Q*)/Q*	relative deviation of manufacturing output from trend of output
CUI	capacity utilization index
DUM1	Korean War dummy (1950:3-51:1 = 1, all others = 0
$(\Sigma \Delta S)$*CUI	sales change adjusted for capacity utilization levels
t	time trend
UI	unemployment rate index
ULCN	normal (standard) unit labor costs
PE	price expectations
DUM2	wage-price guidepost dummy (1963:2 = 1, other periods = 0)
K	capital stock
Y	income of purchasers of manufactured goods
PG	price index for other final goods and services
UNF/Q*	unfilled orders−capacity output ratio

Table 3-10 (cont.)

Symbol	Definition
A	age of nonfarm equipment
ER	employment rate in man-hours
PWM	world price index of exports of raw materials
PFM	WPI for farm products
UNFPD/EPD	UNF/SHP ratio for producer durables equipment
D	real consumption or real investment
WAGE	wages, salaries, and supplements—private nonfarm economy
URI	inverse of the civilian worker unemployment rate
TOT COMP/W	ratio of total compensation per man-hour to the wage index
DUMMY	excise tax dummy (1965:3 = 1, all other periods = 0)
$W - W_{COMM}$	sector wage index minus private, nonfarm economy wage index
AWH	average weekly hours
$(GNP - GNP^*)/GNP^*$	ratio of actual minus trend GNP to trend GNP
+UMC, −UMC	increases(+) and decreases(−) in unit material cost
UNF	unfilled orders
PMN	normal (standard) material price index
+CUI, −CUI	positive and negative deviations of CUI normalized from CUI
INVMAT	material inventory
SHP	shipments
CUID	desired CUI
CUIE	equilibrium CUI
(UNF/SHP)MAT	unfilled orders-shipments ratio of materials
PUS	United States price index
INVE − INV	equilibrium minus actual inventories
WS	total hourly employment cost
CS	steel industry ingot capacity
YS	weighted product of steel-using industries
INV	inventories
ULCPR	production workers ULC
ULCO	nonproduction workers ULC
UK	stockholders' equity per unit of output
UMCN	normal (standard) unit material costs
(SHP/INV) − MA	sales-inventory ratio minus its two-year moving average
tx	corporate income tax-profits ratio
PREQ	profit-equity ratio
S	corporate sales
PPN	normal (standard) productivity
CAP	capacity in manufacturing
NOR	new orders

equation in studies by Moffat and by Eckstein and Wyss. Also normalized *UMC* is used as a regressor in the Schultze and Tryon (Brookings), Rippe, and Moffat price equations. Neither *UKC* nor *UMCN* is employed in the sector or economy price equations. Furthermore, there is more use of desired and long-term *DED* measures in the price equations at the industry level than in those at other levels. The target return theory of pricing along with emphasis on short-term demand movements in relation to desired long-term movements become more predominant as lower levels of aggregation are analyzed. This result seems consistent with the decision process by which business prices at the microeconomic levels of activity are formulated. (Studies of business pricing are mentioned in the first section of Chapter 2 as well as in this section.)

4

Reexamination of Selected Price Formation Studies

Those studies that are being reestimated on the bodies of data particular to the present research are discussed in more detail here than in Chapter 3. The major studies include those by Klein and Ball[35], Liu[111], Nield[44], Schultze and Tryon[51], Fromm and Eckstein[81], Laden[172], and Eckstein and Wyss[159]. In addition, other studies will be discussed that are related to the major studies, in particular, the study by Courchene[73] in conjunction with Liu and the studies by Rushdy and Lund[136], McCallum[116], and Phipps[182] in conjunction with Nield.

The studies selected are quite representative of research on price formation in four main respects. First, they cover work on price formation at the major levels of aggregation (economy, sector, and industry). Two studies, those by Nield and by Schultze and Tryon, analyze price formation at both the sector and industry levels whereas the others fit models to only one level. Second, the selected studies specify models that cover nearly all combinations of short-run cost, long-run cost, direct excess demand, and indirect excess demand hypotheses discussed in Chapter 2. Furthermore, lagged price is introduced as a regressor in certain of the studies, as are other variables (e.g., tax) not directly contained in any of the hypotheses. A broad representation of hypotheses is important when the results of all the models reestimated on new data bodies are compared and analyzed. Third, the studies chosen represent fairly broad coverage of the research concerning the lagged relationships of various regressors with price. Simple lagged and unlagged regressor-price relationships, as well as Koyck, Pascal, and other distributed lags, are discussed. Finally, what I consider to be the best multiequation price models (Klein and Ball, Liu) and the best single-equation price models (Fromm and Eckstein, Schultze and Tryon, Eckstein and Wyss) developed over the past 15 years are contained in the selected studies.

For each study, the complete specification of the model employed is explained and related to the hypotheses of Chapter 2. A brief discussion of the results of each study is included. However, the major empirical discussion is contained in Chapter 6, where the fits of each of the selected models to the present data bodies are compared with one another, and in Chapter 7, where the fits of these models are compared with the fits of the final industry price equations that are developed.

The Klein and Ball Study

The Klein and Ball study, published in 1959, represents the first multiequation explanation of price behavior. A four-equation submodel, which was specified to

45

study the movements of absolute prices and wages, is incorporated into a full-scale econometric model of the United Kingdom. The price-wage model is fitted to quarterly level data over the 1948-56 period, with the consumer price index (British) being the price of interest. In the total model other price equations, for components of the overall consumer price index (food, nondurables less food, and durables) as well as for producer durables and exports, also are included. However, the major function of these additional price equations is in completing the model, with their specifications all including P as a regressor.

Specification of the submodel explaining price and wage behavior is as follows.

$$AWR - AWR(-4) = \alpha_0 + \alpha_1 \left(\frac{U + U(-1) + U(-2) + U(-3)}{4} \right) \qquad (4.1.1)$$

$$+ \alpha_2 \left[\frac{(P - P(-4)) + (P(-1) - P(-5)) + (P(-2) - P(-6)) + (P(-3) - P(-7))}{4} \right]$$

$$+ \alpha_3 F + \alpha_{s1} D_1 + \alpha_{s2} D_2 + \alpha_{s3} D_3 + \mu_1$$

$$AWE - AWR = \beta_0 + \beta_1 AWH + \beta_2 PP + \beta_{s1} D_1 + \beta_{s2} D_2 \qquad (4.1.2)$$

$$+ \beta_{s3} D_3 + \mu_2$$

$$AWH = \gamma_0 + \gamma_1 IPI + \gamma_2 \left(\frac{U + U(-1) + U(-2) + U(-3)}{4} \right) \qquad (4.1.3)$$

$$+ \gamma_{s1} D_1 + \gamma_{s2} D_2 + \gamma_{s3} D_3 + \mu_3$$

$$P = \delta_0 + \delta_1 AWE + \delta_2 PI(-2) + \delta_3 T + \delta_{s1} D_1 + \delta_{s2} D_2 \qquad (4.1.4)$$

$$+ \delta_{s3} D_3 + \mu_4$$

where AWE = quarterly average of index of weekly earnings
  AWH = average weekly hours
  AWR = quarterly average of index of weekly wage rates
  D = quarterly seasonal dummies
  F = political factor (1948-51 = zero; 1952-56 = one)
  IPI = output
  PI = import prices
  PP = productivity
  T = ratio of indirect taxes, less subsidies, to consumer expenditures
  U = index of unemployment

Note that data not adjusted for seasonal variation are used and the seasonal dummies are entered explicitly into each equation. Equation (4.1.1) explains the behavior of the change in weekly wage rates (which are based on a full-time standard work week) as a function of moving averages of both unemployment and price changes. The political factor is entered as a regressor to indicate the party change in Britain in 1952. This equation is a Phillips curve formulation. Equation (4.1.2) explains the spread between the average weekly earnings index and the average weekly wage rate index in terms of weekly hours worked and productivity. As both AWH and PP increase, the spread between AWE and AWR increases. Equation (4.1.3) explains AWH in terms of output and a moving average of unemployment. The price equation (4.1.4) includes only three cost variables (AWE, PI, and T) as regressors. It is evident that equations (4.1.1), (4.1.2), and (4.1.3) are together concerned with explaining the behavior of AWE, which in turn enters the price equation as a regressor. This price equation represents the short-run cost hypothesis of pricing (2.2) without including productivity variables as regressors. AWE indicates the full labor costs and PI is a proxy for material input prices, since a large proportion of Great Britain's material inputs are imported. The model (4.1.1 to 4.1.4) is solved by limited information, maximum likelihood ($LIML$), which takes account of all the predetermined variables in the model in the solution for the coefficients of a particular equation. The principle behind $LIML$ is that the coefficients in the price equation should be selected in such a manner that the addition of the excluded predetermined variables should make a minimal improvement in the explained sum of squares of the dependent variable. Therefore, the price equation when estimated by $LIML$ takes into account an IED measure (U), a DED measure (IPI), productivity, and the other excluded predetermined variables that appear in other equations of the model. However, the estimates for (4.1.4) from $LIML$ and ordinary least squares (OLS) are not significantly different from one another, indicating that the excluded predetermined variables do *not* make a significant contribution toward explaining price formation. This results in the Klein and Ball submodel containing essentially a pure cost explanation of price formation. One reason given for the similarity of results from OLS and $LIML$ estimation is the overall high correlation (and good fit) of (4.1.4). The excluded variables are highly correlated with the included variables in (4.1.4); thus no significant contribution is made to explaining price formation when the excluded variables are considered. This high correlation among variables is attributed mainly to the fact that level data are being used in the analysis, in which strong common trends are exhibited for all variables.

A productivity variable was entered directly into the price equation. However, PP entered with a positive sign, contrary to a priori expectations, and was insignificant. The coefficient of determination of the price equation is over .99, with the coefficients of AWE and PI being highly significant and having their expected positive signs. T is not significant in (4.1.4) whereas the seasonal dummies are significant.

Nerlove[125] in a critique of the United Kingdom model comments that the commodity markets are not directly represented in the price formation process.

Klein and Ball argue that stock of goods data are not available or are of too poor quality to be entered as a regressor in the price equation. However, if the entire model had been solved for the derived, reduced form price equation, the influence of *DED* and *IED* measures in other equations of the model would have been taken into account in explaining price formation. In light of the purpose of the model, namely, to analyze and predict short-run changes in key endogenous variables (including the price level), the solution for the derived, reduced form price equation would have been a valuable extension of the analysis.

The Liu Study

Ta-Chung Liu built a quarterly econometric model of the United States in 1963. One of its unique features in comparison with other models (including present-day models) is its analysis of price formation by use of a submodel on inventory and price movements. The specification of the submodel is given in Equations (4.2.1 to 4.2.7).

$$\%P = \alpha_0 + \alpha_1 (INVD - INV) + \alpha_2 \%P(-1) \qquad (4.2.1)$$
$$+ \alpha_3 \%P(-2) + \alpha_4 \%AHE + \mu_1$$

$$\Delta INVD = INVD - INV(-1) \qquad (4.2.2)$$

$$\Delta INV = \beta_0 + \beta_1 S + \beta_2 rr + \beta_3 LA + \mu_2 \qquad (4.2.4)$$

$$\Delta INV = INV - INV(-1) \qquad (4.2.3)$$

$$\Delta INVD = \gamma_1 (INVE - INV(-1)) + \gamma_2 INV(-1) \qquad (4.2.5)$$
$$+ \gamma_3 INV(-2) + \mu_3$$

$$\Delta INV = Q - S - \Delta INVF \qquad (4.2.6)$$

$$Q = \delta_1 (INVD - INV) + \delta_2 Q(-1) + \delta_3 \%P \qquad (4.2.7)$$
$$+ \delta_4 \%AHE + \mu_4$$

where AHE = average hourly earnings
INV = inventory
$INVD$ = desired inventory
$INVE$ = equilibrium inventory
$INVF$ = farm inventory
LA = liquid assets
Q = output
rr = short-term real rate of interest
S = sales

The endogenous variables in the model are P, INV, ΔINV, $INVD$, $\Delta INVD$, $INVE$, and Q, with three of these variables being unobservable ($INVE$, $INVD$, and $\Delta INVD$). The price decision function (4.2.1) expresses rate of change of price ($\%P$) as a function of its past values, rate of change of wages, and the deviation of actual inventories from desired inventory levels. Equations (4.2.2 to 4.2.5) are necessary in order to derive time series for $INVE$ and $INVD$ so that the price decision function may be estimated. Liu was able to estimate β_2 and β_3 indirectly from certain of the parameter estimates obtained by solving the reduced form equation for ΔINV. The estimates for β_1 and β_0 in (4.2.4) are set on the basis of an assumption that the inventory-sales ratio does not exhibit a trend but is instead an oscillation around an average value. Therefore, β_1 was set equal to the mean inventory-mean sales ratio over the 1947-59 period. A further assumption was made that the mean equilibrium inventory-mean sales ratio was also equal to β_1 over that period. From this information β_0 (mean equilibrium inventories) can be derived. An $INVE$ series may now be generated. Liu next solves (4.2.5) for the change in desired inventories, the rationale behind the equation being that inventories are adjusted at some desired speed (γ_1) between actual and equilibrium levels. Modifying this speed of adjustment to equilibrium levels is the changing mood of business, which he represents with two previous lag values of actual inventory change. The coefficients γ_2/γ_3 and γ_3/γ_1 are available from the reduced form results of ΔINV. Therefore, dividing through (4.2.5) by γ_1, a series for $\Delta INVD/\gamma_1$ may be generated. Utilizing identities (4.2.2) and (4.2.3) along with the series $\gamma_1 \cdot INVD^* = \Delta INVD$, the price decision function (4.2.1) may be respecified as follows.

$$\%P = \alpha_0 + \alpha_1 \gamma_1 \Delta INVD^* - \alpha_1 \Delta INV + \alpha_2 \%P(-1) \qquad (4.2.8)$$
$$+ \alpha_3 \%P(-2) + \alpha_4 \%AHE + \mu_1$$

The expected sign of α_1 can be either positive or negative depending on whether the cost of holding inventories is considered. The coefficients on the $\%P$ and $\%AHE$ regressors have expected positive signs.

Liu fitted this price equation to quarterly data over the 1947-59 period, his price variable being the rate of change in the gross national product deflator. An R_2 of .46 and only one t-value (for α_4) greater than 2 does not make the results impressive. Note that α_1 is positive but insignificant in the final equation. Liu states in his paper that price-inventory relationships should be studied not for the economy as a whole but instead for individual industrial sectors. He did preliminary work on the durable and nondurable sectors which yielded results more promising than those stated above.

Thomas Courchene studied price-inventory behavior for selected Canadian manufacturing industries over the 1956-62 period. He mentions in a footnote that his work estimates a price equation that is similar to that of Liu but fitted over more disaggregate data. Courchene's price equation assumes the following form.

$$\Delta P = \alpha_0 + \alpha_1 (INVE - INV) + \alpha_2 \Delta AHE \qquad (4.2.9)$$
$$+ \alpha_3 \Delta USP + \alpha_4 \Delta PM + \mu_1$$

where PM = material price index
               USP = relevant United States wholesale price

Courchene does not include lagged values of the dependent variable as regressors as does Liu, stating that it is short-term price movements he is examining. Including lagged price as a regressor takes all past behavior of the exogenous variables into account in explaining present period price change. Courchene includes as regressors material prices and import price. Courchene's equation does emphasize cost factors more than Liu's; however, the principal determinant of price change is the inventory variable in both cases. However, Courchene uses equilibrium inventories minus actual inventories as his regressor and does not consider desired inventories as did Liu. One advantage of Courchene's form of the inventory variable is that only one variable ($INVE$) has to be constructed whereas in Liu's study two variables ($INVE$ and $INVD$) must be generated. For this reason, Courchene's inventory variable may be less subject to data errors and less constrained by assumptions than is Liu's hypothetical inventory series.

Courchene analyzed specific production to stock (PTS) and production to order (PTO) industries as well as the total Canadian manufacturing sector. The fit of (4.2.9) was in general better for the PTO industries, with the coefficient of determination ranging between .70 and .80 and the t-values of the coefficients greater than 2. The coefficients of $INVE - INV$ and ΔPM were the most significant in the price equations for each of the industries studied. However, they are insignificant (as are those for ΔAHE and ΔUSP) in the equations for the PTS industries. In all cases, the coefficient for $INVE - INV$ is positive. It should be noted that Courchene entered many other DED and IED measures as regressors in the price equation, including UR, URI, NOR, UNF, and other forms of INV. In general, his selected regressor ($INVE - INV$) is more significant than the others in explaining price change.

Both Liu's and Courchene's final price equations include variables that reflect short-run cost hypothesis (2.2) and market hypothesis (2.10). The emphasis in both equations is placed on the importance of market forces, as represented by the inventory variables, in explaining price change.

The Nield Study

Nield's book, *Pricing and Employment in the Trade Cycle* (1963), contains the first detailed analysis of the influence of lagged regressors on price formation. His study fitted cost-oriented price equations both to the British manufacturing sector and to selected manufacturing industries. One of Nield's major conclusions from the study, that demand has no influence on British manufacturing prices, triggered three subsequent studies of these prices since 1967. All three took Nield's basic hypotheses but expanded them to include emphasis on excess demand and alternative lag distributions for both cost and demand regressors. The Rushdy and Lund (1967) and McCallum (1970) studies reexamined the sector results whereas the Phipps (1969) study reexamined the industry results. These studies all found demand to be important in explaining price behavior, thus rejecting the Nield conclusion.

Nield hypothesizes that price depends on both past and present unit labor and material costs. The specification of his basic hypothesis and distributed lags is given in (4.3.1 to 4.3.5).

$$P = \alpha_0 + \alpha_1 C + \mu_1 \tag{4.3.1}$$

$$C = (1/PP) \cdot AHE + (M/Q) \cdot PM \tag{4.3.2}$$

$$P = \alpha_0 + \alpha_1 \cdot (1/PP) \cdot AHE + \alpha_1 (M/Q) \cdot PM + \mu_1 \tag{4.3.3}$$

$$AHE \approx (1-\lambda)AHE + (1-\lambda)\lambda AHE(-1) + (1-\lambda)\lambda^2 \tag{4.3.4}$$
$$AHE(-2) + \ldots$$

$$PM \approx \delta_0 PM + \delta_1 PM(-1) + \delta_2(1-\lambda)PM(-2) \tag{4.3.5}$$
$$+ \delta_2(1-\lambda)\lambda PM(-3) + \ldots$$

where $\quad AHE$ = average hourly earnings
$\qquad C$ = cost
$\qquad M/Q$ = material-output ratio
$\qquad PM$ = material price index
$\qquad \lambda$ = Koyck lag coefficient, indicating speed of adjustment

$$(1-\lambda)(1+\lambda+\lambda^2+\lambda^3+\ldots) = 1$$

$\qquad \delta$ = distributed lag weights on PM

$$\delta_0 + \delta_1 + \delta_2 = 1$$

In (4.3.1), price is expressed as a function of cost, where cost is defined in (4.3.2) to be the sum of unit labor and unit material costs. Substituting (4.3.2) into (4.3.1) yields (4.3.3), which is a simple price equation including only the present values of unit labor and unit material costs as regressors. This equation can be expanded into a more complex form through substitution of the distributed lags on AHE and PM given in (4.3.4) and (4.3.5). The lag on AHE is a distributed lag that has the weights declining geometrically, with the sum of the weights equal to 1. This formulation indicates a steadily declining importance of past *AHE* on present *P* as periods further in the past are considered. The lag on *PM* is different from that on *AHE*, with the smooth geometric weight structure being modified by the introduction of the additional weights δ_0, δ_1, and δ_2 in the first three time periods. The difference in these lag structures is meant to reflect the more immediate effect of *AHE* on *P*. This reasoning is based on the supposition that materials enter manufacturing mainly in the earlier stages of processing so that there is a longer lag relating *PM* to *P*. Therefore, small values of δ_0 and δ_1 along with a large value for δ_2 make the past values more important in affecting present price than if a straight geometric distributed lag is employed.

The speed of response coefficient (λ) is assumed to be the same for both *AHE* and *PM* although it is applied to each over different periods. This assumption is questioned by Phipps since it implies that the reaction pattern of prices to wages and material prices is the same. Phipps considers that at industry and firm levels of aggregation all industries and firms will not react the same to *AHE* and *PM*, much less have the same λ for both *AHE* and *PM*. However, at aggregate levels of analysis one response coefficient for each of the cost variables is reasonable, resulting in different weighting schemes over time for each cost variable. This is essentially what Nield has, since he introduces the δ weights in addition to λ for *PM*.

Making the substitution of (4.3.4) and (4.3.5) into (4.3.3) yields (4.3.6).

$$
\begin{aligned}
P = \alpha_0 &+ \alpha_1(1/PP)\,[(1-\lambda)AHE + (1-\lambda)\lambda AHE(-1) & \text{(4.3.6)} \\
&+ (1-\lambda)\lambda^2 AHE(-2) + \ldots] + \alpha_1(M/Q)\,[\delta_0 PM \\
&+ \delta_1 PM(-1) + \delta_2(1-\lambda)PM(-2) + \delta_2(1-\lambda)\lambda PM(-3) \\
&+ \ldots] + \mu_1
\end{aligned}
$$

By taking λ times the lagged version of (4.3.6) and subtracting the result from (4.3.6), the price equation in (4.3.7) is obtained.

$$
\begin{aligned}
P = \gamma_0 &+ \gamma_1(1/PP)AHE + \gamma_2(M/Q)PM + \gamma_3(M/Q)PM(-1) & \text{(4.3.7)} \\
&+ \gamma_4(M/Q)PM(-2) + \gamma_5 P(-1) + \mu_1
\end{aligned}
$$

where
$$
\begin{aligned}
\gamma_0 &= \alpha_0(1-\lambda) \\
\gamma_1 &= \alpha_1(1-\lambda) \\
\gamma_2 &= \alpha_1\delta_0 \\
\gamma_3 &= \alpha_1(\delta_1 - \lambda\delta_0) \\
\gamma_4 &= \alpha_1(1-\lambda)\delta_2 - \lambda\delta_1 \\
\gamma_5 &= \lambda
\end{aligned}
$$

All of structural parameters, α_0, α_1, λ, δ_0, δ_1, and δ_2, can be derived from the parameters of (4.3.7). Nield assumes M/Q to be constant and of little importance in explaining price behavior, so that its influence is felt through the regression coefficients on PM and its lagged values. Several forms of PP are introduced. In one case, actual productivity is used, with the resultant ULC term reflecting all short-term movements. Three forms of long-run productivity are introduced which tend to normalize ULC: (1) $(1.025)^{t/4}$, reflecting a constant rise of 2.5 percent per year; (2) $AHE \cdot t$ variable, with its coefficient reflecting the productivity trend; and (3) different-length moving averages of PP. The lagged price is both included and excluded as a regressor in all equations but is retained in the final formulation because of its high degree of significance. The expected signs of the parameters in (4.3.7) are all positive except for the constant term. Short-run cost hypothesis (2.2) is reflected in this price equation. An IED measure similar to an unemployment rate index is introduced as a regressor in cumulative form but is found insignificant for both sector and industry price formation.

Nield used this form of the IED measure in order to be consistent with supply-demand market theory of price, which hypothesizes price change as a function of excess demand. Since his data are in level form, Nield makes price level a function of cumulative excess demand. There is extensive discussion of this point and of the distributed lag interpretation of both cumulative IED and IED in Rushdy and Lund and in McCallum. This point will not be further discussed in this section. The insignificance of the IED variable is not surprising, since level data are used and high collinearity exists between cost and price variables. Nield does state that any demand influence present is probably affecting price through the cost terms. The use of first difference data would increase the significance of the explicit IED measure, as discussed by Rushdy and Lund, and by McCallum.

The sector price equations are run on quarterly data over two time periods, 1950-60 and 1953-60. The best fit generally is obtained using the following equation.

$$P = \gamma_0 + \gamma_1 ULCN + \gamma_2 PM + \gamma_3 PM(-1) + \gamma_4 P(-1) + \mu_1 \qquad (4.3.8)$$

where $ULCN = AHE/(1.025)^{t/4}$

The time forms of the distributed lags on $ULCN$ and PM reflect as expected a higher weight for several lagged PM than for the same lagged AHE. The R^2 is nearly 1.0, which is not surprising because level data are used and a strong collinearity exists between price and cost levels.

The industry price equations are run on quarterly data over the 1957:2 to 1961:4 time period. In general, equation (4.3.9) has the best fit and reflects only short-run cost hypothesis (2.2).

$$P = \gamma_0 + \gamma_2 PM + \gamma_4 P(-1) + \mu_2 \qquad (4.3.9)$$

The coefficients of determination are all above .92 except for that of the chemical industry (.70). Wages are significant only in the equation for the paper industry. The time period of the analysis is not of sufficient length for any strong conclusions to be drawn, however. In both the sector and the industry results, strong positive autocorrelation is evident; therefore, the coefficients are both biased and inconsistent, since (4.3.8) and (4.3.9) contain lagged price as a regressor and have autocorrelated residuals.

Rushdy and Lund extend Nield's analysis by further considering the excess demand measure. They fit price equations on quarterly, first difference data over the same two time periods as are used in the Nield analysis. However, only the manufacturing less food, beverages, and tobacco sector is analyzed. Koyck-type distributed lags are not used; instead, several different combinations of lagged and unlagged cost and demand variables are tried. The best equation resulting from this analysis is given in (4.3.10), reflecting short-run cost hypotheses (2.2) and (2.3) and market hypothesis (2.10).

$$\Delta P = \alpha_0 + \alpha_1 \Delta ULC(-1) + \alpha_2 \Delta PM(-1) + \alpha_3 UI(-1) + \mu_1 \qquad (4.3.10)$$

where $\quad UI = IED$ measure similar to unemployment rate index
$\qquad ULC = AHE/PP$

Note that short-run ULC is used in (4.3.10) whereas $ULCN$ is used in (4.3.8). The coefficient for UI is significant and positive, and the cost variables are more significant in lagged form than they are in unlagged form. Rushdy and Lund do not include the lagged price change as a regressor.

McCallum reestimates a simultaneous version of (4.3.10), which includes lagged price change as a regressor and excludes the constant term, over the same data and time period as Rushdy and Lund. UI is now insignificant while $\Delta P(-1)$ is highly significant. McCallum's major contribution, however, involves the development of a price equation that is based solely on market hypothesis (2.10). His model is specified in (4.3.11) to (4.3.13).

$$\Delta P = (1-\lambda)\gamma\, DED + \lambda\Delta P(-1) \qquad (4.3.11)$$

$$UI = (1-\delta)DED(-1) + \delta\, UI(-1) \qquad (4.3.12)$$

$$\Delta P = \frac{(1-\lambda)\gamma}{1-\delta}\, UI(+1) - \delta\frac{(1-\lambda)\gamma}{1-\delta}\, UI + \lambda\Delta P(-1) + \mu_1 \qquad (4.3.13)$$

where $\quad \gamma$ = adjustment coefficient of price to excess demand situation
$\qquad \lambda$ = time response coefficient of ΔP to DED
$\qquad \delta$ = time response coefficient of UI to DED

McCallum extends the simple hypothesis that price change is a function of excess demand in the product market (4.3.11) by incorporating response lags in this relationship in the form of geometrically distributed lags. In (4.3.12), conditions in the labor market (IED) are hypothesized to be related in this way to previous conditions in the product market (DED). Furthermore, price change is hypothesized to be related in this way to excess demand in the product market. Solving (4.3.12) for DED and substituting this result into (4.3.11) yields the price equation given in (4.3.13).

The constant term is excluded from (4.3.13) in order to be consistent with the Classical market theory. When McCallum does include the constant, it proves insignificant. When fitted over the 1950-60 period, the coefficients of (4.3.13) are all highly significant, with the R^2 being .06 lower than that from the Rushdy and Lund Equation (4.3.10) run over the same period. The response coefficients λ and δ, derived from the coefficients of $UI(+1)$ and UI, are both larger than .80, indicating very slow responses of both ΔP to DED and UI to DED. For this reason, McCallum respecifies (4.3.11) to (4.3.13) using second-order Pascal lag distributions instead of the Koyck lag distributions. This enables weights to increase for several periods before decreasing. The results indicate a faster response of ΔP to DED but not of UI to DED. Therefore, no definite conclusion as to the superiority of one lag distribution over another may be drawn. Still, however, using only lagged price and UI McCallum has developed a price equation that measures up strongly to Nield's (4.3.8) and Rushdy and Lund's (4.3.10) equations.

Phipps extended the Nield analysis into the market hypothesis of pricing. However, instead of using UI he used a DED measure along with cost variables. The DED measure chosen is the demand rachet variable developed by Kuh. Phipps does his analysis on six-month data over the 1957-67 period for four British industries (all of Nield's except food). In general, the best equation is given in (4.3.14).

$$P = \alpha_0 + \alpha_1 ULC + \alpha_2 PM + \alpha_3 DR + \alpha_4 DR(-1) \qquad (4.3.14)$$
$$+ \alpha_5 P(-1) + \mu_1$$

$$DR = Q/(QP \cdot g^{t-p})$$
g = growth rate in capacity
Q = output
QP = peak output in a previous period
p = peak time period

ULCN is substituted for ULC in some regressions but in general is not as significant. Rate of change in output is included instead of DR and has approximately the same significance. Both of these variables have an expected positive influence on prices and reflect market hypothesis (2.10). A version of

(4.3.14) is run which excludes $P(-1)$; however, the fit of this equation is not nearly as good. Equation (4.3.14) has a better fit for the industries studied than does (4.3.8). It must be remembered that both Nield and Phipps fitted their industry equations to very small samples ($n = 19$ for Nield; $n = 20$ for Phipps). However, Phipps has demonstrated the importance of a *DED* measure, in addition to the cost variables that are in Nield's formulation, in explaining price formation.

Schultze and Tryon:
The Brookings Model Study

Schultze and Tryon developed the price and wage equations of the Brookings econometric model in the early 1960s. One interesting aspect is that price formation at two different levels of aggregation, sector and industry, is studied. Furthermore, at the sector level, nonmanufacturing and other sectors are studied in addition to manufacturing sectors (see Table 3-8). Thus, the coverage of price formation is broader than in prior econometric models (most notably Liu, and Klein and Ball), providing insight into price behavior that was not previously possible. Only the price equations developed for manufacturing sectors and industries will be discussed in this section. These equations are all fitted to quarterly data in level form over the 1948-60 period. Using data in level form results in a higher collinearity among costs and prices than when data in change form are used and thus can tend to make price behavior appear to be more cost-dependent than it actually is. Furthermore, the period studied includes the Korean War years, a time during which prices exhibited unusual behavior.

The general equation explaining sector price formation is given in (4.4.1).

$$P = \alpha_0 + \alpha_1 ULCN + \alpha_2 (ULCN + UCCAN) \qquad (4.4.1)$$
$$+ \alpha_3 (ULC - ULCN) + \alpha_4 PM + \alpha_5 PMN$$
$$+ \alpha_6 [(-)(CUI - CUIN)] + \alpha_7 [(+)(CUI - CUIN)]$$
$$+ \alpha_8 [(INV/Q) - (INV/Q)^T] + \mu$$

where CUI = capacity utilization index
$CUIN$ = normal capacity utilization index
INV/Q = inventory-output ratio
$(INV/Q)T$ = trend of inventory output ratio
PM = material price
PMN = normal materials price
$UCCAN$ = normal unit capital consumption allowances (CCA per unit of gross product originating)

ULC = unit labor cost
$ULCN$ = normal unit labor cost

This formulation expresses the primary relationships between price and both long-run and short-run cost factors as well as deviations of actual excess demand measures from their long-run normal levels. Material price is included in both short-run and long-run forms whereas unit labor costs enter in both normal and deviation of actual from normal forms. This manner of including labor cost regressors does enable short-run productivity behavior to influence price formation. Capital cost is represented by the term $UCCAN$, which represents depreciation spread over a long period of time. Asymmetrical demand influence is tested by entering separate regressors for positive and negative deviations of actual capacity utilization from its normal level. The other excess demand indicator, the inventory-output ratio, is believed to have its normal behavior represented by its trend value over time. The a priori signs for all coefficients except α_0 and α_8 are positive, with α_7 expected to be greater than α_6 if the asymetrical behavior of prices and capacity utilization is borne out. However, one could argue for α_8 assuming a positive sign if a firm views increased inventories in terms of increased costs of holding inventories and adjusts its price accordingly. A ratio of unfilled orders to inventories also is entered as a regressor but is found insignificant. Equation (4.4.1) embodies modified versions of several of the price hypotheses from Chapter 2; namely, short-run cost hypotheses (2.2) and (2.3), long-run cost hypothesis (2.6) and market hypothesis (2.10). The inventory-output ratio was formed using both current and constant dollar data. The constant dollar formulation, with a higher level of significance, was retained. The inventory-output term used is actually an inventory-value added term. Since sales is not explained in the Brookings model, the inventory-sales ratio, which may be conceptually superior especially at the industry level, could not be used.

The best equations found for the durables and nondurables manufacturing sectors are given in (4.4.2) and (4.4.3), respectively.

$$P = \beta_0 + \beta_1 \, ULCN + \beta_2 \, (ULC - ULCN) \tag{4.4.2}$$

$$+ \beta_3 \, [(\frac{INV}{Q(-1)}) - (\frac{INV}{Q(-1)})^T] + \mu_1$$

$$P = \gamma_0 + \gamma_1 \, ULCN + \gamma_2 \, PM \tag{4.4.3}$$

$$+ \gamma_3 \, [(\frac{INV}{Q(-1)}) - (\frac{INV}{Q(-1)})^T) + \mu_2$$

The fit of the durables equation (R^2 = .97) is superior to that of the nondurables equation (R^2 = .90). The term $ULC - ULCN$ is highly significant in the durable goods equation and insignificant in the nondurable goods equation. $ULCN$ is significant in both equations although it is twice as significant in the durable goods price equation. PM is significant only in the nondurable goods price equation. However, the insignificance of PM in (4.4.2) could be attributed to the data series used, which is the imported materials price index. In (4.4.3) the agricultural output price series is used for PM and is highly significant. Refinements in the materials price indexes used in both sectors are necessary in order to more closely represent the actual materials that go into the production of the final products. The asymmetrical relationship of capacity utilization and price is not significant, with the CUI terms often entering with negative signs. Therefore, the CUI terms were dropped from the final equation. However, if full capacity is defined as the output of the firm when it is operating at the minimum point on its average cost curve, then a negative sign is quite plausible if the firm is operating below full capacity. The inventory-output term has approximately the same significance in explaining price behavior in both sectors. All regressors in the final equations as well as all rejected variables are introduced in both lagged and unlagged form. Only the lagged version of the excess demand variable is more significant than its unlagged form.

The general price equation that best describes industrial price formation, at mainly the SIC two-digit level of aggregation, differs slightly from the sector price equation given in (4.4.1). It may be expressed as follows:

$$P = \delta_0 + \delta_1 ULCN + \delta_2 (ULCN + UCCAN) \qquad (4.4.4)$$
$$+ \delta_3 (ULC - ULCN) + \delta_4 PM$$
$$+ \delta_5 [(-)(CUI - CUIN)] + \delta_6 [(+)(CUI - CUIN)]$$
$$+ \delta_7 [(-)(CUIS - CUISN)]$$
$$+ \delta_8 [(+)(CUIS - CUISN)] + \mu$$

where $CUIS$ = capacity utilization index of the principal supplying industry
$CUISN$ = normal form of $CUIS$

Equation (4.4.4) differs from (4.4.1) in its exclusion of the inventory-output ratio regressor and the introduction of a form of the capacity utilization index based on the operations of the principal supplying industry. This variable is meant to represent the case where excess demand for materials (i.e., for the products of the supplying industry) is not fully adjusted by a price change (i.e., in PM if PM is a good indicator of material price) in the supplying industry so that its capacity limitations act as a capacity limit on the industry producing the final product. The $CUIS$ term is therefore an indirect measure of capacity utilization in the final product industry. The final product industry has an excess demand for materials from the supplying industry, which if not completely covered by *PM* adjustments will be reflected by the *CUIS,P* relationship in (4.4.4).

The explanation of price formation at the industry level is dominated by cost factors, as it was at the sector level. The cost factors *ULCN* and *PM* are most significant in nondurable goods industries whereas the cost factors *ULCN* + *UCCAN*, *ULC* – *ULCN*, and *PM* are most significant in the durable goods industries. Furthermore, the coefficient of *PM* is in general more significant and a higher value than that of *ULC* – *ULCN*, indicating that short-run changes in material costs are more readily passed on as final product price increases than are short-run changes in labor costs. However, at the industry level *PM* is highly collinear with *ULCN*, which makes it difficult to attain good estimates of the coefficients. The significance of the regressor that includes a measure of capital costs in the durable goods industries is to be expected, given the more capital intensive structure of those industries. The capacity utilization variables in general are insignificant. Schultze and Tryon admit the incompleteness of their industry price analysis, because of time constraints. Still, their study is the first to specify general price equations for a large number of two-digit SIC industries. The Eckstein and Wyss study, examined in a following section, goes considerably beyond this study in the analysis of industry price formation.

The Fromm and Eckstein Study

The price equations specified in the Fromm and Eckstein study are similar to those in the Brookings model. However, there are three notable differences in their structures. First, the excess demand variables are not specified in the Fromm and Eckstein equations in a form that reflects asymmetrical price-excess demand relationships. Second, the Fromm and Eckstein study considers lagged price as a regressor. Third, Fromm and Eckstein include the profit rate on capital, explicitly representing target rate of return pricing, as a regressor. Schultze and Tryon, in considering *UCCAN*, are instead representing fixed cost in their price equation. A general price equation of Fromm and Eckstein (which is not estimated) is given in (4.5.1).

$$P = \alpha_0 + \alpha_1 P(-1) + \alpha_2 ULC + \alpha_3 ULCN \qquad (4.5.1)$$
$$+ \alpha_4 (ULC - ULCN) + \alpha_5 PM + \alpha_6 CUI$$
$$+ \alpha_7 ((UNF/S)(-1)) + \alpha_8 PR + \mu$$

where CUI = capacity utilization index
         PM = material price

PR = profit rate on capital (= after-tax rate of return on real capital, corrected by CUI)

UNF/S = unfilled orders-sales ratio

ULC = unit labor cost

$ULCN$ = normal unit labor costs

Equation (4.5.1) embodies several of the price hypotheses described in Chapter 2. Short-run cost hypothesis (2.2) is represented in part by PM whereas short-run cost hypothesis (2.3) is represented in part by ULC. Long-run cost hypotheses (2.6) and (2.7) are expressed by PR and $ULCN$, respectively. Finally, market hypothesis (2.10) is represented by both CUI and the lagged (UNF/S) term. The a priori signs for all coefficients except α_0 and α_8 in (4.5.1) are positive. Note that besides including $ULCN$ and $ULC - ULCN$ as regressors, ULC itself is also considered. Fromm and Eckstein view the cost-price relationship as shifting gradually as the complexion of industry changes from highly competitive to highly oligopolistic. In highly competitive situations, ULC is the relevant variable, since prices respond to both cost and productivity considerations. As industry conditions become mildly oligopolistic, both actual ULC and normal ULC (short-run productivity changes netted out) may each be partially influential in explaining price behavior. The regressor $ULC - ULCN$ may be the most reasonable cost indicator for this situation. Of course, if ULC and $ULCN$ are the same, it has a zero effect. For this reason, ULC is also included as a regressor. Finally, in the highly oligopolistic case, prices are set on the basis of only long-run costs and $ULCN$ is the appropriate regressor. The price index for materials is included in place of a unit material cost measure because of the lack of accurate data regarding materials consumed per unit of output.

Fromm and Eckstein fit variants of Equation (4.5.1) to quarterly data over the 1954-65 period for total, durables, and nondurables manufacturing. The price equations were fitted to three different forms of data, first difference data being the preferred form. Even though problems of autocorrelation and multicollinearity are reduced by using data in first difference form, errors of measurement are large relative to actual price movements, since the quarter-to-quarter price movements are so small.

Fromm and Eckstein include PR as a regressor representing the target return on capital. It is significant in the price equation for the durables sector. However, they treat this as "one intriguing novelty in these equations to which we would not wish to attach excessive weight." They also discuss the role in the price equation of the capital-standard output ratio as a regressor, with its coefficient being the estimate of the target return. However, this approach is not pursued further because of a lack of sufficient data. The best price equation for the durables and total manufacturing sectors is nearly identical and is given in (4.5.2). The best price equation for the nondurables sector is given in (4.5.3).

$$\Delta P = \alpha_0 + \alpha_1 \Delta P(-1) + \alpha_2 \Delta ULCN + \alpha_3 \Delta ULCN(-1) \qquad (4.5.2)$$
$$+ \alpha_4 (ULC - ULCN) + \alpha_5 \Delta PM + \alpha_6 CUI + \mu$$

$$\Delta P = \beta_0 + \beta_1 \Delta ULC + \beta_2 \Delta PM + \beta_3 \Delta PM(-1) \qquad (4.5.3)$$
$$+ \beta_4 CUI + \mu$$

Equation (4.5.2) when fitted to durables or total manufacturing has an R^2 between .60 and .70, and all the coefficients are significant (with t-values of at least 2.00). Note that PR enters the durables equation significantly whereas UNF/S enters the total manufacturing equation significantly. However, the overall fit of the equations containing these variables is not significantly better than that of (4.5.2). The coefficient of determination of (4.5.3), when fitted to nondurables manufacturing, is less than .50, and all variables except ULC are significant. The labor cost variable is more significant in the durable goods equation whereas the materials cost variable is more significant in the nondurable goods equation.

The constant terms in (4.5.2) and (4.5.3) are negative, reflecting the downward movement in prices resulting from increased productivity and technological change. Whereas Schultze and Tryon tested for asymmetrical behavior in the price-excess demand relationship, Fromm and Eckstein perform similar tests on the price-cost relationship. First, $ULC - ULCN$ is divided into two variables, depending on sign. The coefficient on $+(ULC - ULCN)$ is larger in value and twice as significant as that on $-(ULC - ULCN)$ for durables manufacturing, but the other results are mixed. Equations (4.5.2) and (4.5.3) are also reestimated over sample periods in which quarters of estimated price decline are omitted. In general, the coefficients of the cost variables are larger in the latter runs, indicating a larger than average price response to cost increases.

Despite a thorough theoretical discussion of target return pricing, the only long-run effects on price behavior that are sufficiently tested are those relating to $ULCN$ versus ULC. Further analysis, including other long-run costs (e.g., interest cost on fixed capital) and target rate of return considerations, would enable more careful distinctions between different pricing hypotheses to be made. By extending their present work to less aggregate data (i.e., industries), Fromm and Eckstein could have made a valuable contribution concerning this aspect.

The Laden Study

In the earlier of his two studies, Laden[172] specifies a multiequation model of the output market for the manufacturing sector. He develops structural demand, production, and price equations along with the cost minimization conditions for production. The model is essentially a supply-demand representation of the pricing process, in which the resulting reduced form price equation has the exogenous variables in the demand and supply functions as its regressors. His model takes the following form.

$$Q = f(P,Y,POG) \tag{4.6.1}$$

$$Q = g(H,MATO,K) \tag{4.6.2}$$

$$f_H \cdot PM = f_{MATO} \cdot AHE \tag{4.6.3}$$

$$P = h(AHE,PM,K,Q) \tag{4.6.4}$$

where $\quad AHE$ = average hourly earnings
f_H = marginal productivity of labor
f_{MATO} = marginal productivity of materials
H = labor in man-hours
K = capital stock
$MATO$ = materials produced outside the manufacturing sector
PM = material price
POG = price index for other final goods and services
Q = output
Y = income of purchasers of manufactured goods

Equation (4.6.1) is the demand function, which includes price, income, and substitute goods price as regressors. (4.6.2) is a production function, which includes both variable inputs (H and $MATO$) and fixed capital as regressors. (4.6.3) is derived from the first-order conditions of cost minimization, subject to the production function given in (4.6.2). Equation (4.6.4) is the structural price equation in the model and is consistent with both marginal cost and average cost pricing theories. The regressors are justified as follows: (1) output determines the position on a selected set of cost curves; (2) capital stock determines the relevant set of short-run cost curves; and (3) variable factor prices determine the height of the cost curves for a given capital stock. P, Q,H, and $MATO$ are considered endogenous in the model. Solving the model (4.6.1) to (4.6.4) yields the following derived, reduced form price equation in first difference form.

$$\Delta P = \alpha_0 + \alpha_1 \Delta AHE + \alpha_2 \Delta PM + \alpha_3 \Delta K + \alpha_4 \Delta Y \tag{4.6.5}$$

Laden also allows lagged P to enter (4.6.5) as a regressor if the adjustment to equilibrium is not made fully within the market period. (4.6.5) reflects short-run cost hypothesis (2.2) and market hypothesis (2.10). The inclusion of POG and K

as regressors sets this equation apart from others developed in major price studies.

Equation (4.6.5) is fitted to quarterly data in both the first difference and the first difference of the log forms over the 1954-66 period. The dependent variable in the analysis is the finished goods price in United States manufacturing. The coefficients of ΔP lagged and ΔPOG are insignificant. The insignificance of POG may be partly attributable to the high level of aggregation of the data in this study, making it difficult to show a relationship between substitute products. The insignificance of P lagged is a common empirical result, given that change data and not level data are being used in the analysis. The coefficients of ΔAHE, ΔPM, ΔK, and ΔY are all significant, with all but that for ΔY being positive. The signs for ΔY and ΔK are consistent with average cost pricing if one assumes that the firm is operating on the downward-sloping portion of its average cost curve. In this case, higher demands will mean lower unit costs and lower price whereas expanding K implies higher fixed cost, with higher average fixed cost, average total cost, and therefore higher price. The coefficients of determination from the equations fitted are around .74. An interesting point concerning Laden's study is the price data used. He uses the stage of processing wholesale price indexes in order to specify output-input price relations. The use of wholesale output price indexes for sectors and industries makes such an explicit specification more difficult to make unless input price indexes for each sector and industry are developed (see the Eckstein and Wyss study). Laden tested the additional DED measures INV, NOR, UNF, INV/S and CUI to determine both the significance of each and whether or not each affects the significance of the variables included in (4.6.5). Only INV is significant, as it enters with a positive sign, consistent with average cost pricing. Only CUI affects significantly the coefficients of other included variables, being highly correlated with Y. However, CUI is insignificant, and Laden argues that Y alone should be included in the price equation, since it is contained in the structural demand equation from which, along with the supply equation, is derived the reduced form price equation. (Note that CUI is a measure of the effect of demand pressure on price.)

The Eckstein and Wyss Study

Eckstein and Wyss analyze industrial price formation at the two- and three-digit SIC levels of aggregation. The study is noteworthy in the following respects. (1) It is the first thorough study of the relationship between pricing and market structure since the Yordon study on four-digit SIC industries in 1961; (2) macro variables are in all cases rejected as having an influential effect on industrial price formation in favor of industry-specific cost and demand variables; and (3) the final equations for each industry are corrected for autocorrelation (where present) by a nonlinear regression technique.

Single-equation price models are fitted to quarterly data in the form of two-quarter change on the average over the period 1954 to 1969. Equations containing various combinations of short-run cost variables (*AHE* and *PM*), long-run cost variables (interest rate and profit-equity ratio), *DED* variables (*CUI*, ΔCUI, and *SHP*), and lagged price as regressors are run for each industry. In addition to these industry-specific variables, the macro variables *GNP, Y,* and *PA* are entered as regressors. This analysis results in three general price equations being specified. Each of the equations has special relevance in explaining price formation within a particular type of industry, the types being determined on the basis of the degree of market concentration within the industry. The price equations for each of the three industry divisions follow. Not all of the industries within each type have exactly these price equations. A particular industry may best be represented by a price equation of another type. However, the majority of industries within each type assume the following specifications:

$$P = \alpha_0 + \alpha_1 AHE + \alpha_2 r + \alpha_3 (\pi/EQ) + \mu_1 \qquad (4.7.1)$$

$$P = \beta_0 + \beta_1 AHE + \beta_2 PM + \beta_3 CUI + \mu_2 \qquad (4.7.2)$$

$$P = \gamma_0 + \gamma_1 AHE + \gamma_2 PM + \gamma_3 P(-1) + \mu_3 \qquad (4.7.3)$$

where AHE = average hourly earnings
 CUI = capacity utilization index
 PM = material price
 r = interest rate
 (π/EQ) = profit-equity ratio

Many variables, both industry and macro, have been excluded from the equations on the basis of significance levels of less than .05.

Equation (4.7.1) explains price formation best in highly concentrated industries (SICs 371, 21, and 333). This equation contains short-run cost hypothesis (2.2) as well as long-run cost hypotheses (2.5) and (2.7) in its specification. Note that both a long-run cost variable (i.e., r) and a long-run desired return variable (i.e., π/EQ) are contained in (4.7.1). Industries characterized by high degrees of concentration do not seem to be influenced by demand factors. Equation (4.7.2) explains price formation in moderately concentrated, oligopolistic industries (SICs 26, 28, 30, 36, 331, and 348) whereas Equation (4.7.3) best explains price formation in low-concentration, competitive industries (SICs 20, 22, 23, 24, 25, 32, and 35). This division by Eckstein and Wyss is confusing in that four of the industries placed in the competitive category (SICs 20, 22, 32, and 35) have concentration ratios of a high enough level that they classify better as oligopolistic. The only difference in specification between

(4.7.2) and (4.7.3) is the inclusion of CUI in (4.7.2), reflecting market hypothesis (2.10), and the exclusion of market measures in (4.7.3) in favor of the price adjustment mechanism ($P(-1)$). Short-run cost hypothesis (2.2) is reflected in both equations. Eckstein and Wyss feel that CUI is not significant in the price equation for competitive industries because the supply and demand are never far from equilibrium and therefore the CUI does not vary in a significant manner. The correction for first-order autocorrelation by means of nonlinear estimation is most common in the price equation (4.7.2) for oligopolistic industries.

The DED measure SHP is significant in the price equation for several industries (SICs 28, 371, 24, 26, and 35). The argument given for its significance is that these industries are highly capital intensive, so that a change in shipments (i.e., output) will raise their marginal cost curves more than it would in industries of less capital intensity.

The standard error of regression is much higher for the price equation (4.7.1) run on highly oligopolistic industries than for the others. Also, the coefficients of determination from (4.7.1) being fitted to SICs 371, 21, and 333 are lower ($R^2 \approx .55$) than those from (4.7.2) and (4.7.3) being fitted to the other industries ($R^2 \approx .75$). The fits of (4.7.2) and (4.7.3) to the appropriate industries are similar in terms of standard error of regression and R^2.

There are three weaknesses in the Eckstein and Wyss study. One is that no consideration is given to productivity as a regressor in the price equations. All three equations reflect strongly the relationship that price is a markup over factor prices; the relevance of different costs depends on the type of industry studied. It seems that productivity considerations may alter the price-cost relationship, especially in the competitive industries. Second, no IED measures are considered as regressors in the price equations. A variable such as the unemployment rate may be highly significant in explaining price formation in industries subject to large cyclical fluctuations (e.g., SIC 35, Machinery). Third, the PM variable for each industry is constructed using appropriate information from both the input-output table and the four-digit SIC price indexes regarding the inputs to each industry. Therefore, each PM is industry-specific, as is the wage variable. It would be more interesting if multiequation models for each industry had been developed with PM and AHE also endogenous. In this way price and wage behavior could have been thoroughly studied with regard to the factors that simultaneously underlie their behavior.

5

Industry Selection, Model Selection and Modification, and Organization of the Analysis

The preanalysis aspects of this research, including experimental design and data formation are highlighted in this chapter. It is divided into three sections: selection of sectors and industries, selection of models and modification of variables, and organization of the analysis. Additional discussions relating to market categorization of industries, sources of data, and preliminary analyses are contained in appendixes.

Sector and Industry Selection

This research concentrates exclusively on analyzing price behavior in selected industries of manufacturing sectors. The initial division of manufacturing activity is into two broad sectors, nondurables less food (*NGEF*) and durables (*DG*). Food is excluded throughout the analysis, since its price behavior, especially at the raw stage and for unprocessed consumer foods, has been found to be unlike that of other nondurables and often affected to a large extent by noneconomic factors (e.g., the weather). A further subdivision into subsectors within each of these main sectors is then made. *NGEF* is divided into consumer nondurables less food (*NCG*) and mixed nondurables less food (*NMG*). *DG* is divided into consumer durables (*DCG*), producer durables (*PDG*), and mixed durables (*DMG*). The mixed categories include industries whose output either is used in the production of or is appropriate as final output for both consumer goods and nonconsumer goods (i.e., materials, producer goods). Within each of these divisions, industries can be categorized according to the type of goods each produces. Therefore, each industry can be considered as being either a final products industry (*FP*), intermediate products industry (*IP*), or mixed (i.e., both final and intermediate) products industry (*MP*). This division by type of product is based on the market classification codes for SIC manufacturing industries (see Appendix B) and relates directly to the stage of processing concept.

The division of total manufacturing as described above is depicted in Table 5-1. Within each of the cells are placed industries that represent the different combinations of categorization factors. The industries are selected from the two-, three-, and four-digit SIC industry classifications in order to be as representative as possible of the various cells in Table 5-1. It is apparent that at the two-digit level most industries are of the mixed product type whereas at the

Table 5-1

Sector and Industry Cross-Classification

		Product Divisions		
		Final Product (FP)	Intermediate Product (IP)	Mixed Product (MP)
Sector Divisions — Nondurable Goods except Food (NGEF)	Nondurable consumer goods except food (NCG)	SICs 21, 227, 23, 2111, and 3141	(Not Applicable)	(Not Applicable)
	Nondurable mixed goods except food (NMG)	SIC 301	SIC 29	SICs 22 and 30
Durable Goods (DG)	Durable consumer goods (DCG)	SICs 251 and 3263	(Not Applicable)	(Not Applicable)
	Durable producer goods (DPG)	SIC 3541	SICs 331, 341, 3562, and 333	SIC 35
	Durable mixed goods (DMG)	SIC 25	SIC 24	SICs 34, 36, and 371

three- and four-digit levels of aggregation the designation of an industry as strictly a final or an intermediate product industry becomes more appropriate. It follows that more homogeneity is to be expected in the products of an industry at the lower levels of aggregation. The industries shown in the various categories in Table 5-1 were chosen over others in the same categories on the basis of the availability and reliability of their data. Note that all consumer goods are considered as final products, which results in four "not applicable" cells in Table 5-1.

Table 5-2 contains selected characteristics for each of the industries included in Table 5-1. In addition to the information for each concerning type of good, type of product, and level of aggregation, Table 5-2 also contains the 1967 four-firm concentration ratio for each industry and relative rankings of the industries with regard to capital intensity and the production to stock-production to order distinction. The footnotes for Table 5-2 contain detailed descriptions of the methods used in ranking these industries. Tables 5-1 and 5-2 suggest that a broad spectrum of U.S. manufacturing activity is represented by the industries selected for the analysis. The next section will review the specifications of the price models that will be reestimated on these industries.

Model Selection and Variable Modification

The specifications of the models chosen for reestimation on the industries discussed in the preceding section are reviewed in Table 5-3; a summary of each model is given in Table 5-4. The models are arranged according to 10 hypothesis categories, and the original study in which each model was formulated is noted. These hypothesis categories and the models in each are broadly representative of the various pricing hypotheses, both individually and in combination, that are discussed in Chapter 2. This is in fact the major reason for selecting the models listed in Table 5-3 for reestimation in this research. Certain hypothesis categories are absent because of the lack of well-formulated models to represent them; most notably absent is a category representing a hybrid of the *LRC* and *DED* hypotheses. The analysis in Chapter 7 will conclude, however, that the price behavior of certain industries is best explained by a formulation representing this hypothesis.

The lag structure specified in the original study (see Chapter 4) for each equation in Table 5-3 is retained. In most cases, the procedures used in specifying the lags are not clear. Therefore, pending the results of further work on strict empirical specification of the best lag structure in each equation for each industry in Table 5-2, the original specifications were adopted.

Whenever possible, the variables contained in the models reestimated are constructed in the same manner and represent the same cost or excess demand measures as they do in their original studies. However, there are certain exceptions, as follows, in which a different variable is more appropriate.

1. *PM* in the original Klein and Ball study[35] is an import price variable, since a large proportion of the inputs into British manufacturing are imported. This variable is not appropriate for U.S. manufacturing, so various stages of processing material prices (macro) and industry-specific material prices (micro) are used instead.

2. *TAX* in the Klein and Ball study is represented as the indirect business tax-personal consumption expenditure ratio. However, indirect business taxes are in general levied at the retail level, and the corporate tax is the more appropriate tax to consider in the analysis of manufacturing prices. Therefore, the tax variable used is similar to that of Moffat[118] and is formulated as the ratio of provision for federal income tax to total sales. The expected sign is positive, reflecting an increase in the rate of change of price as taxes become a larger proportion of sales.

3. *FDQ* is the only *DED* measure used in the Phipps[182] equation. In his original work, the Kuh demand rachet was also tried, but the results with the two variables were nearly identical and *FDQ* was chosen as the *DED* measure.

4. *ULC* and *ULCN* for the models in which one or both appear are constructed in this research using *AHE*, *PP*, and *PPN*, the latter being a 12-term moving average of *PP*. The *ULC* and *ULCN* formulations are the same as those in a majority of the studies. Exceptions are the Fromm and Eckstein study[81], in which *ULCN* is based on a regression on *CUI* and not *PPN*, and the Nield study, in which a specified growth rate of *PP* is used instead of *PPN*.

5. Normalized inventories are used in place of desired and equilibrium

Table 5-2
Industry Characteristics

SIC	Industry	Type of Product[a]	Type of Good	K/TMH[b] (Avg.)	INV/UNF[c] (Avg.)	Concentration[d] Ratio
21	Tobacco	FP	NCG	.250		72.5
2111	Cigarettes	FP	NCG	.343		80.0
22	Textile mill products	MP	NMG	.194	1.912	34.8
227	Floor covering mills	FP	NCG	.286	4.092	33.3
23	Apparel and related products	FP	NMG	.040		17.6
24	Lumber and wood products	IP	DMG	.165	2.525	15.4
25	Furniture and fixtures	FP	DMG	.107	1.756	16.2
251	Household furniture	FP	DCG	.099	2.175	13.4
29	Petroleum and coal products	IP	NMG	1.797		31.9
30	Rubber and plastic products	MP	NMG	.286		36.8
301	Tires and tubes	FP	NMG	.534		71.0
3141	Shoes, except rubber	FP	NCG	.033	1.981	27.0
3263	Fine earthenware and food utensils	FP	DCG	.083	4.136	51.0
331	Primary ferrous metals	IP	DPG	.758	1.192	51.0
333	Primary nonferrous metals	IP	DPG	.558	1.718	53.0
34	Fabricated metal industries	MP	DMG	.210	.859	27.9
341	Metal cans	IP	DPG	.434	.600	70.0
35	Machinery, except electrical	MP	DPG	.243	.891	35.9
3541	Machine tools—metal-cutting types	FP	DPG	.263	.589	21.0
3562	Ball and roller bearings	IP	DPG	.333	.830	54.0
36	Electrical machinery	MP	DMG	.206	.601	41.2
371	Motor vehicles and parts	MP	DMG	.393	1.174	93.0

aSee Table 5-1.

bK/TMH is the average total man-hours worked–capital stock ($) ratio for each industry over the 1958-69 period. This ratio serves to rank the industries relative to one another regarding capital and labor intensities. The larger the K/TMH, the more capital intensive the industry and vice versa. These numbers are not meant to be interpreted in the absolute sense. Man-hours is used instead of compensation in order to remove any upward or downward bias that might exist due to significant differences in the wage rate and/or other compensation from industry to industry. Man-hours is felt to be a truer measure of the labor input in an industry with which to compare the capital stock used. The capital stock series for each industry is generated by the method used by Laden[172] and is explained later in this section.

cThe average inventory-unfilled order ratio over the 1958-69 period is used (when possible) to rank the industries with regard to the production to stock (PTS) and production to order (PTO) distinction. This distinction was originally advanced by Zarnowitz and later used by Courchene. The higher the ratio, the more PTS is the industry.

dAll of the concentration ratios are based on 1967 data except for SIC 2111, for which only 1958 data are available. Furthermore, all ratios represent 100 percent of the shipments of the industry except for the following: SIC 22, 95 percent; SIC 23, 95 percent; SIC 30, 90 percent; SIC 333, 60 percent; SIC 34, 96 percent; and SIC 35, 98 percent.

Table 5-3
Classification of Price Models by Hypothesis Categories

Hypothesis Category	Model	Regressors
1. SRC	Klein and Ball 1	AWE, PM(−2), TAX
	Nield 2	PM, P(−1)
	Eckstein and Wyss 1	AHE, PM, P(−1)
2. LRC,SRC	Nield 1	ULCN, PM, PM(−1), P(−1)
	Eckstein and Wyss 2	AHE, RLT, PREQ
3. SRC,DED(Micro)	Phipps	ULC, PM, FDQ, FDQ(−1), P(−1)
	Eckstein and Wyss 3	AHE, PM, SHP, P(−1)
	Fromm and Eckstein 2	ULC, PM, PM(−1), CUI
	Eckstein and Wyss 4	AHE, PM, CUI, SHP
4. SRC,DED(Macro)	Laden 1	AHE, PM, Y
5. SRC,DED(Micro,Macro)	Laden 2	AHE, PM, K, Y
6. SRC,DED(SR and LR Micro)	Liu	AHE, FDINV, FDINVN, P(−1), P(−2)
	Courchene	AHE, PM, FD(I−IN)
7. SRC,IED	Rushdy and Lund	ULC(−1), PM(−1), URI(−1)
8. IED	McCallum	URI, URI(+1), P(−1)
9. SRC,DED,IED	Klein and Ball 2	PM(−2), TAX, 4TMAUR, Q, PP, 4TMAP(−1)
10. SRC,LRC,DED	Schultze and Tryon 1	ULCN, ULC−ULCN, FDIST(−1)
	Schultze and Tryon 2	ULCN, PM,FDIST(−1)
	Eckstein and Wyss 5	AHE, RLT, PREQ, SHP
	Fromm and Eckstein 1	ULCN, ULCN(−1), ULC−ULCN, PM, CUI

Table 5-4
Summary of Characteristics of Selected Price Models

Model	Aggregation	Frequency	Data Form
Klein and Ball 1	Economy	Q	Level
Nield 2	Industry	Q	Level
Nield 1	Sector	Q	Level
Phipps	Industry	6-month Obs.	Level
Eckstein and Wyss 3	Competitive industries (low-concentration)	Q	Weighted PCH
Fromm and Eckstein 2	Nondurables subsector	Q	Level,FD,4Q–PCH
Eckstein and Wyss 2	Oligopolistic industries (moderate-concentration)	Q	Weighted PCH
Laden 1	Sector	Q	FDLN
Laden 2	Sector	Q	FDLN
Liu	Economy	Q	PCH
Courchene	Sector, industry	Q	FD
Rushdy and Lund	Sector	Q	Level,FD
McCallum	Sector	Q	FD
Klein and Ball 2	Economy	Q	Level
Schultze and Tryon 1	Durables subsector	Q	Level
Schultze and Tryon 2	Nondurables subsector	Q	Level
Eckstein and Wyss 1	Highly-concentrated industries	Q	Weighted PCH
Fromm and Eckstein 1	Durables subsector	Q	Level,FD,4Q–PCH

Note: Additional facts regarding these studies are given in Tables 3-1 through 3-9.

inventories in reestimating the Liu[111] and Courchene[73] models. A 12-term (i.e., 3 years for quarterly data) moving average is used to construct the normalized inventory variable, after experimentation with moving averages of other lengths. The Liu equation with desired and equilibrium inventories is estimated for nine of the industries analyzed and compared with the results of the equation containing normalized inventories. The fits of the equations are very similar, as is discussed in detail in Chapter 6. Because of the less complex nature of *INVN*, it was chosen for use in the analysis. (See "The Liu Study" in Chapter 4 for a thorough description of Liu's and Courchene's inventory variables.)

Other than these exceptions, all variables used in reestimating the selected models of price formation are constructed in this research as they were originally, although the forms they assume may differ.

Table 5-5
Form of Regressors

Regressor	Meaning	Form(s)[a]	Influence
PM	material price index	PCH	SRC
TAX	ratio of provision for tax to sales	ratio	Tax
AWE	average weekly earnings	PCH	SRC
ULC	unit labor cost	PCH	SRC
ULCN	standard unit labor cost	PCH	LRC
P(−1)	lagged price	PCH	Lagged price adjustment
FDQ	change in output	FD(PCH)	DED
AHE	average hourly earnings	PCH	SRC
SHP	shipments	PCH	DED
CUI	capacity utilization index	Level	DED(capacity pressure)
Y	disposable income	PCH(FD)	DED(macro)
K	capital stock	PCH(FD)	DED
FDINV	change in inventories	FD(PCH)	DED
FDINVN	change in standard inventories	FD(PCH)	DED(LR)
FDI,IN(≡FD(I − IN))	change in difference between INV and INVN	FD(PCH)	DED(LR,SR)
URI	inverse of unemployment rate	Inverse	IED(macro)
4TMAP(−1)	four-term moving average of lagged price	PCH	Lagged price
Q	output	PCH	DED
PP	productivity	PCH	SRC

75

4TMAUR	four-term moving average of the unemployment rate	Rate	IED(macro)
DULC,N($\equiv$ ULC − ULCN)	difference between actual and standard unit labor costs	Difference(PCH)	SRC and LRC
FDIST(−1)	first difference of inventory− sales ratio minus the lagged trend value of inventory−sales ratio	Difference in ratios	DED(LR,SR)
PREQ	ratio of profit after tax to stockholders' equity	Ratio	LRC(target return)
RLT($\equiv$ r)	long-term interest rate (Moody's AAA bond rate)	FD(Level,PCH)	LRC

aForms in parentheses are alternative forms that were tried.

Organization of the Analysis

All regressions to reestimate previous models on the new data bodies (see Chapter 6) and to improve upon specifications of the previous models (see Chapter 7) are run on quarterly, seasonally adjusted data, with the regression in percentage change form. The method of estimation used is ordinary least squares; the maximum time period analyzed is 1958:1 to 1969:2. The time period coverage is limited mainly because of (1) the lack of *SEC-FTC* data prior to 1958, (2) the unavailability of *SHP, INV*, and *Q* prior to 1953 at best, and (3) the lack of price data for the SIC two-digit and selected three-digit industries beyond 1969:2. For some industries, the time period for analysis is considerably less. Descriptions of both the data and the time period of analysis for each industry are given in Appendix A.

The structural explanation of price behavior in each of the selected manufacturing industries, including examination of the varying rates of inflation which have been most apparent since 1965, is the main focus of this research. Price equations are not estimated for the sectors and subsectors of Table 5-1, since the emphasis of this study is on price behavior in the two-, three-, and four-digit industries. Given a solid structural explanation of each industry's price movements, various policies that would serve to dampen inflationary price movements can be hypothesized and simulated. The emphasis on inflation rates and policy analysis makes the quarterly percentage change in price the most relevant dependent variable to use. Further, the use of percentage change data tends to lessen the effects of multicollinearity and autocorrelation, which are so apparent when level data are used. In most cases, the regressors also are expressed in percentage change form. However, certain excess demand variables (e.g., *CUI* and *UR*), ratio variables (e.g., *PREQ*), and variables that deviate from a trend or normal level are not in percentage change form. A complete description of the final form of each variable and of alternative forms tried is given in Table 5-5. The source and construction of all variables used in the final analysis are described in Appendix A. Furthermore, in some cases more than one formulation was possible for a given variable (e.g., output); these alternative formulations are described and reasons for their rejection given in Appendix A.

The analysis that follows is divided into three parts. In Chapter 6, the models shown in Table 5-3 are reestimated on percentage change data for each of the industries shown in Table 5-2, the time period of analysis varying to some extent among industries. The results are discussed according to industry coverage of a hypothesis category and in terms of the best combinations of hypotheses for explaining price behavior in various categories of industries. The results from each of the reestimated price equations in this study can not be directly compared to each equation's results from its original study unless the original study was also performed on percentage change data. Therefore, for only the Laden and Liu equations may such a comparison be made. The results can not be compared because nonlinear data transformations occur between the level, log, and percentage change forms which can significantly change a regressor's effect on price. Therefore, cost variables that are extremely important when level data are used (see the Schultze and Tryon original results) are not necessarily as important when percentage data are used (see "Category Ten" in Chapter 6).

A "best equation" is chosen for each industry from those reestimated, and tentative conclusions are drawn. The best equation for each industry is in general the one with the highest R^2. However, the proper signs and significance of the regressors is of utmost importance. The best equations are in turn divided into two groups, one for "best-fitting industries" and one for "worst-fitting industries" (see the introduction of Chapter 6). The analysis of Chapter 6 is extended in Chapter 7; the best price equation for each manufacturing industry is improved where possible through the use of modified lag specifications and alternative hypothesis combinations. Some of the final industry price equations that result are similar to those estimated in Chapter 6 whereas others are quite different.

Chapter 8 combines the results of Chapter 7 with consumer price index (*CPI*) equations (for the consumer goods industries) and/or material price index (*PM*) equations where appropriate (for those industries that contain *PM* in their price equations) into a stage of processing price model for each selected industry. The *CPI* and *PM* specifications are based on the results of previous analyses of price behavior. Details of these specifications are discussed by Popkin and Earl.[133] Ex post simulations within each industry are performed over the 1965:1 to 1969:2 period in order both to study the varying rates of inflation across industries and to examine the ability of the different industry pricing models to explain the respective rates of inflation. Policy simulations are then performed for the 1967:1 to 1969:2 period.

Reestimation of Existent Price Models

The 18 models from previous studies that are reestimated in this research have been grouped into the 10 general hypothesis categories shown in Table 5-3 on the basis of the hypotheses that each equation's specifications represent. Even though equations in the same category may have different regressors, these variables represent the price formation hypotheses of Chapter 2. Each model was fitted, using ordinary least squares, to each of the data bodies selected.

The results of the analysis are presented in this chapter in three ways. Initially, the results are discussed for all industries under each hypothesis category. An adjusted R^2 of .40 or higher is considered sufficient for an industry to be considered one of the best-fitting industries. In the hypothesis categories that include more than one price equation, some industries may have more than one price equation with an $R^2 \geqslant .40$. In these cases, the equation with the highest R^2 is chosen unless the coefficient signs in the other equations are more consistent with a priori notions. (Best-fitting equations are also termed "well explained.") The best-fitting industries are discussed in terms of category regarding (1) the most important determinant(s) of price change; (2) the significance of regressors; and (3) the expected and actual sign of each regressor. In the determination of the significance of regressors, a $t > 1.7$ is the criterion adopted. Given the average number of degrees of freedom in the analysis, this places the risk of Type I error at .10 or less for a one-tail test on each regression coefficient (i.e., given the expected sign of a coefficient, we are testing whether it is significantly different from zero). When possible, the industries are grouped within hypothesis categories using the information of Tables 5-1 and 5-2 (e.g., the second hypothesis category (LRC,SRC) may best explain price formation in consumer durables industries). This will allow tentative conclusions to be drawn concerning explanation of price behavior in certain types of industries.

Secondly, the best equation for each industry will be selected from among the 18 run on each. This will enable tentative conclusions to be drawn regarding which hypothesis categories best explain industrial price formation. These conclusions are tentative in that the hypothesis categories are only those formulated on the basis of previous studies. These results will be further improved in Chapter 7 for both individual industries and categories of industries, making use of (1) new combinations of hypotheses which were not contained in the models reestimated in this chapter but which are apparent after this analysis; (2) more careful specification of lag structure; (3) discussion of individual regressors and their significance in different industries; and (4) industry characteristics.

Finally, the industries will be grouped according to their characteristics, given in Tables 5-1 and 5-2. This results in the industries, represented by their best equations, being categorized in seven ways. Tentative conclusions are then drawn regarding differences in price behavior based on differences in industry characteristics.

Analysis by Hypothesis Categories

Category One: SRC

Three studies, by Klein and Ball, Nield, and Eckstein and Wyss, developed price equations representative of only the short-run cost (SRC) hypothesis. All three models include material cost as a regressor. The Klein and Ball model also includes labor cost and a tax variable, whereas Eckstein and Wyss include labor cost and a lagged price variable and Nield includes only the lagged price variable. All costs in this category are factor prices. The expected signs for all coefficients are positive. The term "all coefficients" does not include the constant term. The constant in many equations is positive, in many other equations negative. The sign it will assume depends on the regressors in a particular specification and their effect on the rate of change of price. If the estimated price equation overpredicts the average price change based on the average values of each of the regressors, then the constant will be negative, as seen by $\hat{\beta}_0 = \overline{Y} - \sum\limits_{i}^{k} \beta_i \overline{X}_i$.

The equations for the industries whose price behavior is well explained by one of these specifications are given in Table 6-1. No clear distinction can be drawn by type of product or type of good. However, all of the industries except SIC 22 have concentration ratios less than 28 percent and have a large number of establishments, indicating relatively competitive industries. Actual costs are more significant than normalized costs in such industries, which is to be expected.

The signs of the coefficients are as expected except those for $PM(-2)$ in industries 24 and 3541, which are negative but also insignificant. AWE is only marginally significant in SIC 24 but insignificant in industries 23 and 3541. Interpreting the effect of this variable in the pricing process is difficult, since it is the product of AHE and AWH. The tax variable is the most significant regressor in the three industries that follow the Klein and Ball specification. The price behavior of both SIC 25 and SIC 251 is explained well by the Nield equation, whereas the price behavior of only SIC 34 (but not 341) and SIC 3541 (but not 35) is explained well by the Klein and Ball and the Nield price equations. This contrast in the explanation of price behavior at different levels of aggregation within an industry could be attributed in part to the relationship of the part to the whole. SIC 251 accounts for nearly 65 percent of the value of shipments of SIC 25, whereas SICs 341 and 3541 account for only 8 percent and 4 percent,

Table 6-1

Hypothesis Category One (SRC): Best Industry Price Equations

SIC Industry	Regressors[a]							R², SEE, DW	Model
	Constant	AWE	PM(−2)	TAX	PM	P(−1)	AHE		
23	−1.747 (4.1)	.044 (1.2)	.032 (.6)	119.21 (4.6)				.486 .255 1.86	Klein and Ball 1
24	−5.028 (3.9)	.593 (1.8)	−.198 (.8)	255.116 (4.7)				.422 2.204 2.01	Klein and Ball 1
3541	−2.99 (3.4)	.070 (1.4)	−.052 (.2)	86.647 (4.1)				.472 .454 1.57	Klein and Ball 1
22	−0.591 (4.2)				.093 (.9)	.478 (5.2)	.666 (6.1)	.648 .595 1.27	Eckstein and Wyss 1
25	−0.005 (.1)				.033 (1.9)	.511 (4.3)	.223 (2.2)	.564 .280 2.44	Eckstein and Wyss 1
251	.148 (2.3)				.065 (3.8)	.544 (5.0)		.503 .305 2.35	Eckstein and Wyss 1
34	.102 (1.5)				.435 (3.4)	.385 (2.9)		.416 .347 1.86	Eckstein and Wyss 1

[a]The entries for each industry under each regressor are the regression coefficients and t-values (in parentheses). The adjusted coefficient of determination (R^2), standard error of the estimate (SEE), and Durbin-Watson statistic (DW) are also given.

respectively, of the value of shipments of SICs 34 and 35. The price equation of Eckstein and Wyss, which is rule of thumb modified by the inclusion of the lagged price, is superior in overall fit to the other two equations in this category.

Generally, the SRC hypothesis modified by TAX or $P(-1)$ does not explain industry price behavior very well. The adjusted R^2 for all industries not in Table 6-1 (with the exception of industries 35, 22, and 333) is less than .25 and in some cases negative. The SRC cost variable PM is itself significant in a wider range of industries than given in Table 6-1.

Category Two: SRC,LRC

Two price equation specifications from Nield and from Eckstein and Wyss represent this category of combined short-run and long-run (normalized) costs. The labor cost variable is normalized unit costs ($ULCN$) whereas the material cost is factor price (PM) in the Nield equation. However, the argument has been made that the material output ratio does not vary significantly in the short run, so that PM also is a proxy for unit material costs. Given this assumption, the Nield price equation is expressed in unit cost terms with the lagged price included. The Eckstein and Wyss equation includes a factor price labor regressor, a cost of capital variable ($FDRLT$), and a target rate of return variable ($PREQ$). The expected signs on all cost variables as well as on the lagged price are positive.

For all of the industries included in Table 6-2, the Nield specification is superior to that of Eckstein and Wyss. Neither specification fits well for the excluded industries. All of the industries in Table 6-2 except SIC 22 are durable goods industries. Assuming on the basis of previous results that durable goods prices are cost-dependent and less subject to market behavior, long-run costs can be expected to be an important regressor in these industries. However, this specification best fits SIC 22, the nondurable goods industry, with $ULCN$ also being most significant in this industry. Among the durable goods industries, in only SIC 25 is $ULCN$ significant. The signs of the coefficients are as expected for all variables except $PM(-1)$, which enters with a negative sign in some cases. This result is most probably caused by multicollinearity with PM. Both the long-run and short-run coefficients of the cost variables are lower than expected in all industries except SIC 22. The good explanation of SIC 22 price behavior is in contrast to the poor explanation of SIC 227 price behavior ($\overline{R}^2$ = .169; coefficient of $ULCN$ is negative); SIC 227 represents less than 10 percent of the value of shipments of SIC 22. Note in the case of industries 35 and 3541 that their adjusted R^2s are approximately equal whereas the standard error of estimate of SIC 3541 (.475) is considerably larger than that of SIC 35 (.290). This indicates a larger variance in the price of SIC 3541, which can be expected at lower levels of aggregation. As in hypothesis category one, the price behavior of both SIC 25 and SIC 251 is well explained by the same price equation.

Table 6-2
Hypothesis Category Two (LRC,SRC): Best Industry Price Equations

SIC Industry	Regressors[a]						
	Constant	ULCN	PM	PM(−1)	P−1)	R²,SEE,DW	Model
22	.090	.528	.119	−.208	.527	.629	Nield 1
	(.9)	(4.9)	(1.1)	(2.0)	(5.4)	.612	
						1.32	
25	.104	.291	.032	−.006	.493	.601	Nield 1
	(1.3)	(2.6)	(1.7)	(.3)	(3.4)	.287	
						2.50	
251	.230	.061	.067	−.009	.518	.454	Nield 1
	(1.6)	(.4)	(2.7)	(.3)	(2.3)	.356	
						2.12	
35	.294	.024	.142	.350	.086	.429	Nield 1
	(4.0)	(.3)	(1.8)	(2.3)	(.5)	.290	
						2.28	
3541	.359	.044	.014	.411	.483	.421	Nield 1
	(2.0)	(.5)	(.1)	(1.6)	(3.2)	.475	
						2.11	

[a]The entries for each industry under each regressor are the regression coefficients and t-values (in parentheses). The adjusted coefficient of determination (R^2), standard error of the estimate (SEE), and Durbin-Watson statistic (DW) are also given.

The price behavior of industries not included in Table 6-2 is in general poorly explained by this hypothesis category specification. However, there appears to be a slight improvement in the fits for most industries over those in hypothesis category one.

Category Three: SRC,DED

There are four price equations that represent this general specification. Two of these are from the Eckstein and Wyss study, and the others are from the Phipps and the Fromm and Eckstein studies. All four equations contain labor and material cost variables, with factor prices (*AHE* and *PM*) in the Eckstein and Wyss equations and unit costs (*ULC* and *PM*, assuming *UMC* = *B*PM*) in the Phipps and the Fromm and Eckstein equations. The expected signs of the coefficients on these cost variables are positive. The *DED* variables are different in each of the equations. The Phipps equation includes *FDQ* and *FDQ*(−1) whereas both of the Eckstein and Wyss equations have percentage change in shipments (*SHP*) as a regressor. The Fromm and Eckstein equation and one of the Eckstein and Wyss equations both include the *CUI*, with its expected sign being positive, indicating that as a firm approaches or exceeds its capacity (*CUI* is in level form), its rate of change in price increases. This tends to stabilize the excess demand situation that exists, the extent of the price change depending on the elasticities that exist in the supply and product markets. The Phipps equation, and the Eckstein and Wyss equation without *CUI*, also contain the lagged price as a regressor.

Table 6-3 contains the results for those industries explained well by these types of price equations. The Phipps equation provides a good fit for industries 34 and 3541, both durable goods industries. However, only cost variables are significant, so that neither *FDQ* nor *FDQ*(−1) appears to be a significant *DED* measure. The Eckstein and Wyss equation with *CUI* and the Fromm and Eckstein equation provide the best fits in industries 333 and 35, respectively, both of which are producer durable goods industries. Both of these industries are ranked in the upper two thirds of the capital-intensity range (SIC 333 is third), which indicates that capital considerations may be more important than labor considerations in making price decisions. This is evidenced by the strong significance of *CUI* in both cases. The *SHP* term enters and is highly significant in only SIC 333. This industry faces a relatively inelastic demand schedule for its products and is powerful in its markets as evidenced by a concentration ratio of 53 percent. Given these conditions, one would expect the negative sign on *SHP*'s coefficient but would not interpret *SHP* as a *DED* measure.

Even though *CUI* and/or *SHP* are significant with or without cost variables for industries other than those shown in Table 6-3, the overall fits in these industries of the various price equations included under category three do not meet the criterion of $R^2 \geqslant .40$. All industries in Table 6-3 except SIC 22 are durable goods industries. As under hypothesis category two, industries 35 and 3541, and 25 and 251, are all well explained.

Category Four: SRC,DED

This category of price behavior is similar to the previous one in that *SRC* and *DED* hypotheses of price behavior are represented in the equations. However, the *DED* measure now is a macro measure, either *GNP* or *DY*, instead of one of the micro *DED* measures from hypothesis category three. Only the study by Laden develops a price equation similar to this type. It is interesting to include this formulation in order to compare the significance of industry-specific versus macro *DED* measures in explaining price behavior for various types of industries. The Laden equation includes as regressors the factor prices for both labor and materials along with GNP. The equation is modified for this study, in that *DY* is used in place of GNP for consumer goods industries. Both *DED* variables are entered in nominal and constant dollar forms. The nominal form is used by Laden and generally is most significant in this analysis. Therefore, the *DED* measure is actually the product of real product or income and the general price level.

Table 6-3
Hypothesis Category Three (SRC,DED): Best Industry Price Equations

SIC Industry	Constant	ULC	PM	FDQ	FDQ(−1)	P(−1)	AHE	SHP	PM(−1)	CUI	R²,SEE,DW	Model
22	−.260 (2.2)	.187 (2.5)	.082 (.7)	.254 (3.8)	.044 (.6)	.515 (4.9)					.626 .613 1.76	Phipps
25	.073 (1.0)	.010 (.2)	.039 (1.8)	.033 (.9)	.002 (.1)	.677 (5.6)					.505 .298 2.56	Phipps
251	.208 (2.3)	.075 (1.5)	.059 (2.9)	−.004 (.1)	.006 (.2)	.440 (3.2)					.496 .308 2.21	Phipps
34	.096 (1.3)	.066 (1.0)	.467 (3.3)	−.030 (1.1)	.014 (.6)	.368 (2.7)					.412 .349 1.73	Phipps
3541	.346 (2.4)	.132 (2.8)	.114 (1.2)	.028 (.5)	.073 (1.2)	.434 (3.5)					.570 .410 2.43	Phipps
35	−1.015 (2.4)	.021 (.6)	.115 (1.7)						.231 (1.9)	.016 (3.1)	.547 .258 2.39	Fromm and Eckstein 2
333	−5.433 (2.8)		.638 (5.7)				.009 (.02)	−.252 (5.3)		.066 (3.3)	.709 1.009 2.04	Eckstein and Wyss 4

[a]The entries for each industry under each regressor are the regression coefficients and t-values (in parentheses). The adjusted coefficient of determination (R²), standard error of the estimate (SEE), and Durbin-Watson statistic (DW) are also given.

A positive effect on industry prices is to be expected from macro demand measures. However, the results in Table 6-4 indicate that for both industries explained well by this equation the macro *DED* measure enters with a negative sign. Furthermore, *DY* is not significant in the equation for SIC 22. The significance of GNP in determining price change in SIC 35 indicates that P35 and the overall price level may be out of phase with one another, thus leading to the negative sign on GNP even though the relationship between *P35* and GNP58 may be positive. In a majority of the cases where *DY* or GNP is insignificant, both current and constant dollar forms of the variables have the same sign, usually negative. In those industries where *DY* or GNP is significant (SICs 24, 25, 331, 301, 30, and 36), the signs of both constant and current dollar forms of GNP or *DY* are the same in all cases, with a negative sign present in SICs 25, 35, and 36. Therefore, SIC 35 may be leading or lagging the overall economy with regard to direction of price change. Of all the industries excluded from Table 6-4, GNP is significant in one industry (SIC 25). In only SIC 301 does this *DED* measure have a positive effect on price change. It is clear that this price equation is not as widely applicable in explaining price behavior in several industries as are the price equations in the preceding hypothesis categories.

Category Five: SRC,DED

This category includes both industry-specific and macro *DED* measures along with *SRC* in terms of factor prices. Another variant of the Laden equation represents this category, the price equation of category four being expanded to include an industry-specific capital stock variable. (As indicated in Table 3-6, Laden's equation also included a price of substitutes (*PUS*) variable as a regressor; however, that variable is left out of both categories four and five because of the difficulty of defining substitutes at the levels of aggregation concerned with in this study. The *PUS* regressor is insignificant in Laden's

Table 6-4
Hypothesis Category Four (SRC,DED): Best Industry Price Equations

SIC Industry	Constant	AHE	PM	DY	GNP	R^2,SEE,DW	Model
			Regressors[a]				
22	−.513 (2.2)	.819 (5.5)	.259 (2.0)	−.130 (.8)		.445 .764 .83	Laden 1
35	.255 (2.7)	.231 (2.2)	.569 (5.5)		−.135 (2.8)	.513 .246 1.92	Laden 1

[a]The entries for each industry under each regressor are the regression coefficients and t-values (in parentheses). The adjusted coefficient of determination (R^2), standard error of the estimate (SEE), and Durbin-Watson statistic (DW) are also given.

results.) Capital stock represents the supply side of the market and according to Laden would assume a negative sign in the price equation because of the effects of increased productivity resulting from an expansion of capital. However, an expansion of capital also results in higher average costs, which will lead to an increase in price if the firm or industry is an average cost pricer. Therefore, a positive sign is feasible.

It can be seen in Table 6-5 that the price behavior of only four industries is well explained by this equation. The cost variables have the expected signs whereas DY and GNP take on negative signs in all cases. In three durable goods industries (25, 35, and 3541), the coefficient on the capital term (K) has a positive sign, indicating that those industries follow average cost pricing. However, in SIC 22 the sign of the coefficient on K is negative, reflecting the productivity effects. In all of the industries K is significant. Also note that these industries had their price behavior well explained by price equations in hypothesis category two, which includes both short-run and long-run cost terms. This is consistent with the above results, since capital expansion is a long-run concept. The long-run cost variables included in the equations of Table 6-2 are either $ULCN$ or RLT, and in all industries except for SIC 35 the explanation of price behavior is better than that in Table 6-5. Note that the concentration ratios of the industries in Table 6-5 are all less than 36 percent and they are all relatively low in the range of industries classified according to capital intensity (see Table 5-2). Both of these findings are the converse of what is expected in

Table 6-5
Hypothesis Category Five (SRC,DED): Best Industry Price Equations

SIC Industry	Regressors[a]							
	Constant	AHE	PM	DY	GNP	K	R²,SEE,DW	Model
22	−.314	.803	.385	−.018		−.187	.515	Laden 2
	(1.1)	(5.7)	(3.0)	(.1)		(3.0)	.699	
							1.07	
25	.094	.421	.029	−.148		.095	.452	Laden 2
	(.8)	(3.7)	(1.5)	(1.9)		(2.4)	.313	
							1.36	
35	.108	.255	.177		−.034	.074	.477	Laden 2
	(.9)	(2.1)	(2.5)		(.6)	(3.5)	.278	
							2.20	
3541	.518	.287	−.043		−.072	.141	.412	Laden 2
	(2.9)	(2.5)	(.4)		(.8)	(5.1)	.485	
							1.49	

[a]The entries for each industry under each regressor are the regression coefficients and t-values (in parentheses). The adjusted coefficient of determination (R^2), standard error of the estimate (SEE), and Durbin-Watson statistic (DW) are also given.

industries in which *LRC* or capital stock is important in explaining price behavior (see Eckstein and Wyss[159]). The fit for SIC 35 is worse than under category four, with GNP becoming insignificant when *K* is introduced. The price behavior of industries excluded from Table 6-5 is poorly explained by this type of price equation. Note that industries 35 and 3541 are both well explained by this type of price equation.

Category Six: SRC,DED

This is the final *SRC,DED* category and is represented by modifications of price equations from the Liu and Courchene studies. The *SRC* terms are again factor prices, with *AHE* and *PM* in the Courchene equation and only *AHE* in the Liu equation. In addition, the Liu specification contains two lagged price change variables as regressors. The *DED* measures in both are industry-specific inventory variables and are distinguished from the other *DED* measures (hypothesis categories three, four, and five) in that they represent long-run (normalized) excess demand pressure as well as present pressure (*SR-DED* and *LR-DED*). The *FDINV, FDINVN,* and *FDI,IN* variables for industries 301, 3541, and 227 are based on inventory data from their respective two-digit industries. Inventory data are not available for SIC 301; however, this industry accounts for a sizeable portion of SIC 30 so that the latter inventory data may be a good proxy for the former. Unpublished data are available for SIC 354 and SIC 227. In both cases, however, the fits of the Liu and Courchene price equations are much better when the two-digit inventory data are used. Especially in the case of the unpublished data, the accuracy of the three-digit data is open to question.

As noted in Chapter 5, the original Liu price equation for the U.S. private deflator included the change in desired inventories (*FDID*) as a regressor instead of *FDINVN*. In arriving at *FDID*, the concept of equilibrium inventories is also used. The assumptions made by Liu concerning the inventory-sales ratio and the use of indirect least squares in deriving a *FDID* series are explained in detail in Chapter 4. It was felt that the use of *FDINVN* as a regressor in industry price equations would be much more flexible than the use of *FDID*, because of its simpler formulation, and would in actuality better approximate the type of variable on which business pricing decisions are based. However, the exact Liu formulation was fitted to several two-digit industries and compared with the modified Liu equation results. They compare as seen below.

The adjusted R^2s for two of the better-fitting industries (SICs 22 and 29) are greater for the modified Liu equation. Further, whenever *FDID* is significant, *FDINVN* is also significant, whereas the converse is not necessarily true (note SIC 29 results). On the basis of both the above results and practical considerations, it was decided to use *FDINVN* as a regressor in the Liu equation and *FDI,IN* as a regressor in the Courchene equations.

Industry	Adjusted R²		Sign and Significance	
	Original Liu	Modified Liu	FDID	FDIN
SIC 21	.326	.304	+ No	− No
SIC 22	.737	.738	+ No	− No
SIC 29	.578	.603	+ No	− Yes
SIC 30	.567	.506	− Yes	+ Yes
SIC 32	.330	.356	+ No	− No
SIC 34	.386	.284	+ Yes	+ Yes
SIC 36	.077	.067	− No	+ No
SIC 371	−.002	−.008	+ No	+ No

The expected signs on all cost and lagged price variables are positive. Arguments for either negative or positive signs on the inventory terms may be made. Increased excess demand in the product market will force a firm to draw down inventories in order to meet demand (i.e., some inventories would become shipments) if output does not increase enough to eliminate the excess demand. In this case, the direction of change in inventories would be the opposite of that in excess demand, resulting in price increases when inventories decrease. However, this interpretation conflicts with the negative sign on the shipments term (but, this is a cost interpretation) in the category three equations discussed above. If output can be shown to change sufficiently to allow for simultaneous expansion or contraction in both inventories and shipments, then the negative signs on both *SHP* in Tables 6-3 and 6-10 and *FDI* (*DED* interpretation) in Table 6-6 are consistent with one another. Therefore, in this case inventory change does not contribute to shipments change. A study of the correlations between *Q, FDINV,* and *FDINVN* with both the level and the percentage change in *SHP* reveals positive correlations among these variables in most industries (two negative correlations between *SHP* and *FDINV* in SIC 24 and SIC 21 are both less than .10 in value). Therefore, *FDINV* and *SHP* do generally move in the same direction. The negative signs on both *FDINVN* and *FDI,IN* may also be explained by these same reasons.

If the inventory movements are construed as a proxy for the costs of holding inventories, then price and inventories will move in the same direction, with the resultant sign on the inventory coefficient being positive. This may be especially true in industries that base pricing decisions on long-run costs, in which case the coefficient on *FDINVN* would be expected to be positive. Also, it is most likely that decisions on expansion of facilities in which to hold inventories are based on normalized inventories.

Interpretation of *INV* and forms of it as regressors in a price equation at disaggregate levels of data is difficult to make because of the uncertainty about why inventories change (i.e., voluntary versus involuntary changes). Neverthe-

Table 6-6
Hypothesis Category Six (SRC,DED): Best Industry Price Equations

SIC Industry	Constant	AHE	FDINV	FDINVN	P(-1)	P(-2)	PM	FDI,IN	R², SEE, DW	Model
				Regressors[a]						
22	-.300 (1.8)	.563 (5.1)	-.002 (2.6)	-.0006 (.4)	.627 (6.1)	-.214 (2.1)			.726 .526 2.03	Liu
24	.336 (.5)	.040 (.1)	-.021 (6.4)	-.026 (.6)	.282 (1.3)	.138 (.6)			.788 1.590 1.79	Liu
29	.385 (1.4)	.157 (.9)	-.010 (7.3)	-.014 (2.1)	.201 (1.9)	-.034 (.3)			.553 1.116 2.27	Liu
30	-1.04 (2.6)	.095 (.6)	-.008 (5.3)	.029 (4.3)	.188 (1.6)	-.235 (2.1)			.509 .889 1.64	Liu
301	-.783 (1.2)	-.034 (.2)	-.015 (7.8)	.030 (3.1)	.186 (1.9)	-.197 (2.0)			.623 1.292 1.33	Liu
333	2.204 (5.0)	.132 (.5)	-.008 (10.7)	-.014 (2.8)	-.032 (.3)	-.049 (.5)			.822 .790 1.53	Liu
35	-.014 (.1)	.261 (2.3)	.00009 (.9)	.0007 (3.0)	.068 (.4)	-.044 (.3)			.443 .286 2.33	Liu
3541	.051 (.2)	.207 (1.4)	-.0002 (.8)	.0007 (1.2)	.423 (2.1)	.167 (.9)			.415 .478 1.71	Liu
227	-.043 (.3)	-.143 (.9)					.989 (3.6)	-.005 (5.1)	.523 .816 1.66	Courchene

[a]The entries for each industry under each regressor are the regression coefficients and t-values (in parentheses). The adjusted coefficient of determination (R^2), standard error of the estimate (SEE), and Durbin-Watson statistic (DW) are also given.

less, it is apparent from Table 6-6 that the price behavior of a greater number of industries is well explained by the equations in this than in any other hypothesis category. The Liu formulation is superior for all industries in Table 6-6 except SIC 227. This equation is preferable, since it explicitly accounts for change in current and change in normalized inventories. In the equations for industries 29, 30, 333, and 301, both *FDINV* and *FDINVN* are significant and have negative signs on their coefficients except for *FDINVN* in SIC 301 which is positively significant. In only SIC 35 are the coefficients on *FDINV* and *FDINVN* both positive, reflecting a possible cost interpretation for inventories. *AHE* is negative in the SIC 301 equation whereas $P(-1)$ is negative in the equation for SIC 333. The negative sign on the coefficient of $P(-2)$ and its significance in industries 22, 30, and 301 indicate cyclical behavior of prices in these industries with respect to their past price changes. The coefficient on *AHE* in SIC 227 is negative but insignificant. Much of the trouble with actual signs being different from expected signs can perhaps be attributed to multicollinearity. Of the industries included in Table 6-6, those with the poorest fits (SICs 35 and 3541) are lower relative to the others regarding the inventory-unfilled orders ratio, both having ratios less than 1 (see Table 5-2). This might indicate that the inclusion of inventory variables as *DED* measures is more relevant in production to stock (PTS) industries than in production to order (PTO) industries. However, this contention is in doubt because of the insignificance of the inventory variables in industries SIC 25 and SIC 251, both relatively high in the PTS industry range.

More of the industries excluded from Table 6-6 have their price behavior better explained by the Liu and Courchene equations than was the case in the preceding categories. Therefore, it appears that this type of formulation, including *SRC*, long-run *DED*, and short-run *DED*, provides a better explanation of price change for a wider range of industries than do the price equations in the other categories. Furthermore, these equations are more generally applicable to industries at all levels of aggregation—with special notice to small three- and four-digit industries (i.e., SICs 3541, 227, and 301)—than are the price equations in any of the other categories. In the case of SICs 22, 30, and 35, both the two-digit industry and a selected subindustry in each (SICs 227, 301, and 3541) have their price formation explained well by the same type of price equation.

Category Seven: SRC,IED

A price equation from the study by Rushdy and Lund represents this category. The excess demand measure is now an indirect one, the inverse of the unemployment rate lagged one time period. The form of this variable is consistent with Phillips curve theory, and has an expected positive sign, since rate of price change and the unemployment rate are hypothesized to be inversely related to one another. Lagged unit labor costs and the lagged material price index are the cost terms.

The three industries given in Table 6-7, whose price behavior is well explained by this specification, are all durable goods industries. The $URI(-1)$ term is highly significant in all three industries, with its coefficient having the expected positive sign. In all instances, the coefficients on the $ULC(-1)$ term are negative but insignificant. The importance of the IED pricing hypothesis in explaining price behavior in these industries is expected. Assuming UR to be a proxy for income, a higher UR will be accompanied by lower income, which can result in consumers' postponing the purchase of durable items such as furniture. Therefore, with an easing of demand pressure the rate of inflation tends to decline. Furthermore, a high unemployment rate and slack in production is often cause for a decrease in capital expenditures, thus easing demand pressures and reducing inflation rates in industries such as SIC 35 (nonelectrical machinery). The $URI(-1)$ regressor is significant in several industries not included in Table 6-7, a majority of these being durable goods industries. However, the overall fit of this specification, which includes SRC and IED hypotheses, is not generally good in the excluded industries.

Category Eight: IED

The equation from the McCallum study, representing this category, explicitly includes only the present and expected URI and the lagged price. The derivation of this formulation, based on the hypothesis that today's labor market reflects yesterday's product market, is given in Chapter 4.

Table 6-7
Hypothesis Category Seven (SRC,IED): Best Industry Price Equations

SIC Industry	Constant	ULC(−1)	PM(−1)	URI(−1)	R²,SEE,DW	Model
			Regressors[a]			
25	−1.032 (5.0)	−.009 (.2)	.006 (.3)	7.080 (6.8)	.611 .264 1.82	Rushdy and Lund
251	−1.156 (3.9)	−.070 (1.3)	.010 (.5)	7.637 (5.3)	.531 .297 1.78	Rushdy and Lund
35	−.457 (2.3)	−.038 (1.0)	.335 (3.2)	4.119 (4.1)	.559 .255 2.35	Rushdy and Lund

[a]The entries for each industry under each regressor are the regression coefficients and t-values (in parentheses). The adjusted coefficient of determination (R^2), standard error of the estimate (SEE), and Durbin-Watson statistic (DW) are also given.

All industries with equations in Table 6-8 except SIC 22 are durable goods industries. SICs 22 and 34 have the poorest fits of the industries in this category. The price behavior of industries 25 and 251 is better explained and that of SIC 35 is not as well explained as in the equations of category seven. Industries 25, 251, 34, and 35 are cyclical in their behavior, demand for their products fluctuating depending on general economic conditions. Therefore, one would expect a macro indicator such as the civilian unemployment rate to be significant in explaining price behavior in these industries. In many cases the insignificance and negative signs of the coefficients on URI and $URI(+1)$ are attributed to a high degree of multicollinearity among URI, $URI(+1)$, and $P(-1)$. The fits for all excluded industries except SICs 23, 331, and 3541 are extremely poor ($R^2 < .25$). Furthermore, URI and $URI(+1)$ are not significant regressors in any of the excluded industries (except SIC 331), again resulting in part from multicollinearity.

Category Nine: SRC,DED,IED

The specification that combines the *SRC, DED*, and *IED* pricing hypotheses is the reduced form price equation from the Klein and Ball model. The $PM(-2)$ and *TAX* variables are present in the Klein and Ball structural equation under

Table 6-8
Hypothesis Category Eight (IED): Best Industry Price Equations

SIC Industry	Regressors[a]					
	Constant	URI	URI(+1)	P(−1)	R²,SEE,DW	Model
22	−.216	−29.008	29.814	.570	.416	McCallum
	(.4)	(2.5)	(2.5)	(4.8)	.767	
					1.72	
25	−.887	6.505	−.515	.157	.627	McCallum
	(4.0)	(1.5)	(.1)	(1.1)	.258	
					2.14	
251	−.840	5.041	.788	.137	.534	McCallum
	(3.5)	(1.1)	(.2)	(.9)	.296	
					2.04	
34	−.762	−2.274	7.195	.233	.420	McCallum
	(2.8)	(.4)	(1.3)	(1.5)	.346	
					1.77	
35	−.752	1.707	4.047	.032	.516	McCallum
	(3.6)	(.4)	(1.0)	(.2)	.267	
					2.01	

[a]The entries for each industry under each regressor are the regression coefficients and t-values (in parentheses). The adjusted coefficient of determination (R^2), standard error of the estimate (SEE), and Durbin-Watson statistic (DW) are also given.

category two. The *IED* measure is a moving average of the unemployment rate whereas the *DED* measure is output (Q). The productivity term (*PP*) should assume a negative sign, with productivity gains exercising a dampening effect on price increases caused by cost and excess demand pressures. A moving average of past prices ($4TMAP(-1)$) is also included as a regressor.

As in hypothesis categories seven and eight, most of the industries whose price behavior is explained well by this type of equation (see Table 6-9) are durable goods industries. The only exception is SIC 23. Where significant, the *PP* term does have a negative influence on price change in all cases except that of SIC 24. Since *AHE* is not included as a regressor, it is not unreasonable for *PP* to enter a price equation with a positive sign if in fact it is reflecting an increase in *AHE*. In all cases, the coefficient on $4TMAUR$ is as expected (negative), whereas the coefficient on Q is positive for all industries except SIC 24, indicating a *DED* interpretation for this variable. Where significant, the coefficients on $PM(-2)$ and *TAX* are positive. In the equations for SIC 24 and SIC 34, the coefficient on $4TMAP(-1)$ is negative and significant. With the exception of industries 21, 2111, 22, and 30, each of the industries excluded from Table 6-9 has an adjusted R^2 less than .25. Note that the industries present in Table 6-9 are all two-digit or large three-digit industries, with the exception of SIC 3541. This indicates that a macro measure such as $4TMAUR$ may be a better explanatory variable for price change than industry-specific variables in industries where many of the characteristics of the units composing the industry are neutralized through aggregation. It will be seen later, however, that the price behavior of only one industry, SIC 331, is best explained by this specification.

Category Ten: SRC,LRC,DED

Four equations from three studies are representative of this category. Two equations by Schultze and Tryon from the Brookings model differ in only the short-run cost terms included. In the one, normalized unit labor costs (*ULCN*) and the deviation of normal from actual unit labor costs (*DULC,N*) are the cost regressors; in the other, *PM* is included along with *ULCN*. The *DULC,N* term has an expected positive sign, since any costs above normal will reduce the profit margin and thus result in a higher price in order to restore the normal margin. The *DED* measure in both equations is the lagged difference between the inventory-sales ratio and its trend value. Assuming that industries have a desired tradeoff between inventories and sales (or output or shipments), any ratio above that tradeoff means either excess inventories and/or slack sales. In this case, any excess demand pressures that may have been present are reduced and prices decline. The $FDIST(-1)$ term therefore has an expected negative sign. If *INV/S*, *INV/SHP*, or *INV/Q* does not follow a trend for a particular industry, regressing these ratios on time and then forming $FDIST(-1)$ will result in a meaningless

Table 6-9
Hypothesis Category Nine (SRC,DED,IED): Best Industry Price Equations

SIC Industry	Regressors[a]							R² ,SEE,DW	Model
	Constant	PM(−2)	TAX	4TMAUR	Q	PP	4TMAP(−1)		
23	−1.688 (2.1)	.032 (.5)	141.43 (3.7)	−.060 (.8)	.015 (.3)	−.049 (1.3)	−.374 (1.0)	.459 .262 1.83	Klein and Ball 2
24	−8.180 (1.7)	.081 (.3)	676.34 (5.2)	−.978 (1.2)	−.699 (1.5)	.835 (1.9)	−2.201 (4.0)	.744 1.749 2.30	Klein and Ball 2
25	.626 (.8)	.034 (1.5)	22.051 (1.1)	−.190 (2.5)	.023 (1.1)	.064 (1.2)	.287 (1.5)	.631 .257 1.82	Klein and Ball 2
251	1.348 (1.5)	.042 (1.6)	5.000 (.2)	−.229 (2.7)	.032 (1.5)	−.026 (.4)	.190 (.8)	.525 .299 1.75	Klein and Ball 2
331	.846 (2.9)	.052 (.9)	9.292 (1.8)	−.212 (3.2)	.0008 (.2)	−.007 (.5)	.492 (3.0)	.409 .325 1.57	Klein and Ball 2
34	2.962 (3.3)	−.212 (1.6)	23.728 (1.3)	−.568 (5.9)	.019 (1.0)	−.027 (.4)	−1.251 (3.6)	.516 .316 1.64	Klein and Ball 2
35	3.048 (3.0)	.175 (1.4)	−23.154 (1.6)	−.308 (3.8)	.089 (3.3)	−.081 (1.9)	.008 (.03)	.517 .267 2.25	Klein and Ball 2
3541	−1.004 (.6)	.164 (.7)	38.983 (1.4)	−.050 (.4)	.119 (2.7)	−.138 (2.6)	.349 (1.8)	.629 .381 2.29	Klein and Ball 2

[a]The entries for each industry under each regressor are the regression coefficients and t-values (in parentheses). The adjusted coefficient of determination (R^2), standard error of the estimate (SEE), and Durbin-Watson statistic (DW) are also given.

variable. Therefore, the trend regression results for all industries, and whether or not $FDIST(-1)$ is significant in a price equation, must be carefully examined. It may be that the deviation of one of the ratios from its normalized value is a more accurate representation of this DED influence. This is further examined in fitting the final industry price equations in Chapter 7.

The Fromm and Eckstein equation includes all of the cost terms from both of the Schultze and Tryon equations, as well as $ULCN(-1)$. The capacity utilization index is the excess demand measure in this equation. The Eckstein and Wyss formulation is a modified version of the equation discussed under category two, with SHP entering as the DED measure.

Table 6-10 includes the industries well explained by the models in this category. Each of the Schultze and Tryon equations explains only one industry's price behavior better than do the other models. All regressors are significant in the two equations although the $DULC,N$ term in the SIC 22 equation has a negative sign. The Eckstein and Wyss specification provides the best fit only for industry 34, for which the coefficient on SHP is negative and significant, indicating either the average cost or market power interpretations for the effect of SHP on P. Since SIC 34 has a concentration ratio less than 30 percent, the argument that market power allows prices to increase when shipments decrease (assuming relatively inelastic demand) in order to maintain total profits does not appear to hold in this case. The Fromm and Eckstein equation provides a good fit for the price behavior of four durable goods industries. However, the $DULC,N$ term has a negative coefficient but is insignificant in all industries except SIC 251, in which it is positive and marginally significant.

All industries whose price behavior is well explained by equations in this category are durable goods producers, except for SIC 22. This finding is similar to that for category two, which also included LRC regressors. With the exception of SIC 331, all industries excluded from Table 6-10 have poor fits, using any of the equations in this category.

Best Price Equation From Past Specifications
for Each Industry

Price equations covering a wide range were discussed in the first section of this chapter. The results of estimating these price equations were given for those industries best fitted within designated hypothesis categories. In this section, the best equation for each industry will be selected from all those in the previous section. (The equations selected are generally those with the highest adjusted R^2s for each industry. However, in selected cases (e.g., SIC 251), a higher adjusted R^2 is sacrificed in order to have significant coefficients with the expected signs.) These equations will then be discussed in terms of the hypotheses represented and the most common regressors found in a majority of the industry price equations.

Table 6-10
Hypothesis Category Ten (SRC,LRC,DED): Best Industry Price Equations

SIC Industry	Constant	ULCN	DULC,N	FDIST(-1)	PM	AHE	FDRLT	PREQ	SHP	ULCN(-1)	CUI	R^2,SEE,DW	Model
22	-1.136 (3.2)	.700 (6.4)	-.190 (3.7)	-4.182 (4.0)								.611 .626 1.04	Schultze and Tryon 1
3541	.695 (7.2)	.440 (5.2)		-5.159 (6.0)	.276 (2.5)							.588 .401 1.96	Schultze and Tryon 2
34	-.501 (2.7)					.170 (1.8)	.489 (1.2)	30.805 (4.2)	-.058 (3.1)			.437 .341 1.39	Eckstein and Wyss 5
25	-1.412 (1.2)	.322 (3.2)	-.054 (1.4)		.032 (1.8)					.262 (2.8)	.014 (1.2)	.496 .300 1.45	Fromm and Eckstein 1
251	-2.638 (2.3)	.119 (1.4)	.048 (1.7)		.050 (2.5)					-.033 (.4)	.033 (2.9)	.441 .324 1.18	Fromm and Eckstein 1
333	-8.718 (2.9)	.208 (.5)	-.109 (1.8)		.467 (2.7)					.105 (.3)	.090 (3.1)	.457 1.379 1.76	Fromm and Eckstein 1
35	-1.560 (3.6)	.047 (.5)	-.027 (1.1)		.146 (2.2)					.164 (1.8)	.021 (4.6)	.552 .257 2.22	Fromm and Eckstein 1

[a]The entries for each industry under each regressor are the regression coefficients and t-values (in parentheses). The adjusted coefficient of determination (R^2), standard error of the estimate (SEE), and Durbin-Watson statistic (DW) are also given.

Table 6-11 contains the best reestimated price equation for each of the best-fitting industries (i.e., those with $R^2 \geqslant .40$). The equations representing industries 30, 301, 227, 29, and 331 are the only ones for those industries to have an adjusted R^2 greater than .40. The price behavior of all other industries shown in Table 6-11 is well explained by equations in at least two hypothesis categories. Hypothesis category six, which best represents seven industries, is predominant; it contains the modified versions of Liu and Courchene equations. Both *SR-DED* and *LR-DED* are represented along with *SR* factor prices and lagged price. The Klein and Ball specification in hypothesis category nine is the best reestimated price equation for five industries. This equation includes regressors for the *SRC, DED,* and *IED* hypotheses. The Eckstein and Wyss and the Fromm and Eckstein equations under hypothesis category ten include *SRC, LRC,* and *DED* hypotheses in their formulations and each best represents only one industry's price behavior.

Eleven of the 14 industry equations in Table 6-11 include the lagged price(s) or a form of it as a regressor, with its significance apparent in only 6 cases. The factor price of labor (*AHE*) is present in 8 of the industry equations as either the only or one of the *SRC* regressors. However, *AHE* is significant only in the SIC 22 and SIC 34 price equations. All of the industry equations in Table 6-11 contain both the *SRC* hypothesis and some form of the *DED* hypothesis. In all cases, the *DED* hypothesis is represented by industry-specific (as opposed to macro) regressors. Recall, however, that for most three- and four-digit industries studied (exceptions: SICs 331, 333, and 371), the *INV, SHP,* and $FDIST(-1)$ variables included are the appropriate two-digit industry data and not the specific three- or four-digit industry data.

Table 6-12 contains the best results for those industries whose price behavior is not explained well (i.e., $R^2 < .40$) by any of the equation specifications in hypothesis categories one to ten. As in Table 6-11, hypothesis category six has the most widespread significance in explaining price behavior, best explaining six out of these eight worst-fitting industries. Four of these industries are best explained by the modified Courchene equation, with *FDI,IN* being significant with a negative coefficient in all cases and both *AHE* and *PM* being generally insignificant. In the two industries best explained by the modified Liu equation, *AHE* and *FDINVN* are insignificant whereas *FDINV* is significant with a negative sign and $P(-1)$ is significant and positive. The adjusted R^2s for the six industries best explained by hypothesis category six range from .205 to .365. The other two worst-fitting industries included in Table 6-12 both have the *LRC* regressor *ULCN* in their specifications, with SIC 36 best explained by the Nield equation (hypothesis category two) and SIC 371 best explained by the Fromm and Eckstein equation (hypothesis category ten). In both equations, *ULCN* is significant; $PM(-1)$ also is significant in the SIC 36 equation.

Two possible reasons for the poor explanation of price behavior in the industries of Table 6-12 are lack of variability in the price variable itself and the

Table 6-11
Optimum Reestimated Equation for Each of Best-Fitting Industries

Best Reestimated Industry Price Equations	R^2, SEE, DW	Time Interval	Model

Hypothesis category six (SRC,DED):

P30 $= -1.040 + .095*AHE30 - .008*FDINV30 + .029*FDINVN30 + .188*P30(-1) - .235*P30(-2)$
$\quad$ (2.6) $\quad$ (.6) $\qquad$ (5.2) $\qquad\quad$ (4.2) $\qquad\quad$ (1.6) $\qquad\quad$ (2.1)
$\qquad$ .509, .889, 1.64 $\qquad$ 1958:2-1969:2 $\qquad$ Liu

P227 $= -.043 - .143*AHE227 + .989*PM22 - .005*FDI,IN22$
$\quad$ (.2) $\quad$ (.9) $\qquad\quad$ (3.6) $\qquad$ (5.1)
$\qquad$ .523, .816, 1.66 $\qquad$ 1958:2-1969:2 $\qquad$ Courchene

P29 $= .385 + .157*AHE29 - .010*FDINV29 - .014*FDINVN29 + .201*P29(-1) - .034*P29(-2)$
$\quad$ (1.4) $\quad$ (.9) $\qquad$ (7.3) $\qquad\quad$ (2.0) $\qquad\quad$ (1.9) $\qquad\quad$ (.3)
$\qquad$ .553, 1.116, 2.27 $\qquad$ 1958:2-1969:2 $\qquad$ Liu

P301 $= -.783 - .034*AHE301 - .015*FDINV30 + .030*FDINVN30 + .186*P301(-1) - .197*P301(-2)$
$\quad$ (1.2) $\quad$ (.2) $\qquad$ (7.8) $\qquad\quad$ (3.1) $\qquad\quad$ (1.9) $\qquad\quad$ (2.0)
$\qquad$ .623, 1.292, 1.33 $\qquad$ 1958:2-1969:2 $\qquad$ Liu

P22 $= -.300 + .563*AHE22 - .002*FDINV22 + .0006*FDINVN22 + .627*P22(-1) + .214*P22(-2)$
$\quad$ (1.8) $\quad$ (5.1) $\qquad$ (2.6) $\qquad\quad$ (.4) $\qquad\qquad$ (6.1) $\qquad\quad$ (2.1)
$\qquad$ .726, .526, 2.03 $\qquad$ 1958:2-1969:2 $\qquad$ Liu

P24 $= .336 + .040*AHE24 - .021*FDINV24 - .026*FDINVN24 + .282*P24(-1) + .138*P24(-2)$
$\quad$ (.5) $\quad$ (.1) $\qquad$ (6.4) $\qquad\quad$ (.6) $\qquad\qquad$ (1.3) $\qquad\quad$ (.6)
$\qquad$ .788, 1.590, 1.79 $\qquad$ 1964:2-1969:2 $\qquad$ Liu

P333 $= 2.204 + .132*AHE333 - .008*FDINV333 - .014*FDINVN333 - .032*P333(-1) - .049*P333(-2)$
$\quad$ (5.0) $\quad$ (.5) $\qquad$ (10.7) $\qquad\quad$ (2.8) $\qquad\qquad$ (.3) $\qquad\qquad$ (.5)
$\qquad$ .822, .790, 1.53 $\qquad$ 1961:3-1969:2 $\qquad$ Liu

Hypothesis category nine (SRC,DED,IED):

P331 $= .846 + .052*PM331(-2) + 9.292*TAX331 - .212*4TMAUR + .0008*Q331 - .0065*PP331 + .492*4TMAP331(-1)$
$\quad$ (2.9) $\quad$ (.9) $\qquad\qquad$ (1.8) $\qquad$ (3.2) $\qquad\quad$ (.2) $\qquad\quad$ (.5) $\qquad$ (3.0)
$\qquad$ .409, .325, 1.57 $\qquad$ 1958:2-1969:2 $\qquad$ Klein and Ball 2

P3541 $= -1.004 + .164*PM3541(-2) + 38.983*TAX35 - .050*4TMAUR + .119*Q3541 - .139*PP3541 + .349*4TMAP3541(-1)$
$\quad$ (.6) $\quad$ (.7) $\qquad\qquad$ (1.4) $\qquad$ (.4) $\qquad\quad$ (2.7) $\qquad\quad$ (2.6) $\qquad$ (1.8)
$\qquad$ .629, .381, 2.29 $\qquad$ 1961:2-1969:2 $\qquad$ Klein and Ball 2

P23 $= -1.688 + .032*PM23(-2) + 141.43*TAX23 - .06*4TMAUR + .015*Q23 - .049*PP23 - .374*4TMAP23(-1)$
$\quad$ (2.1) $\quad$ (.5) $\qquad\qquad$ (3.7) $\qquad$ (.8) $\qquad\quad$ (.3) $\qquad\quad$ (1.3) $\qquad$ (1.0)
$\qquad$ .459, .262, 1.83 $\qquad$ 1961:2-1969:2 $\qquad$ Klein and Ball 2

P25 $= .626 + .034*PM25(-2) + 22.051*TAX25 - .19*4TMAUR + .023*Q25 + .064*PP25 + .287*TMAP 25(-1)$
$\quad$ (.8) $\quad$ (1.5) $\qquad\qquad$ (1.1) $\qquad$ (2.5) $\qquad\quad$ (1.1) $\qquad\quad$ (1.2) $\qquad$ (1.5)
$\qquad$ .631, .257, 1.82 $\qquad$ 1958:2-1969:2 $\qquad$ Klein and Ball 2

P251 $= 1.348 + .042*PM25(-2) + 5.0*TAX25 - .229*4TMAUR + .032*Q251 - .026*PP251 + .190*4TMAP251(-1)$
$\quad$ (1.5) $\quad$ (1.6) $\qquad\qquad$ (.2) $\qquad$ (2.7) $\qquad\quad$ (1.5) $\qquad\quad$ (.4) $\qquad$ (.8)
$\qquad$ .525, .299, 1.75 $\qquad$ 1958:2-1969:2 $\qquad$ Klein and Ball 2

Hypothesis Category Ten (SRC,LRC,DED):

P34 $= -.501 + .170*AHE34 + .489*DRLT + 30.805*PREQ34 - .058*SHP34$
$\quad$ (2.5) $\quad$ (1.8) $\qquad$ (1.2) $\qquad$ (4.2) $\qquad$ (3.1)
$\qquad$ .437, .341, 1.39 $\qquad$ 1958:2-1969:1 $\qquad$ Eckstein and Wyss 5

P35 $= -1.560 + .047*ULCN35 + .164*ULCN35(-1) - .027*DULC,N35 + .146*PM35 + .021*CUI35$
$\quad$ (3.6) $\quad$ (.5) $\qquad\qquad$ (1.8) $\qquad\quad$ (1.1) $\qquad\qquad$ (2.2) $\qquad$ (4.6)
$\qquad$ .552, .257, 2.22 $\qquad$ 1958:2-1969:2 $\qquad$ Fromm and Eckstein 1

Notes:
*Best-fitting industries are categorized as those which appear at least once in Tables 6-1 to 6-10 (i.e., $R^2 \geq .40$ at least once).
The entries for each industry with the regressors are the regression coefficients and t-values (in parentheses).

Table 6-12
Optimum Reestimated Equation for Each of Worst-Fitting Industries

Best reestimated industry price equations	R^2,SEE,DW	Time Interval	Model
Hypothesis category two (SRC,LRC):			
P36 = -.023 + .294*ULCN36 - .205*PM36 + .567*PM36(-1) + .087*P36(-1) (.2) (2.0) (1.4) (3.3) (.6)	.275, .601, 2.13	1958:2-1969:2	Nield 1
Hypothesis category six (SRC,DED):			
P3141 = .889 - .028*AHE3141 + 1.158*PM31 - .011*FDI,IN31 (1.9) (.1) (1.9) (2.2)	.205, 1.071, 1.53	1964:2-1969:2	Courchene
P2111 = .344 - .022*AHE2111 - .003*FDINV21 + .0001*FDINVN21 + .271*P2111(-1) - .201*P2111(-2) (2.1) (.2) (3.1) (.1) (1.8) (1.4)	.251, .660, 1.98	1958:2-1969:2	Liu
P341 = .174 + .247*AHE341 - .058*PM341 - .001*FDI,IN34 (1.2) (2.5) (.9) (3.8)	.251, .705, 1.86	1958:2-1969:1	Courchene
P3562 = -.155 - .263*AHE3562 + .327*PM35 - .001*FDI,IN35 (.6) (1.5) (1.4) (4.1)	.263, 1.115, 2.01	1958:2-1969:2	Courchene
P21 = .266 + .006*AHE21 - .002*FDINV21 - .00003*FDINVN21 + .489*P21(-1) - .323*P21(-2) (2.3) (.1) (3.1) (.03) (3.3) (2.3)	.345, .512, 1.81	1958:2-1969:2	Liu
P3263 = .284 + .051*AHE3263 + .681*PM3263 - .004*FDI,IN32 (1.4) (.2) (2.2) (4.7)	.365, .775, 1.84	1958:2-1969:2	Courchene
Hypothesis category ten (SRC,LRC,DED):			
P371 = .526 + .151*ULCN371 + .151*ULCN371(-1) - .026*DULC,N371 + .043*PM371 - .006*CUI371 (.8) (2.8) (2.8) (1.2) (.9) (.9)	.183, .546, 2.38	1958:2-1969:2	Fromm and Eckstein 1

Notes:
Worst-fitting industries are categorized as those which do not appear in Tables 6-1 to 6-10 (i.e., $R^2 < .40$ in all cases).
The entries for each industry with the regressors are the regression coefficients and t-values (in parentheses).

importance of seasonal movements. The lack of variability argument does not seem valid for most of the industries in question. The table of means, standard deviations, and coefficients of variation in Appendix C indicates that the price variables of the worst-fitting durable goods industries are among the most variable of all durable goods prices. The worst-fitting nondurable goods industries (SICs 21, 2111, and 3141), however, exhibit small price variability relative to the other nondurable goods industries. In these latter cases, explaining price movements is most difficult, since the price change is slight and in the limit, the dependent variable being explained by various behavioral relationships is a constant term. Therefore, lack of variability in price is a reasonable explanation for the poor fits exhibited by the nondurable goods industries in Table 6-12. The importance of seasonal movements has not been considered in the analysis of the industries of this study. However, if seasonal fluctuations are extremely important in explaining the price behavior for any of the industries in Table 6-12, then seasonally adjusted data, which smooth out any seasonal fluctuations, would not be the proper data set to use. Furthermore, if the seasonal behavior of the industry price is different from that of the regressors in its price equation, it may be best to use unadjusted data, in order to capture the true relationship between the variables, and to enter selected seasonal dummies only when necessary. This problem is especially important in the food sector, particularly consumer unprocessed foods and crude foods, because of the many uneconomic factors (e.g., weather) that affect food prices.

From the above comments it is evident that the explanation of price behavior can be significantly improved in a majority of the industries of Table 6-12. This matter will be further explored in Chapter 7 through the use of alternative specifications and lag structures.

Tentative Conclusions Regarding Price Behavior within Different Industry Groupings

The conclusions drawn in this section are based exclusively on the results of reestimating price equation specifications of past studies, grouped into ten hypothesis categories, on the selected industries. Since extensions to these past models in terms of lag structures and alternative hypothesis formulations have yet to be made, the conclusions are termed tentative. The analysis of Chapter 7 should further confirm or cast doubt upon the comments made here.

The industries of this study can be grouped in seven different ways, according to the information contained in Table 5-2. Specifically, the industries may be analyzed relative to one another according to (1) durability of product; (2) type of goods; (3) type of product; (4) degree of industry concentration; (5) level of aggregation; (6) degree of capital intensity; and (7) the production to stock-production to order distinction. Groupings of the industries into each of these seven categories are shown in Tables 6-13 to 6-19, respectively; each industry is ranked relative to the others within each table according to the adjusted R^2 from its best equation (given in Tables 6-11 and 6-12). Tentative conclusions regarding the explanation of price behavior by industry groupings, are as follows.

Durability of Product

There appears to be a more uniform explanation of nondurable goods industry prices than of durable goods industry prices, with all but one of the former (SIC 23) best explained by the modified Liu or Courchene equations of hypothesis category six (see Table 6-13). Six out of the 9 nondurable goods industries have

Table 6-13

Industry Price Behavior by Durability of Product (On the basis of optimum reestimated price equations)

	SIC Industry	Hypotheses	Adj. R^2
Nondurable goods:	22	SRC,DED	.726
	301	SRC,DED	.623
	29	SRC,DED	.553
	227	SRC,DED	.523
	23	SRC,DED,IED	.459
	30	SRC,DED	.509
	21	SRC,DED	.345
	2111	SRC,DED	.250
	3141	SRC,DED	.205
Durable goods:	333	SRC,DED	.822
	24	SRC,DED	.788
	25	SRC,DED,IED	.631
	3541	SRC,DED,IED	.629
	251	SRC,DED,IED	.525
	35	SRC,LRC,DED	.552
	34	SRC,LRC,DED	.483
	331	SRC,DED,IED	.409
	3263	SRC,DED	.365
	36	SRC,LRC	.275
	3562	SRC,DED	.263
	341	SRC,DED	.251
	371	SRC,LRC,DED	.183

an adjusted $R^2 > .50$ for their best price equations whereas only 7 out of the 14 durable goods industries have best price equations with an adjusted $R^2 > .50$. The 2 best explained durable goods industries (SIC 333 and SIC 24) both are fitted by the modified Liu equation of hypothesis category six. Five of the 8 best-fitting durable goods industries have their price behavior best explained by the Klein and Ball equation that includes a form of UR in its specification. This result is reasonable, given the more pronounced cyclical behavior of most durable goods industries.

Type of Goods

The price behavior of mixed goods industries is better explained in general than that of either the consumer goods or producer goods industries, with 8 out of 10 mixed goods industries having adjusted R^2s $> .40$ for their best price equations (see Table 6-14). One third of the mixed goods industry price equations are from hypothesis categories containing SRC, LRC, and in certain cases DED. No hypothesis category is predominant in the producer goods industries. The price behavior of 5 out of the 7 consumer goods industries is best explained by equations from hypothesis category six. However, in all of those industries except SIC 227, the adjusted R^2 is less than .40.

Type of Product

There does not appear to be a significant difference in the explanations of price behavior in final products, intermediate products, and mixed product industries (see Table 6-15). Industries with good and poor fits are found in all three categories. It is interesting that all mixed product, durable goods industries have both SRC and LRC in their best price equations.

Degree of Industry Concentration

The price behavior of industries with four-firm concentration ratios of less than 50 percent is better explained than is that of industries with concentration ratios of over 50 percent (see Table 6-16). There is no uniform explanation in terms of hypothesis categories of price behavior within any of the three concentration ratio categories. However, in the lowest category, DED and IED hypotheses are contained in four of the seven equations, indicating a greater effect of market forces. This finding of better explanation of price behavior in the lower-concentration industries is consistent with the results of Eckstein and Wyss. However, in concluding that the more highly concentrated industries exercise more discretion in both the timing and magnitude of their price change, Eckstein and Wyss classify these highly concentrated industries as target return pricers with $FDRLT$ and $PREQ$ as significant regressors. In general this conclusion is not supported by the results of this study (see Table 6-10).

Table 6-14

Industry Price Behavior by Type of Goods (On the basis of optimum reestimated price equations)

	SIC Industry	Hypotheses	Adj. R²
Consumer goods:	251	SRC,DED,IED	.525
	227	SRC,DED	.523
	23	SRC,DED,IED	.459
	3263	SRC,DED	.365
	21	SRC,DED	.345
	2111	SRC,DED	.250
	3141	SRC,DED	.205
Producer goods:	333	SRC,DED	.822
	3541	SRC,DED,IED	.629
	35	SRC,LRC,DED	.552
	331	SRC,DED,IED	.409
	3562	SRC,DED	.263
	341	SRC,DED	.251
Mixed goods:	24	SRC,DED	.788
	22	SRC,DED	.726
	25	SRC,DED,IED	.631
	301	SRC,DED	.623
	29	SRC,DED	.553
	30	SRC,DED	.509
	34	SRC,LRC,DED	.483
	36	SRC,LRC	.275
	371	SRC,LRC,DED	.183

Level of Aggregation

Price behavior is explained significantly better, the higher the level of aggregation of the industry (see Table 6-17). Of the 10 two-digit industries examined, the price behavior of only SIC 21 and SIC 36 is explained poorly. Of the 7 industries examined at the three-digit level, the price behavior of SICs 341 and 371 is poorly explained and SIC 331 barely meets the minimum criterion for well explained. Finally, at the four-digit level of aggregation only SIC 3541 is well explained out of the 5 such industries studied. Note that the four-digit industries not well explained all have price equations from hypothesis category six as their best equations. There is no single equation specification that seems to best explain price formation for all two-digit industries. These results are consistent with the poor quality of data for the industries at lower levels of

Table 6-15
Industry Price Behavior by Type of Product (On the basis of optimum reestimated price equations)

	SIC Industry	Hypotheses	Adj. R²
Final product:	25	SRC,DED,IED	.631
	3541	SRC,DED,IED	.629
	301	SRC,DED	.623
	251	SRC,DED,IED	.525
	227	SRC,DED	.523
	23	SRC,DED,IED	.459
	3263	SRC,DED	.365
	21	SRC,DED	.345
	2111	SRC,DED	.250
	3141	SRC,DED	.205
Intermediate product:	333	SRC,DED	.822
	24	SRC,DED	.788
	29	SRC,DED	.553
	331	SRC,DED,IED	.409
	3562	SRC,DED	.263
	341	SRC,DED	.251
Mixed product:	22	SRC,DED	.726
	35	SRC,LRC,DED	.552
	30	SRC,DED	.509
	34	SRC,LRC,DED	.483
	36	SRC,LRC	.275
	371	SRC,LRC,DED	.183

aggregation. Note also that the fit of a two-digit industry as compared with that of its three- and four-digit components, varies greatly from industry to industry. A major reason for the differences is based on the relative size of the two-digit industry and the component considered. For example, SIC 2111 comprises nearly 90 percent of SIC 21; therefore, one would expect similar specifications and fits of their price equations.

Degree of Capital Intensity

There is no evidence to support the contention that the price behavior of the more highly capital intensive industries is best explained by an equation that includes capital quantity (K) or cost (RLT), target return ($PREQ$), and/or capacity (CUI) variables as regressors (see Table 6-18). Eckstein and Wyss[159]

Table 6-16

Industry Price Behavior by Concentration Ratio (CR) (On the basis of optimum reestimated price equations)

	SIC Industry	Hypotheses	Adj. R^2
CR ⩾ 50%	333	SRC,DED	.822
	301	SRC,DED	.623
	331	SRC,DED,IED	.409
	3263	SRC,DED	.365
	21	SRC,DED	.345
	3562	SRC,DED	.263
	2111	SRC,DED	.250
	341	SRC,DED	.251
	371	SRC,LRC,DED	.183
50% > CR ⩾ 30%	22	SRC,DED	.726
	29	SRC,DED	.553
	35	SRC,LRC,DED	.552
	227	SRC,DED	.523
	30	SRC,DED	.509
	36	SRC,LRC	.275
CR < 30%	24	SRC,DED	.788
	25	SRC,DED,IED	.631
	3541	SRC,DED,IED	.629
	251	SRC,DED,IED	.525
	23	SRC,DED,IED	.459
	34	SRC,LRC,DED	.483
	3141	SRC,DED	.205

comment that *SHP* also should enter significantly in the price equation for capital intensive industries, on the basis of the assumption that the marginal cost curve in these industries is likely to rise more with an increase in production. This finding is not supported by these results, since those industries which have *SHP* in their optimum price equations (SICs 23 and 34) are on the lower portion (*KI* < .30) of the *KI* scale. There is no equation within any of the hypothesis categories which explains well all of the industries within either of the capital intensity ranges.

Production to Stock Versus Production
to Order Industries

Of those industries which have an inventory-unfilled order ratio (*INV/UNF*) equal to or greater than 1.0, the price behavior of more than one half is best

Table 6-17

Industry Price Behavior by Aggregation (On the basis of optimum reestimated price equations)

	SIC Industry	Hypotheses	Adj. R^2
Two-digit:	24	SRC,DED	.788
	22	SRC,DED	.726
	25	SRC,DED,IED	.631
	29	SRC,DED	.553
	35	SRC,LRC,DED	.552
	23	SRC,DED,IED	.459
	30	SRC,DED	.509
	34	SRC,LRC,DED	.483
	21	SRC,DED	.345
	36	SRC,LRC	.275
Three-digit:	333	SRC,DED	.822
	301	SRC,DED	.623
	251	SRC,DED,IED	.525
	227	SRC,DED	.523
	331	SRC,DED,IED	.409
	341	SRC,DED	.251
	371	SRC,LRC,DED	.183
Four-digit:	3541	SRC,DED,IED	.629
	3263	SRC,DED	.365
	3562	SRC,DED	.263
	2111	SRC,DED	.250
	3141	SRC,DED	.205

explained by the modified Liu or Courchene equations of hypothesis category six (see Table 6-19). However, of these industries, 3141 and 3263 are poorly explained. Of the industries with $INV/UNF < 1.0$, both 36 and 3562 are best (but poorly) explained by the equations of hypothesis category six. Courchene[73] draws the conclusion from his research that an excess demand variable incorporating a form of inventory behavior is best for explaining price behavior regardless of the INV/UNF ratio of the industry. The present result seems to indicate that the price equation specifications that include as regressors $FDINV$ and $FDINVN$, or FDI,IN, are most significant in explaining price behavior in those industries which are more PTS than PTO in their behavior.

Table 6-18
Industry Price Behavior by Capital Intensity (KI) (On the basis of optimum reestimated price equations)

	SIC Industry	Hypotheses	Adj. R^2
KI $\geqslant$ .30	333	SRC,DED	.822
	301	SRC,DED	.623
	29	SRC,DED	.553
	331	SRC,DED,IED	.409
	3562	SRC,DED	.263
	341	SRC,DED	.251
	2111	SRC,DED	.250
	371	SRC,LRC,DED	.183
KI < .30	24	SRC,DED	.788
	22	SRC,DED	.726
	25	SRC,DED,IED	.631
	3541	SRC,DED,IED	.629
	251	SRC,DED,IED	.525
	35	SRC,LRC,DED	.552
	227	SRC,DED	.523
	23	SRC,DED,IED	.459
	30	SRC,DED	.509
	34	SRC,LRC,DED	.483
	3263	SRC,DED	.365
	21	SRC,DED	.345
	36	SRC,LRC	.275
	3141	SRC,DED	.205

Table 6-19

Industry Price Behavior by Production to Stock, Production to Order Distinction (On the basis of optimum reestimated price equations)

	SIC Industry	Hypotheses	Adj. R^2
(INV/UNF) $\geqslant$ 1.0	333	SRC,DED	.822
	24	SRC,DED	.788
	22	SRC,DED	.726
	25	SRC,DED,IED	.631
	251	SRC,DED,IED	.525
	227	SRC,DED	.523
	331	SRC,DED,IED	.409
	3263	SRC,DED	.365
	3141	SRC,DED	.205
	371	SRC,LRC, DED	.183
(INV/UNF) < 1.0	3541	SRC,DED,IED	.629
	35	SRC,LRC,DED	.552
	34	SRC,LRC,DED	.483
	36	SRC,LRC	.275
	3562	SRC,DED	.263
	341	SRC,DED	.251

7

Estimation of Final Industry Price Equations

This chapter introduces a new set of industry price equations that are specified in an attempt to improve upon the best reestimated price equations given in Tables 6-11 and 6-12. The first section explains the modifications of previous models that were considered, the formation of selected long-run cost and *DED* measures, and the approach taken in constructing the final industry price equations. The next section parallels the first and third sections of Chapter 6 by discussing the results with regard to the hypothesis categories represented and the price behavior exhibited by selected industry groupings. The third section then compares the final industry price equations of Tables 7-1 and 7-2 with the best reestimated equations of Tables 6-11 and 6-12 with respect to hypothesis categories represented and overall fits of the equations. The final section presents specific conclusions regarding the final price equation for each industry. The equations developed in this chapter are the final industry price equations from which equations will be selected to be used in the simulations in Chapter 8.

Specification of Final Industry Price Equations

The initial step in specifying the final industry price equations is the extension of the list of regressors contained in past models to include certain long-run measures representing both cost and direct excess demand.

A long-run material price variable (*PMN*), which is a 12-quarter moving average of *PM*, is constructed. Schultze and Tryon constructed similar normalized *PM* variables in the price block of the Brookings model. However, their formulations are not industry-specific but are instead based on aggregate price indexes for imports, agricultural products, and construction materials. It is considered that the industry-specific *PM* and *PMN* will in general be more significant than macro (or more aggregate) material prices. This is tested by also using stage of processing durables and nondurables material price indexes (*WMDM* and *WMNM*), both short-run and normalized, in the correlation and regression analysis. The *PMN* variable represents long-run cost hypothesis (2.6) as long as the assumption of a relatively constant material-output ratio is made.

Three long-run *DED* measures are formed. It is supposed that a firm, in making a price decision, considers a series of past market situations and capacity limitations along with the present conditions. Therefore, 12-term moving averages of output (Q) and capacity utilization (CUI) are constructed, resulting in the *LR-DED* measures QN and *CUIN*. A measure similar to QN is included in price equations by Kuh[170] but only at the sector level. Of course, normalized inventory variables have been formed and used in several price studies, most notable Liu's study. *CUIN* has not been used directly in any price equations, although Schultze and Tryon do include the deviation of present utilization from normal utilization in their price equations. This latter specification is also tested in the present research and found inferior to *CUI* and/or *CUIN* for all industries. The third *LR-DED* measure formed is a deviation of the normalized inventory-sales ratio from the actual ratio. Other formulations are also tried, based on inventory-shipments and inventory-output ratios. Schultze and Tryon constructed a similar variable based on trend and not normalized inventory-sales ratios (see Table 6-10). However, it was found that no significant trend in any of these ratios is exhibited by several of the industries studied. Therefore, the construction of an excess demand measure based on deviations around a trend component may be questioned. In general, the normalized version of this excess demand measure is more significant than the trend version in contributing to the explanation of industry price behavior.

The next step in specifying the final industry price equations utilizes correlation analysis to determine both the regressors to include in each industry's equation and the proper lagged relationship of each regressor with the industry price. All industry-specific and macro regressors representing *SRC*, *LRC*, *IED*, and both long-run and short-run *DED* hypotheses (*SR-DED* and *LR-DED*) are correlated with the appropriate output prices on quarterly lagged relationships extending back one year (e.g., $\rho(P, ULC_t)$, $t = 0,-1,-2,-3,-4$, where ρ = correlation coefficient). In choosing between alternative measures of a given influence on price (e.g., *AHE* vs. *ULC, Q* vs. *SHP*), that which has a significantly higher correlation with price is generally chosen. In cases where the regressors are nearly identical in their correlations with price, they are all tested in the regression analysis. In general, regressors with simple correlations less than $\rho = .35$ are not tested in the regressions. The appropriate lag structure between each regressor and price is determined on the basis of the highest correlation. In cases where several lagged values of a regressor have nearly the same correlation with price, as well as in those cases where alternative measures of an influence on price behavior have similar correlations, several combinations of the regressors are hypothesized in the regressions. This allows regressors with lower simple correlations to appear in the final specifications of price equations as a result of higher partial correlations with price in the presence of other regressors. It should be noted that the equations of Tables 6-11 and 6-12 are modified where necessary in order to represent the optimum lag specification, and then reestimated. In one case (SIC 227), the specification in Table 6-11 with a modified lag structure is the final industry price equation.

As a result of this analysis, several new hypothesis categories are derived which best represent the price behavior of certain industries. These categories, which are contained in Tables 7-1 and 7-2, are designated as follows:

Hypothesis category eleven: *SRC, LR-DED*
Hypothesis category twelve: *SRC, LRC, SR-DED*
Hypothesis category thirteen: *SRC, LRC, LR-DED*
Hypothesis category fourteen: *SRC, LRC, IED*

It is apparent that these hypothesis categories place more emphasis on the effect of *LRC* and *LR-DED* regressors in the price formation process than do the categories in the previous models (see Table 5-3). Hypothesis categories twelve and thirteen are special cases of hypothesis category ten, with the *DED* hypothesis being divided into short-run and long-run components.

Hypotheses Represented by Final Price Equations and Pricing Behavior Exhibited by Selected Industry Groupings

The first part of this section discusses the hypotheses represented in the final industry price equations for both the best-fitting and the worst-fitting industries (see the first notes, Tables 7-1 and 7-2). The second part discusses the pricing behavior exhibited, as reflected by the hypotheses contained and the overall fit of the final price equations, by the different industry groupings given in the last section of Chapter 6.

Hypothesis Represented by Final Price Equations

Inasmuch as the discussion now relates to the final industry price equations, there is only one equation for each industry. Therefore, each industry appears in one hypothesis category, and the extensive layout of Chapter 6, where all industries have price equations fitted within each hypothesis category, is absent. Discussion relating to specific regressors contained in each industry price equation is reserved for the final section of this chapter.

Best-Fitting Industries. Table 7-1 contains the final industry price equations for the best-fitting industries. Better-fitting price equations result for industries 23, 24, and 331 by including *RLT* as a regressor. However, the interpretation of *RLT* as a cost regressor in price equations explaining the rate of change of price is difficult to make. Instead, its inclusion represents a monetarist view of the pricing process, which is itself difficult to support at disaggregate levels of analysis. Such equations follow but were not chosen for further analysis in this research (*t*-values are given in parentheses).

Table 7-1
Final Industry Price Equation for the Best-Fitting Industries [a]

Final industry price equations	R² ,SEE,DW	Time Interval
Hypothesis category three (SRC,SR-DED)		
P333 = 1.337 + .066*ULC333(−4) − .683*INV333 　　　(7.7)　(1.7)　　　　　　　　　　(7.3)	.793, .873, 1.33	1962:2- 1969:2
P22 = −.864 + .547*AHE22 + .235*Q22(−1) 　　　(4.9)　(4.3)　　　　　(4.5)	.601, .534, 1.07	1961:3- 1969:2
P29 = .195 + .657*PM29(−2) − .453*INV29 　　　(1.1)　(1.5)　　　　　　(5.8)	.453, 1.234, 1.59	1958:2- 1969:2
P24 = −.038 + 1.097*AHE24(−3) − .687*INV24 　　　(.1)　　(3.8)　　　　　　　　(7.8)	.708, 1.566, 1.36	1961:2- 1969:2
Hypothesis category eleven (SRC,LR-DED)		
P251 = −13.783 + .098*PM25(−2) + .178*AHE251(−3) + .138*CUIN25 　　　　(4.3)　　(3.8)　　　　　　(1.5)　　　　　　　　　(4.3)	.699, .263, 2.23	1962:2- 1969:2
P3141 = −.047 + .215*WMNM + .535*AHE3141(−3) + 1.34*QN3141 　　　　(.2)　　(.6)　　　　　　(2.7)　　　　　　　　　(4.2)	.430, .830, 2.00	1961:1- 1969:2
Hypothesis category six (SRC, SR-DED, LR-DED)		
P227 = 0.361 + .406*PM22 + .294*AHE227(−2) − .0058*FDI,IN22 　　　(1.7)　　(2.6)　　　(1.6)　　　　　　　　(6.0)	.549, .805, 1.57	1961:3- 1969:2
P34 = .146 + .504*PM34 + .19*INVN34 − .027*SHP34(−1) 　　　(1.9)　(3.2)　　　(1.9)　　　　　(1.4)	.518, .312, 1.49	1959:2- 1969:1
P35 = −1.166 + .084*PM35(−1) + .217*AHE35(−1) + .164*INVN35(−3) + .424*UNFSC35 　　　(2.2)　　(.8)　　　　　　(2.4)　　　　　　　(3.3)　　　　　　　　　(2.3)	.670, .213, 2.38	1959:2- 1969:2

Hypothesis category twelve (SRC, LRC, SR-DED)

P23 = .120 + .197*AHE23(−2) + .658*FDRLT(−3) − .034*SHP23
    (1.6) (3.7)   (1.8)   (2.4)
.447, .314, 1.70   1958:2-1969:2

P301 = 1.264 + .263*PM30(−4) + .052*DULC,N301(−2) − .481*INV30
    (3.6) (1.0)   (1.5)   (7.5)
.640, 1.263, 1.18   1958:2-1969:2

P30 = 1.287 + .461*WMNMN(−4) + .117*DULC,N30(−3) − .266*INV30
    (3.7) (1.5)   (2.7)   (4.3)
.441, .949, 1.29   1958:2-1969:2

P3562 = .963 + .932*PMN35(−4) + .072*DULC,N3562(−3) − .338*INV35
    (2.7) (1.5)   (1.5)   (4.2)
.532, .776, 2.29   1962:2-1969:2

Hypothesis category thirteen (SRC,LRC,LR-DED)

P25 = −13.411 + .087*PM25(−2) + .212*ULCN25 + .135*CUIN25
    (4.6) (4.3)   (2.4)   (4.7)
.741, .231, 2.04   1961:1-1969:2

P3541 = −.34 + .479*PM35(−1) + .104*ULC3541 + 17.571*PREQ35 + .268*QN3541
    (1.4) (3.2)   (2.8)   (1.8)   (4.6)
.750, .312, 2.00   1961:2-1969:2

Hypothesis category fourteen (SRC,LRC,IED)

P331 = −.702 + .087*PM331(−1) + .127*ULCN331 + 4.333*URI
    (3.2) (1.6)   (3.6)   (4.3)
.529, .245, 1.86   1962:1-1969:2

Notes:

Best-fitting industries are those which each have an adjusted R^2 of at least .40 (i.e., $\bar{R}^2 \geqslant .40$).

[a]The entries for each industry under each regressor are the regression coefficients and t-values (in parentheses). The adjusted coefficient of determination (R^2), standard error of the estimate (SEE), and Durbin-Watson statistic (DW) are also given.

$$P23 = -1.119 + .105*AHE23(-2) + .289*RLT - .04*SHP23$$
$$(3.5) \quad (2.0) \qquad\qquad (3.9) \qquad (3.3)$$

$$R^2 = .667, SEE = .206, DW = 2.15$$

$$P24 = -7.369 + .598*AHE24(-3) + 1.642*RLT(-3) - .671*INV24$$
$$(4.1) \quad (2.3) \qquad\qquad (4.2) \qquad\qquad (9.5)$$

$$R^2 = .812, SEE = 1.259, DW = 1.65$$

$$P331 = -1.229 + .179*PMN331 + .075*ULCN331 + .247*RLT$$
$$(3.5) \quad (1.1) \qquad\qquad (2.1) \qquad\qquad (3.7)$$

$$+ 13.775*PREQ331$$
$$(2.0)$$

$$R^2 = .496, SEE = .300, DW = 1.60$$

The industries shown in Table 7-11 are representative of six hypothesis categories, four of which are new and two of which (categories three and six) are from the breakdown given in Table 5-3. All of the hypothesis categories are hybrids of various cost and *DED* hypotheses except category fourteen, which contains a hybrid of the cost and *IED* hypotheses.

Hypothesis category three, which is based on *SRC* and *SR-DED* hypotheses, is the specification that underlies the final price equations for industries 333, 22, 24, and 29. The signs of the coefficients are as expected, with most regressors also significant. The durable goods industry SIC 333 contains the longest lag, that of four quarters on *ULC* 333. In general, a longer lag structure is evident for the *SRC* variables than for the *SR-DED* measures. All are either intermediate or mixed product industries. The Durbin-Watson statistic for all four industries is low, indicating a positive relationship between the residuals over time.

Hypothesis category eleven, containing *SRC* and *LR-DED* hypotheses, is the basis for the final price equations for industries 251 and 3141. The signs of the coefficients are again as expected with most regressors significant. The industries best fitted by this category have much in common, in that both are final product, consumer goods industries and each has a concentration ratio less than 30 percent, a low degree of capital intensity, and a high (greater than 1) *INV/UNF* ratio. The labor cost variable (*AHE*) enters both equations with a lag of three quarters. However, the *LR-DED* measures have the longest lag represented within them, since they are moving averages over 12 past quarters.

Hypothesis category six, which is the dominant basis for the reestimated industry price equations in Tables 6-11 and 6-12, provides the best specifications for industries 227, 34, and 35 in Table 7-1. It contains regressors that represent the *SRC* and both the *SR-DED* and *LR-DED* pricing hypotheses. All three industries are low on the capital intensity scale. All coefficients have the expected signs (except the sign on $SHP34(-1)$, which is negative), with most variables being significant. Interpreting $SHP34(-1)$, as a $SR\text{-}DED$ measure is most difficult (see Chapter 2, page 17).

Of all the categories, hypothesis category twelve provides the most generally applicable specification for explaining price behavior. Four industries (23, 30, 301, and 3562) reflect this category in their final price equations. Included are regressors depicting SRC, LRC, and $SR\text{-}DED$ hypotheses. All of the industries in this category have relatively long lag structures with respect to one or more cost variables but have simultaneous relationships between price and the $SR\text{-}DED$ variables. All regressors enter with the expected sign except for $SHP23$, which is again negative as in the SIC 34 equation above. All regressors except $PM30(-4)$ have a t-value of at least 1.5.

Hypothesis category thirteen, which combines SRC, LRC, and $LR\text{-}DED$ hypotheses, provides the best specification for the final price equations of industries 25 and 3541. All regressors in the two equations are significant and have proper signs. Both industries are durable goods and final product industries having concentration ratios less than 30 percent and being low on the capital intensity scale. Note that both industries of hypothesis category eleven, which includes $LR\text{-}DED$, are also final product industries. It appears that accounting for market behavior over a substantial period of time may be of greater importance in the examination of the price behavior of final product industries.

The final hypothesis category in Table 7-1 provides the final price equation for SIC 331. Since it explains only one industry best, the results are discussed in the final section of this chapter under SIC 331.

Worst-Fitting Industries. Table 7-2 contains the estimated final industry price equations for the worst-fitting industries. Five hypothesis categories are represented to best explain price formation in these six industries. All variables enter with their proper signs (except that SHP is again negative) and are almost all significant, although the overall degree of explanation for each industry's price behavior is poor. The lag structure with respect to cost variables is again long relative to that with respect to DED variables. The specific results for each industry will be discussed in the section on industry conclusions.

Pricing Behavior Exhibited by
Selected Industry Groupings

The construction of Table 7-3 to 7-9 is analogous to that of Tables 6-13 to 6-19, with the industries ranked relative to each other within each table according to the adjusted R^2s from their final equations. Groupings of industries include those by durability of product, type of goods, type of product, degree of industry concentration, level of aggregation, degree of capital intensity, and the

Table 7-2
Final Industry Price Equations for the Worst-Fitting Industries [a]

Final Industry Price Equations	R^2, SEE, DW	Time Interval
Hypothesis category three (SRC,SR-DED)		
P3263 = .18 + .644*PM32(−4) + .376*AHE3263 − .132*SHP32 (.8) (2.0) (1.9) (4.1)	.346, .787, 2.40	1958:2-1969:2
Hypothesis category eleven (SRC,LR-DED)		
P341 = .305 + .081*ULC341 + 3.969*FDIQN341(−2) (2.7) (3.5) (1.8)	.229, .715, 1.67	1958:2-1969:1
Hypothesis category twelve (SRC,LRC,SR-DED)		
P21 = −3.36 + .229*WMNM(−4) + .056*ULCN21(−4) + 108.244*PREQ21 − .146*INV21 (1.9) (1.4) (1.1) (2.1) (2.8)	.311, .525, 1.27	1958:2-1969:2
P371 = .297 + .211*PM371(−1) + .028*DULC,N371(−4) − .071*INV371(−2) (2.3) (1.3) (1.5) (4.5)	.385, .474, 1.91	1958:2-1969:2
Hypothesis category two (LRC,SRC)		
P36 = −.183 + .393*PM36(−1) + .440*PM36(−3) + .252*ULCN36(−2) (1.5) (2.6) (2.6) (1.9)	.371, .560, 1.90	1958:2-1969:2
Hypothesis category fifteen (LRC,SR-DED)		
P2111 = −3.885 + .177*ULCN2111(−4) + 121.443*PREQ21 − .182*INV21 (1.9) (2.2) (2.0) (3.1)	.368, .606, 1.57	1958:2-1969:2

Notes:
Worst-fitting industries are those which each have an adjusted R^2 of less than .40 (i.e., $\bar{R}^2 < .40$).
aThe entries for each industry under each regressor are the regression coefficients and t-values (in parentheses). The adjusted coefficient of determination (R^2), standard error of the estimate (SEE), and Durbin-Watson statistic (DW) are also given.

Table 7-3

Industry Price Behavior by Durability of Product (On the basis of final industry price equations)

	SIC Industry	Hypotheses	Adj. R^2
Nondurable goods:	23	SRC,LRC,SR-DED	.529
	301	SRC,LRC,SR-DED	.640
	22	SRC,SR-DED	.601
	227	SRC,SR & LR-DED	.549
	29	SRC,SR-DED	.453
	30	SRC,LRC,SR-DED	.441
	3141	SRC,LR-DED	.430
	2111	LRC,SR-DED	.368
	21	SRC,LRC,SR-DED	.311
Durable goods:	24	SRC,SR-DED	.708
	333	SRC,SR-DED	.793
	3541	SRC,LRC,LR-DED	.750
	25	SRC,LRC,LR-DED	.741
	251	SRC,LR-DED	.699
	35	SRC,SR & LR-DED	.670
	3562	SRC,LRC,SR-DED	.532
	34	SRC,SR & LR-DED	.518
	331	SRC,LRC,IED	.447
	371	SRC,LRC,SR-DED	.385
	3263	SRC,SR-DED	.346
	36	LRC,SRC	.342
	341	SRC,LR-DED	.229

production to stock-production to order distinction. Tentative conclusions were drawn in Chapter 6 concerning each of these groupings with regard to the presence of uniformity in the pricing hypotheses best explaining a certain industry grouping. However, the differences among hypothesis categories one to ten are generally clear, ranging from a category with only *SRC* to one with *SRC, LRC,* and *DED* (see Table 5-3). The hypothesis categories that form the basis for the final industry price equations given in Tables 7-1 and 7-2 are almost all based on cost and excess demand hypotheses, with various combinations of short- and long-run measures composing the categories. A careful examination of the groupings in Tables 7-3 to 7-9 reveals no apparent uniformity in pricing behavior within any of the groups. This result casts doubt on the tentative conclusions drawn in the last section of Chapter 6. However, it does support the contention that even though a *general* cost, excess demand formulation underlies most

Table 7-4
Industry Price Behavior by Type of Goods (On the basis of final industry price equations)

	SIC Industry	Hypotheses	Adj. R²
Consumer goods:	251	SRC,LR-DED	.699
	23	SRC,LRC,SR-DED	.529
	227	SRC,SR & LR DED	.549
	3141	SRC,LR-DED	.430
	2111	LRC,SR-DED	.368
	3263	SRC,SR-DED	.346
	21	SRC,LRC,SR-DED	.311
Producer goods:	333	SRC,SR-DED	.793
	3541	SRC,LRC,SR-DED	.750
	35	SRC,SR & LR DED	.670
	3562	SRC,LRC,SR-DED	.532
	331	SRC,LRC,IED	.447
	341	SRC,LR-DED	.229
Mixed goods:	24	SRC,SR-DED	.708
	25	SRC,LRC,LR-DED	.741
	301	SRC,LRC,SR-DED	.640
	22	SRC,SR-DED	.601
	34	SRC,SR & LR-DED	.518
	29	SRC,SR-DED	.453
	30	SRC,LRC,SR-DED	.441
	371	SRC,LRC,SR-DED	.385
	36	LRC,SRC	.342

industries' price formation processes, there are subtle differences between industries with regard to both the factors that affect price behavior and the time span over which these factors are influential. Thus, uniform explanations of price behavior within selected groupings of industries are difficult if not impossible to make.

One comment based on the results contained in Tables 7-3 to 7-9 can be made with regard to fit. In general, any industry having certain of the following characteristics has its price behavior explained better than others: durable goods, producer goods, intermediate products, low (less than 30 percent) degree of concentration, and high level of aggregation (two-digit industry). Industries with the above characteristics are generally those with low demand elasticities, high margins, and lack of substitutes.

Table 7-5

Industry Price Behavior by Type of Product (On the basis of final industry price equations)

	SIC Industry	Hypotheses	Adj. R²
Final product:	3541	SRC,LRC,LR-DED	.750
	25	SRC,LRC,LR-DED	.741
	251	SRC,LR-DED	.699
	23	SRC,LRC,SR-DED	.529
	301	SRC,LRC,SR-DED	.640
	227	SRC,SR & LR-DED	.549
	3141	SRC,LR-DED	.430
	2111	LRC,SR-DED	.368
	3263	SRC,SR-DED	.346
	21	SRC,LRC,SR-DED	.311
Intermediate product:	24	SRC,SR-DED	.708
	333	SRC,SR-DED	.793
	3562	SRC,LRC,SR-DED	.532
	331	SRC,LRC,IED	.447
	29	SRC,SR-DED	.453
	341	SRC,LR-DED	.229
Mixed product:	35	SRC,SR & LR-DED	.670
	22	SRC,SR-DED	.601
	34	SRC,SR & LR-DED	.518
	30	SRC,LRC,SR-DED	.441
	371	SRC,LRC,SR-DED	.385
	36	LRC,SRC	.342

Comparison of Final and Best Reestimated Price Equations

The results contained in Tables 6-11 and 6-12 are compared in this section with those contained in Tables 7-1 and 7-2. In this way, the final industry price equations may be judged relative to a standard composite of the best results obtained from estimating representative past price models on the same industries.

An initial comparison of the results may be made by examining the overall fits of the two sets of equations relative to one another. The adjusted R^2s for each industry's equations are given in Table 7-10. In 14 out of the 22 industries, the explanation of price behavior is improved considerably in the final industry

Table 7-6

Industry Price Behavior by Concentration Ratio (CR) (On the basis of final industry price equations)

	SIC Industry	Hypotheses	Adj. R^2
CR $\geqslant$ 50%	333	SRC,SR-DED	.793
	301	SRC,LRC,SR-DED	.640
	3562	SRC,LRC,SR-DED	.532
	331	SRC,LRC,IED	.447
	371	SRC,LRC,SR-DED	.385
	2111	LRC,SR-DED	.368
	3263	SRC,SR-DED	.346
	21	SRC,LRC,SR-DED	.311
	341	SRC,LR-DED	.229
50% > CR $\geqslant$ 30%	35	SRC,SR & LR-DED	.670
	22	SRC,SR-DED	.601
	227	SRC,SR & LR-DED	.549
	29	SRC,SR-DED	.453
	30	SRC,LRC,SR-DED	.441
	36	LRC,SRC	.342
CR < 30%	24	SRC,SR-DED	.708
	3541	SRC,LRC,LR-DED	.750
	25	SRC,LRC,LR-DED	.741
	251	SRC,LR-DED	.699
	23	SRC,LRC,SR-DED	.529
	34	SRC,SR & LR-DED	.518
	3141	SRC,LR-DED	.430

price equations. Eight of the final price equations have an adjusted R^2 of at least .60 compared with only 6 of the best reestimated ones. Furthermore, the number of worst-fitting industries has been reduced from 8 to 6. More importantly, there are only 3 final industry price equations with an R^2 of less than .35 whereas there were 7 of the best reestimated equations with an R^2 lower than .35.

Comments are now in order regarding the final industry price equations with overall fits that are inferior to those of the best reestimated equations, namely, SICs 333, 22, 29, 24, 30, 3263, 341, and 21. All of these industries have either the Liu or the Courchene formulation as their best reestimated equation, as indicated in Tables 6-11 and 6-12. The Liu equations, namely, those for SICs 333, 22, 29, 24, 30, and 21, include both $P(-1)$ and $P(-2)$ regressors.

Table 7-7

Industry Price Behavior by Aggregation (On the basis of final industry price equations)

	SIC Industry	Hypotheses	Adj. R^2
Two-digit:	24	SRC,SR-DED	.708
	25	SRC,LRC,LR-DED	.741
	35	SRC,SR & LR-DED	.670
	23	SRC,LRC,SR-DED	.529
	22	SRC,SR-DED	.601
	34	SRC,SR & LR-DED	.518
	29	SRC,SR-DED	.453
	30	SRC,LRC,SR-DED	.441
	36	LRC,SRC	.342
	21	SRC,LRC,SR-DED	.311
Three-digit:	333	SRC,SR-DED	.793
	251	SRC,LR-DED	.699
	301	SRC,LRC,SR-DED	.640
	227	SRC,SR & LR-DED	.549
	331	SRC,LRC,IED	.447
	371	SRC,LRC,SR-DED	.385
	341	SRC,LR-DED	.229
Four-digit:	3541	SRC,LRC,LR-DED	.750
	3562	SRC,LRC,SR-DED	.532
	3141	SRC,LR-DED	.430
	2111	LRC,SR-DED	.368
	3263	SRC,SR-DED	.346

Modifying and estimating the final industry price equations for these industries by including $P(-1)$ as a regressor results in the adjusted R^2s given in the last column of Table 7-10.

It is apparent that the final price equation with the lagged price as a regressor for SIC 29 is equivalent in overall fit to the reestimated Liu equation and for both SIC 21 and SIC 24 is superior in fit to the Liu formulation. Furthermore, the signs of the regressors in the final price equations for all three industries are as expected and the significance is higher than for the regressors of the reestimated Liu equation. The overall fits of the final equations modified to include lagged price as a regressor for industries 333, 22, and 30 are still worse than the fits of the reestimated Liu equation. However, in their final equations all of the regressors are significant with the proper signs; this is not the case for

Table 7-8
Industry Price Behavior by Capital Intensity (KI) (On the basis of final industry price equations)

	SIC Industry	Hypotheses	Adj. R^2
KI ⩾ .30	333	SRC,SR-DED	.793
	301	SRC,LRC,SR-DED	.640
	3562	SRC,LRC,SR-DED	.532
	331	SRC,LRC,IED	.447
	29	SRC,SR-DED	.453
	371	SRC,LRC,SR-DED	.385
	2111	LRC,SR-DED	.368
	341	SRC,LR-DED	.229
KI < .30	24	SRC,SR-DED	.708
	3541	SRC,LRC,LR-DED	.750
	25	SRC,LRC,LR-DED	.741
	251	SRC,LR-DED	.699
	35	SRC,SR & LR-DED	.670
	23	SRC,LRC,SR-DED	.529
	22	SRC,SR-DED	.601
	227	SRC,SR & LR-DED	.549
	34	SRC,SR & LR-DED	.518
	30	SRC,LRC,SR-DED	.441
	3141	SRC,LR-DED	.430
	3263	SRC,SR-DED	.346
	36	LRC,SRC	.342
	21	SRC,LRC,SR-DED	.311

the best reestimated equations (see Tables 6-11 and 7-1). Finally, the other two industries, SICs 3263 and 341, are both specified in Table 6-12 by reestimated Courchene equations. However, none of the regressors in those equations are significant, with *PM* having a negative sign in the SIC 341 equation. The equations for SICs 3263 and 341 given in Table 7-2 include regressors that are all significant with the expected signs. On the basis of these observations, it is considered that the final industry price equations are better specifications for explaining price formation in these industries than are the best reestimated equations even though the former have lower overall fits.

The lagged price $P(-1)$ was entered as a regressor in all final industry price equations. For industries 21, 22, 23, 24, and 29, the $P(-1)$ regressor is significant and the overall fit of each price equation is improved. These modified

Table 7-9

Industry Price Behavior by Production to Stock, Production to Order Distinction (on the basis of final industry price equations)

	SIC Industry	Hypotheses	Adj. R^2
(INV/UNF) ⩾ 1.0	24	SRC,SR-DED	.708
	333	SRC,SR-DED	.793
	25	SRC,LRC,LR-DED	.741
	251	SRC,LR-DED	.699
	22	SRC,SR-DED	.601
	227	SRC,SR & LR-DED	.549
	331	SRC,LRC,IED	.447
	3141	SRC,LR-DED	.430
	371	SRC,LRC,SR-DED	.385
	3263	SRC,SR-DED	.346
(INV/UNF) < 1.0	3541	SRC,LRC,LR-DED	.750
	35	SRC,SR & LR-DED	.670
	3562	SRC,LRC,SR-DED	.532
	34	SRC,SR & LR-DED	.518
	36	LRC,SRC	.342
	341	SRC,LR-DED	.229

equations are given below. The present intent is to explain each industry's price behavior without entering the autoregressive term. However, the autoregressive equations are tried in the ex post simulations of Chapter 8 and employed in the policy simulations whenever they prove superior to the final industry price equations.

$$P21 = -2.431 + .257*WNMN(-4) + .041*ULCN21(-4)$$
$$(1.4) \quad (1.6) \quad\quad\quad (.8)$$
$$+ 78.318*PREQ21 - .123*INV21 + .288*P21(-1)$$
$$(1.5) \quad\quad\quad (2.4) \quad\quad (2.1)$$
$$R^2 = .364, SEE = .505, DW = 1.6$$

$$P22 = -.680 + .564*AHE22 + .125*Q22(-1) + .419*P22(-1)$$
$$(4.7) \quad (4.8) \quad\quad (2.7) \quad\quad (4.3)$$
$$R^2 = .679, SEE = .568, DW = 1.5$$

Table 7-10

Comparison of Optimum Reestimated Price Equations with Final Industry Price Equations (Adj. R²)

SIC Industry	Optimum Reestimated	Final Industry	Final Industry with Lagged Price
333	.822	.793	.788
22	.726	.601	.679
29	.553	.453	.551
251	.525	.699	
3141	.205	.430	
227	.523	.549	
34	.483	.518	
35	.552	.670	
23	.459	.529	
24	.788	.708	.821
301	.623	.640	
30	.509	.441	.428
3562	.263	.532	
25	.631	.741	
3541	.629	.750	
331	.409	.447	
3263	.365	.346	
341	.251	.229	
21	.345	.311	.364
371	.183	.385	
36	.275	.371	
2111	.251	.368	

$$P23 = .100 + .112*AHE23(-2) + .832*FDRLT(-3) - .038*SHP23$$
$$(.14)\ (1.7) \qquad (2.4) \qquad (2.8)$$
$$+ .324*P23(-1)$$
$$(2.1)$$
$$R^2 = .583, SEE = .230, DW = 2.26$$

$$P24 = -.173 + .671*AHE24(-3) - .786*INV24 + .394*P24(-1)$$
$$(2.1)\ (2.7) \qquad (10.9) \qquad (4.5)$$
$$R^2 = .821, SEE = 1.226, DW = 2.07$$

$$P29 = .218 + .619*PM29(-2) - .513*INV29 + .303*P29(-1)$$
$$(1.3)\ (.6) \qquad (7.0) \qquad (3.2)$$
$$R^2 = .551, SEE = 1.118, DW = 2.4$$

A second comparison of the two sets of equations may be made by examining the signs of the regressors in the equations in light of their expected signs. The final industry price equations are definitely superior in this regard. They contain no cost variables with negative signs whereas the best reestimated equations for industries 227, 301, 36, 3141, 2111, and 3562 in Tables 6-11 and 6-12 have negative signs on the *AHE* or *PM* regressors. All *DED* variables in both sets enter with signs consistent with theory, though not necessarily representing an excess demand influence (e.g., *SHP* has a negative sign).

Concerning the significance of the regressors, it is apparent that almost every regressor is significant in the final industry price equations whereas many variables are insignificant in the best reestimated price equations. The combination of correct sign and high significance of each of the regressors in the final industry price equations makes these equations more attractive as structural equations for explaining price behavior.

The final point of comparison regards the hypotheses represented in both the best reestimated price equations and the final industry price equations. The final price equations are almost all hybrid hypotheses that combine cost and excess demand hypotheses. Only in one industry is price behavior best explained by pure cost hypotheses, with the lagged price not contained in any of the final industry price equations. Fourteen of the best reestimated price equations include the lagged price as a regressor and one industry's price behavior is best explained by only cost regressors. Some form of *INV* is included as a *DED* regressor in 13 of the final price equations, with labor cost being represented evenly by both *AHE* and various forms of *ULC*. *PM* is in 10 final price equations.

The *PMN* or *LR-DED* regressors are contained in seven final industry price equations. Therefore, the equations for these industries include either new hypotheses or new formulations of a regressor which did not appear in the best reestimated price equations or in any past price models at the two-, three-, and four-digit levels of aggregation. Furthermore, only two of these industries (SICs 341 and 30) have poorer fits in the final price equations than in the best reestimated price equations, whereas the other five industries exhibit substantially better fits.

In summary, the final industry price equations appear to represent sounder structural formulations for explaining the price behavior of the 22 industries studied, as compared with the best formulations from past studies. They contain a more extensive set of regressors representing cost and excess demand influences in both the short and long run. Thus, many different specifications of hybrid hypotheses are formulated, being differentiated from one another according to the included regressors. This result is indicative of the different factors that influence pricing decisions and their variance from industry to industry.

Industry-Specific Conclusions

In this section are presented industry-specific conclusions based on the final industry price equations of Tables 7-1 and 7-2. Certain information is employed along with these equations in order to thoroughly analyze each industry's price behavior over the period 1965:1 to 1969:2, the most volatile portion of the sample period. Table 7-11 contains the equations in Beta coefficient form for those industries in which all regressors are not in percentage change form (e.g., $AHE25$ vs. $CUIN25$ in SIC 25). The Beta coefficients are interpreted in terms of the standard deviation change in price change which results from a standard deviation change in each of the regressors. They allow the relative effects of various regressors on price to be compared when the regressors are not in the same units. Table 7-12 contains summary facts, based on the period 1965:1 to 1969:2, relating to both the residuals and the movement of the fitted series versus the actual series. The average absolute price change (AAP) is compared with the average absolute residual (AAR) for each industry. The average residual over the 1965:1 to 1969:2 period is approximately zero, so that comparing AAR with AAP seems to be a suitable way of comparing the relative size, regardless of signs, of each industry's price change and each industry price equation's error. Signs are taken into account in evaluating price declines with regard to both the number of actual declines accurately fitted and the number of false price declines that are predicted. The number of positive (underprediction) and negative (overprediction) residuals are given for each industry's equation, along with the proportion of turning points accurately traced over the 1965:1 to 1969:2 period. (Turning points are considered as both changes in the direction of price change and reversals in the magnitudes of price change.) A table of actual price change, the fitted series, and the residual series, along with a plot of the actual versus fitted price change, is given for each industry in Appendix D. In the discussion that follows, the expressions "price change" and "average price change" refer to percentage change in price, whereas the terms "fitted," "predicted," and "simulated" are used interchangeably when referring to the price change series estimated by each final industry price equation. All discussion relating to the information contained in Table 7-12 is in reference to the 1965:1 to 1969:2 period.

Best-Fitting Industries

SIC 333: Primary Nonferrous Metals. This industry bases its pricing decisions primarily on market conditions, with $INV333$ having an effect 10 times as large as that of $ULC333(-4)$ on price change. The coefficient on unit labor cost seems unreasonably low (.066) in magnitude. Price change is underpredicted 12 times and overpredicted 6, with a majority of the positive residuals prior to 1967:3 and 5 out of 6 overpredictions after that period. Price fluctuations over the 1965:1 to 1969:2 period were of large magnitude, with an AAP of 1.585. The simulated price series tracked these changes quite accurately, having an AAR of .656 and picking up 8 out of 10 turning points. However, even though all five

Table 7-11
Beta Equations for Selected Industries of Tables 7-1 and 7-2

(1) (P251/.425) $= -32.642 + .471(PM25(-2)/2.044) + .248(AHE251(-3)/.591) + .605(CUIN25/1.863)$

(2) (P227/1.114) $= -.324 + .308(PM22/.845) + .230(AHE227(-2)/.870) - .722\ (FDI,IN22/138.742)$

(3) (P35/.375) $= -3.109 + .098(PM35(-1)/.439) + .236(AHE35(-1)/.407) + .415(INVN35(-3)/.950) + .258(UNFSC35/.228)$

(4) (P23/.357) $= .336 + .490(AHE23(-2)/.887) + .243(F'DRLT/.132) - .392(SHP23/4.116)$

(6) (P301/2.061) $= .613 + .097(PM30(-4)/.763) + .140(DULC,N301(-2)/5.535) - .240(INV30/3.158)$

(7) (P25/.414) $= -32.394 + .430(PM25(-2)/2.044) + .273(ULCN25/.534) + .608(CUIN25/1.863)$

(8) (P3541/.626) $= -.543 + .336(PM35(-1)/.439) + .337(ULCN3541/2.027) + .337(PREQ35/.012) + .942(QN3541/2.200)$

(9) (P331/.414) $= -1.681 + -.186(PM331(-1)/.886) + .406(ULCN331/1.322) + .502(URI/.048)$

(11) (P30/1.242) $= 1.036 + .141(WMNMN/.380) + .317(DULC,N30(-3)/3.367) - .512(INV30/2.391)$

(12) (P3562/1.106) $= .871 + .195(PMN35(-4)/.231) + .221(DULC,N3562(-3)/3.399) - .594(INV3562/1.943)$

(13) (P341/.788) $= .387 + .478(ULC341/4.654) + .252(FDIQN341(-2)/.050)$

(14) (P21/.619) $= -5.428 + .179(WMNM(-4)/.484) + .136(ULCN21(-4)/1.503) + .350(PREQ21/.002) - .386(INV21/1.636)$

(15) (P371/.598) $= .497 + .175(PM371(-1)/.496) + .202(DULC,N371(-4)/4.304) - .538(INV371(-2)/4.531)$

(16) (P2111/.746) $= -5.208 + .275(ULCN2111(-4)/1.157) + .326(PREQ21/.002) - .406(INV21/1.664)$

Note:
The general form of the equation is $Y/\sigma_y = B_0/\sigma_y + B_1(\sigma_x/\sigma_y)(X/\sigma_x)$, where $B_0^* = B_0/\sigma_y$ and $B_1^* = B_1(\sigma_x/\sigma_y)$ are the Beta coefficients and σ_y and σ_x are the standard deviations of Y and X.

Table 7-12

Residual Analysis and Turning-Point Behavior, Final Industry Price Equations, 1965:1–1969:2

SIC Industry	Average Absolute Price Change (AAP)	Average Absolute Residual (AAR)	Number of Positive Residuals	Number of Negative Residuals	Turning Points, Predicted-Actual	P Declines, Predicted-Actual	False P Declines
333	1.585	.656	12	6	8–10	5–5	3
22	.728	.373	7	11	11–13	6–7	0
29	1.005	.660	12	6	5–9	3–4	3
251	.784	.199	7	11	5–9	0–1	0
3141	1.218	.684	6	12	9–12	1–2	0
227	.766	.615	7	11	4–11	7–11	4
34	.707	.243	8	9	5–5	0–0	0
35	.785	.212	9	9	4–7	0–0	0
23	.454	.204	9	9	6–9	0–1	0
24	3.112	1.239	7	11	7–9	4–5	1
301	1.058	.760	14	4	7–12	3–4	3
30	.871	.558	11	7	7–10	2–3	3
3562	.589	.521	11	7	6–11	8–9	4
25	.793	.196	10	8	7–10	0–0	0
3541	1.233	.251	9	9	5–9	0–0	0
331	.521	.194	9	9	4–7	0–0	0
3263	1.001	.793	8	10	4–11	1–5	0
341	.845	.478	9	8	7–12	1–4	1
21	.724	.516	7	11	7–13	0–4	0
371	.374	.347	7	11	6–11	1–3	1
36	.585	.400	6	12	4–12	2–4	0
2111	.977	.518	8	10	5–11	0–3	0

price declines were properly predicted, three false price decline predictions also resulted.

SIC 22: Textile Mill Products. The results indicate that this industry follows primarily rule-of-thumb pricing based on wage rates, with price change also adjusted on the basis of market conditions as measured through lagged output change. The effect of change in wages on price is over twice that of a comparable change in output. The simulated series overpredicts price change 11 times and underpredicts it 7 times, with the AAP being nearly twice as large as the AAR. The turning points in the actual price series are followed by the simulated series in 11 out of 13 cases. The actual price declines of SIC 22 are predicted six out of seven times by the simulated series.

SIC 29: Petroleum and Coal Products Rule-of-thumb pricing that also allows for adjustments due to market conditions is again apparent. In contrast to SIC 22, however, the short-run cost and *DED* variables are *PM*29(−2) and *INV*29, with the influence of the former on price change one and one-half times that of the latter. As in SIC 333, 12 price changes are underpredicted and only 6 overpredicted, with a AAR of .660 compared with an average price change of 1.005. Price declines are predicted six times and occur only four times, signifying the effect of a large increase in *INV*29 in certain periods. Five out of the nine turning points in the actual price change are correctly tracked.

SIC 251: Household Furniture. Long-run capacity considerations are the most important factor influencing price behavior, with both cost variables reflecting rule-of-thumb pricing. This conclusion is substantiated by examining the Beta coefficients, which indicate that the effect of *CUIN*25 on price change is two and one-half times that of *AHE*25(−3) and one and one-third times that of *P*24(−2). Lags are present on both cost regressors and the coefficient values are lower than expected. The overpredictions outnumber the underpredictions 11 to 7, with an AAR of .199 compared with an AAP of .784. There is only one price decline and it is not picked up by the predicted series. Turning points are correctly tracked only five out of nine times.

SIC 3141: Shoes, Except Rubber. Price change in this industry is influenced most significantly by long-run output changes, reflecting adjustments to long-run market forces, with the influence of *QN*3141 on price change six times that of *WMNM* and two and one-half times that of *AHE*3141(−3). Note that the materials price regressor is highly insignificant. The actual price change is overpredicted 12 times and underpredicted 6 times, with an AAR of .684 compared with an AAP of 1.218. One of two price declines is predicted, with the price decline from 1969:1 to 1969:2 being properly traced. Nine out of 12 turning points are tracked correctly. The AAR,AAP relationship and the turning-point behavior of the fitted series are quite good considering the fit of the equation ($R^2 = .429$).

SIC 227: Floor Covering Mills. Long-run and short-run market forces, as represented by *FDI,IN*22 exhibit the strongest influence on price behavior, being highly significant and having a Beta coefficient more than twice the magnitude of those on *PM*22 and *AHE*227(−2). Both cost regressors once again indicate a rule-of-thumb cost basis for price formation. Eleven price changes are overpredicted and seven underpredicted. The relationship between AAR and AAP, which have values of .615 and .766, respectively, is not as favorable as in the industries examined above. Furthermore, only 4 out of 11 turning points are correctly tracked, with 7 out of 11 price declines predicted correctly and 4 other price declines falsely predicted.

SIC 34: Fabricated Metal Industries. This industry's price behavior is dominated by the behavior of its material price index, with its coefficient about 18 times as large as the coefficient on $SHP34(-1)$ and 3 times as large as that on $INVN34$. The *LR-DED* measure $INVN34$ is significant but the *SR-DED* measure $SHP34(-1)$ is not. Both of these variables might be best interpreted other than in the *DED* sense, given the signs that they assume in the equation. If so, the cost influence on price change reflected by this price equation would be greater than that indicated by $PM34$ alone. The number of over- and underpredictions is nearly even, with all five turning points correctly tracked. All price changes over this period for SIC 34 are positive, as they are predicted. The AAP is nearly three times as large as the AAR. This result, combined with the perfect turning-point tracking, is surprising, given an R^2 of only .518.

SIC 35: Machinery, Except Electrical. Price behavior in SIC 35 is influenced mainly by *DED* factors, assuming $INVN35$ can be interpreted as a *DED* measure (see the above discussion of SIC 34). The Beta coefficients indicate that the strongest effects on price change are from $INVN35(-3)$ and $UNFSC35$. At the same time, $PM35(-1)$ is insignificant, with an unusually low coefficient. The numbers of over- and underpredictions of actual price change are equal, with a very low AAR of .212 compared with an AAP of .785. Only four out of seven turning points are tracked correctly.

SIC 23: Apparel and Related Products. The explanation of price behavior in SIC 23 is dominated by the short-run cost variable $AHE23$. Examination of the Beta coefficients reveals the effect of $AHE23$ on price change is twice that of $FDRLT$ and one and one-third times that of $SHP23$. The over- and underpredictions of actual price change are equal, with an AAR of .204 compared with an AAP of .454. The one decline in the industry price is not picked up whereas six out of the nine turning points in the actual price change series are accurately predicted.

SIC 24: Lumber and Wood Products. This industry's price behavior is marked by highly significant effects of regressors representing the *SRC* and *SR-DED* hypotheses. The effect of $INV24$ is nearly twice that of $AHE24(-3)$. A long lag structure is present on the cost regressor whereas a simultaneous relationship exists between $P24$ and $INV24$. The overpredictions of the actual price change outnumber the underpredicitons 11 to 7, with the AAP almost three times the AAR in value. Seven out of the nine turning points and four out of five price declines are correctly tracked, with only one false price decline being predicted. The $P24$ series is highly volatile; however, the fitted series performs consistently in predicting large and small fluctuations in price. Of the three price declines over the 1966:3 to 1967:1 period, the first two are picked up by the fitted series.

SIC 301: Tires and Tubes. The price behavior of SIC 301, like that of SIC 333, is affected most strongly by short-run market forces, as represented by $INV30$. The SRC regressor is not significant and the combination SRC,LRC regressor is only marginally significant. The Beta coefficients indicate that $INV30$ has almost three times the effect of $PM30(-4)$ and almost twice the effect of $DULC,N301(-2)$ in influencing price change. As in SIC 24 above, a lagged relationship exists between the cost regressors and price whereas a simultaneous relationship exists between the DED measure and price. Underpredictions outnumber overpredictions 14 to 4, with the AAR being .760 compared with an AAP of 1.058. Three false price declines are predicted for the 1968:2 to 1968:4 period, prior to an actual price decline in 1969:1, which is also predicted. Two out of three other price declines are predicted, with 7 out of 12 turning points accurately traced. Given the good overall fit of the price equation, the AAP,AAR relationship and the accuracy of the tracking of the turning points are disappointing.

SIC 30: Rubber and Plastic Products. The price behavior of SIC 30 is very similar to that of SIC 301, with the Beta coefficients indicating that $INV30$ has over three times the effect of $WMNMN$ and nearly twice the effect of $DULC,N30(-3)$ on price change. The lagged relationship between the cost regressors and price is longer than in SIC 301. Eleven price changes are overpredicted by the simulated price series while seven are underpredicted. The AAR is well over half of the AAP. Seven out of 10 turning points are predicted correctly, with false price declines predicted for the 1968:2 to 1968:4 period, prior to the actual decline in 1969:1. This latter result is the same as in SIC 301 and is attributable in both cases to unusually large increases in $INV30$.

SIC 3562: Ball and Roller Bearings. SIC 3562 is similar in its price formation to SICs 30, 301, and 24 in that short-run market forces play the dominant role in causing price change. The lag structure of the cost regressors is quite long, with both variables being only marginally significant. The Beta coefficients indicate that the effect of $INV35$ on price change is three times that of $PMN35(-4)$ and over twice that of $DULC,N3562(-3)$. Eleven of the actual price changes are underpredicted and seven overpredicted, with the AAR and AAP nearly equal at .521 and .589, respectively. The actual price movement in SIC 3562 fluctuates greatly; as a result, four false price declines are predicted which are all continuations of actual price declines that were correctly predicted in the immediately preceding period(s). Turning points in the actual price series are correctly tracked only 6 out of 11 times.

SIC 25: Furniture and Fixtures. As in SIC 251, long-run capacity considerations are the key influence on price change. The Beta coefficients indicate the effect of $CUIN25$ on $P25$ is one and one-half that of $PM25(-2)$ and over twice that of

*ULCN*25. Furthermore, the coefficient on *PM*25(−2) is unrealistically low. Underpredictions outnumber overpredictions 10 to 8. There are no price declines over the period and no declines falsely predicted. The AAP is over four times as large as the AAR. Seven out of 10 turning points in the actual price change series are correctly predicted.

SIC 3541: Machine Tools–Metal Cutting Types. This industry price equation includes a target return pricing regressor, *PREQ*35. However, the overriding influence on price change is the long-run market measure *QN*3541, whose Beta coefficient is nearly three times as great as those for *PM*35(−1), *ULCN*3541, and *PREQ*. Furthermore, the Beta coefficients on these latter three regressors are equal, indicating further the limited effect of the target return hypothesis on SIC 3541 price behavior. The numbers of overpredictions and underpredictions are equal, whereas the AAP is 1.233 compared with an AAR of only .251. *P*3541 increases over the entire period, with the fitted series reflecting this in that no false price declines are predicted. However, only five out of nine turning points are correctly tracked.

SIC 331: Primary Ferrous Metals. The indirect excess demand measure *URI* is the dominant influence affecting price behavior. The Beta coefficients indicate that its influence on *P*331 is nearly three times that of *PM*331(−1) and one and one-quarter times that of *ULCN*331. The numbers of underpredictions and overpredictions are equal, with four out of seven turning points being correctly tracked. There are no actual price declines during this period, nor are any predicted. The AAR is .194, comparing favorably with the AAP of .521.

Worst-Fitting Industries

SIC 3263: Fine Earthenware and Food Utensils. This price equation, which is under hypothesis category three, most strongly represents rule-of-thumb pricing, with both SRC regressors being significant and having reasonable coefficients. The *SR-DED* variable *SHP*32 is highly significant but, as is the case in other industries, enters with a negative sign. The material price regressor has nearly twice the effect of the wage rate in causing price change. Ten price changes are overpredicted whereas eight are underpredicted. Four out of five price declines are not predicted but no false price declines are predicted. Only 4 out of 11 turning points are accurately tracked. The AAR is .793 compared with an AAP of 1.001.

SIC 341: Metal Cans. The price equation for SIC 341 is under hypothesis category eleven and includes regressors that represent *SRC* and *LR-DED* hypotheses. Both *ULC*341 and *FDIQN*341(−2) are significant; however, the coefficient on $ULC341$ is extremely low. Examining the Beta coefficients, it is apparent that $ULC341$ is nearly twice as influential as $FDIQN341(-2)$ in causing price change. The numbers of over- and underpredictions are nearly equal, as was the case for SIC 34. A large price increase ($P341 = 3.196$) is underpredicted by 70 percent in 1968:3. Three actual price declines are not predicted whereas one is falsely predicted. The AAR is .478 compared with an AAP of .845. Seven out of 12 turning points are accurately tracked. The ability of this price equation to simulate the price behavior of SIC 341 over the 1965:1 to 1969:2 period is reasonably good, considering that its fit is the worst of all the final industry price equations.

SIC 21: Tobacco. The price behavior of SIC 21 is best explained by an equation with hypothesis category twelve as a basis, including *SRC, LRC,* and *SR-DED* regressors. Both *WMNM* and $ULCN21$ enter with four-quarter lags. However, both of these regressors have coefficients that are unexpectedly low in value and insignificant. The target return variable $PREQ21$ and the *SR-DED* measure $INV21$ are both significant with the proper signs. An examination of the Beta coefficient reveals a slightly more important role for $INV21$ relative to $PREQ21$ in the pricing process, although the effectiveness of target return pricing is likely to be substantial, given the high degree of concentration in the industry. Eleven price changes are overpredicted and seven underpredicted, with the AAR being large (.516) relative to the AAP (.724). None of the four actual price declines are predicted by the final price equation, whereas 7 out or 13 turning points are tracked.

SIC 371: Motor Vehicles and Parts. The final price equation for SIC 371 is also representative of hypothesis category twelve. As in SIC 21 above, the material and labor cost variables enter in lagged relationships but are insignificant. The *SR-DED* measure $INV371(-2)$ is highly insignificant, with its Beta coefficient being well over twice the value of the Beta coefficients for $PM371(-1)$ and $DULC,N371(-4)$. Therefore, the final price equation for SIC 371 reflects market forces as the key determinant behind pricing behavior. As in SIC 21, 11 overpredictions and 7 underpredictions of price change occur. The AAR of .347 is quite high relative to the AAP of .374. Only 6 out of 11 turning points are correctly tracked. One out of three price declines is correctly predicted whereas one decline is falsely predicted. The false decline occurs in 1965:2, immediately preceding three consecutive actual price declines.

SIC 36: Electrical Machinery. The final price equation for SIC 36 is the only one that contains strictly cost hypotheses, having as a basis hypothesis category two. *SRC* regressors include one-quarter and three-quarter lags of *PM* while the *LRC* regressor is $ULCN36(-2)$. All three regressors are significant and have the proper signs. The material price regressors influence price change relatively more than does normalized labor cost. This equation overpredicts actual price change 12 times and underpredicts it 6 times. Price declines are predicted correctly in two out of four cases, whereas only 4 out of 12 turning points are tracked correctly. The AAR is .400 compared with an AAP of .585.

SIC 2111: Cigarettes. The final price equation for SIC 2111 represents hypothesis category fifteen and includes regressors that depict *LRC* and *SR-DED* hypotheses. It differs from the SIC 21 final price equation because of the absence of a *SRC* regressor. All regressors are significant and have the proper signs. The effects of both *INV*21 and *PREQ*21 are more influential than that of *ULCN*2111(-4) in causing price change, as indicated by the Beta coefficients. This result is the same as that for SIC 21, with the major effects on pricing behavior being derived from both market forces and the target return goal. The actual price change is overpredicted 10 times and underpredicted 8 times. The AAP (.977) is nearly double the AAR (.518). There are three actual price declines, none of which are predicted by the final price equation. Only 5 out of 11 turning points are correctly tracked.

Simulations Using Stage of Processing Industry Price Models

Using the final industry price equations given in Tables 7-1 and 7-2 as the basis, selected industry price models are specified by including price equations that explain price behavior at higher and/or lower stages of processing. Thus price is the key variable in these models for linking the various stages of processing together, resulting in recursive models by stage of process. The link between stages might also be expressed by the higher stage's demand measure affecting the next lower stage's price in some subsequent period. This approach has been used unsuccessfully in sectoral price studies and is not reemployed in this industry analysis. [See Popkin and Earl[133].] The general specifications of the *PM* and *CPI* price equations in this chapter are based on those in the Popkin and Earl study. This approach was taken because the primary intent of this research is the explanation of final industry prices. The industries selected for this analysis (SICs 22, 23, 25, 29, 301, 331, 35, 3541, and 371) are considered to be representative of all the industries from Chapter 7 in terms of both industry characteristics and fits of the final industry price equations. Thus, the simulation results discussed later in this chapter might also be valid for the excluded industries.

The simulation analysis is undertaken for three primary reasons. First, it enables the final price equation results to be compared with model results for each industry in terms of predicting the behavior of the industry price over the 1965:1 to 1969:2 period. Emphasis is placed on turning point behavior and residual analysis. Second, specific policy measures can be tailored to each industry, based in part on the relative contributions of each component (i.e., coefficient times regressor) to the industry price change. These policy measures are addressed at dampening the inflationary price movements over the 1967:1 to 1969:2 period. In consumer goods industries, lessening inflationary pressures at all three stages (i.e., *CPI*, *P*, and *PM*) is of interest whereas in other industries only the *P* and *PM* stages are relevant. By linking together the processing stages of an industry through price relationships, it can be explicitly shown how policies affecting an exogenous regressor in the *PM* equation can significantly lessen consumer price increases, given that *PM* is an important component in the *P* equation and *P* in turn is an important component in the *CPI* equation. Finally, the results of simulating the various industry price models, both with and without policy measures, can be compared. The ex post simulations give an indication of the relative ability of the industry price models to track actual price change. The policy simulations enable the relative effectiveness of both common macro and industry-specific policy measures for slowing inflation to be compared across industries.

The first of four sections in this chapter specifies and estimates the *PM* and *CPI* equations, presenting the estimated results for each. The second section contains the industry stage of processing price models, with a brief description of the regressors included and the lag structure of each. The third discusses the results of the ex post simulations. The final section discusses both the methodology used for developing the series of policy simulations and the results of these simulations.

Material and Consumer Price Equations

The general specification for both the material and the consumer price equations includes the short-run cost (2.2) and the excess demand (2.10) hypotheses. Analysis similar to that in Chapter 7 is performed in order to determine the proper lag structure for each of the regressors. The lagged price is also included as a regressor where its correlation with price is significant. All *CPI* and *PM* equations are estimated on quarterly data over the 1958:2 to 1969:2 period.

Both the wage and the excess demand measures used in the *CPI* and *PM* equations are macro in nature. The wage variables tried are adjusted for both overtime and interindustry shifts, and are available for workers in retail and wholesale (*AHERW*), durable goods (*AHEDG*), and nondurable goods (*AHENG*). The excess demand regressors considered are of both the *DED* type (*CUI*) and the *IED* type (*URI*). The capacity utilization indexes are the Federal Reserve Board indexes for total manufacturing (*CUM*), advanced products (*CUAP*), and primary products (*CUPP*), whereas the unemployment rate is that for all civilian workers.

Reliance on macro regressors for labor cost and excess demand in the *PM* and *CPI* equations may be questioned, especially in light of the emphasis in preceding chapters on industry-specific measures. However, specific wage series for different types of materials have not been developed; therefore *AHEDG* and *AHENG*, even though they include wages paid to workers in final product industries, seem to be the best overall measures available. In regard to the *CPI* equations, all wages except those of the retail workers and middlemen have been accounted for in the lower-stage prices which are included. Therefore, *AHERW* is the logical series to use. Industry-specific demand measures at both the consumer level (e.g., sales and consumption expenditure data) and the intermediate materials level (e.g., industrial production indexes) are available. However, prior research on selected sectors has shown the superiority of *URI* as a retail excess demand measure and a like position for the macro *CUI* indexes as intermediate material excess demand measures. This conclusion is adopted for the present research.

The estimated *CPI* equations are given in Table 8-1. Their general specifications include the proper lagged final industry price and *AHERW* as cost regressors, along with either *URI* or one of the *CUI* measures as the excess demand regressor. The results indicate the presence of *P* as a regressor in all of the *CPI* equations, with its significance high in all equations. *AHERW* is present in all equations except for *C371*, being significant in all but the *C22* equation. *URI* is contained and significant in all but the *CGAS* and *C301* equations. *CUI* is not significant as a regressor in any of the final *CPI* equations. This result supports the contention that *URI* is a good income measure at the retail level and that any effect of capacity is present at the lower stages of processing and affects retail prices through the *P* regressor. The fits of the *CPI* equations are poor in general, with all R^2s less than .400 except those for the SIC 23 and SIC 25 equations. These poor fits may reflect problems in the construction of the consumer prices (see Appendix A).

Table 8-2 presents evidence that the fits of the *PM* equations are in general much better than those of the *CPI* equations. All regressors, including the constant terms, are significant with the proper signs. With the exception of the *PM29* equations, the R^2s are all well above .400. The *SRC* cost regressors *WCNMEF*, and *AHEDG* or *AHENG*, are tried in the *PM* equations. The *WCNMEF* term is a macro stage of processing price index for crude nonfood, nonfuel materials for manufacturing. It is the most appropriate *PM* measure to use as a regressor in the material price equations, given the lack of industry-specific input prices and the general nature of inputs that go into the production of these intermediate materials. *WCNMEF* is included in the final *PM* equation for all industries except SIC 29. A wage variable, always with at least a two-quarter lag, is in all the *PM* equations except that for SIC 371. *CUAP* is the excess demand measure in the SIC 29 *PM* equations whereas *CUPP* is present in all the other *PM* equations except SIC 371, which includes the *IED* measure *URI*. The lagged price term is significant in all *PM* equations except that of SIC 331.

Industry Price Models

This section contains the specifications for each of the industry price models that are simulated. In some cases, more than one consumer, final industry, and/or material price equation is given for a particular industry, resulting in more than one model to be simulated.

SIC 22: Textile Mill Products

This industry is represented by the equations in A221 to A224 below, which include one consumer price equation, three final industry price equations, and

Table 8-1
Estimated Consumer Price Equations [a]

SIC Industry	Estimated Equation	R^2	SEE	DW
22	$C22 = -1.213 + .121*P22(-1) + .207*AHERW(-1) + 6.013*URI$ $\quad\;\;(2.8)\qquad(1.7)\qquad\qquad(.5)\qquad\qquad(3.4)$	.357	.470	2.14
23	$C23 = -1.685 + .278*P23 + .333*AHERW(-1) + 8.377*URI(-1)$ $\quad\;\;(7.5)\qquad(2.3)\qquad(1.9)\qquad\qquad(9.1)$	.823	.225	1.34
25	$C25 = -1.472 + .496*P25 + .426*AHERW + 5.561*URI$ $\quad\;\;(3.6)\qquad(2.2)\qquad(1.5)\qquad\quad(2.8)$	.623	.392	2.08
29	$CGAS = -1.779 + .321*P29 + 1.788*AHERW(-4)$ $\qquad\;\;(1.5)\qquad(2.9)\qquad\quad(1.9)$ $CMOTOIL = -.831 + .161*P29(-3) + .745*AHERW(-1) + 3.186*URI(-4)$ $\qquad\qquad\;(1.8)\quad(3.9)\qquad\qquad(2.0)\qquad\qquad(1.6)$	.167 .335	1.359 .504	2.70 1.85
301	$C301 = -2.418 + .568*P301 + 2.328*AHERW$ $\qquad\;\;(1.6)\qquad(4.4)\qquad\quad(1.9)$	.356	1.778	2.03
371	$C371 = -.735 + .384*P371 + 3.800*URI(-4) + .345*C371(-1)$ $\qquad\;\;(1.5)\qquad(2.2)\qquad\quad(1.6)\qquad\qquad(2.7)$	.370	.616	1.87

Note:
[a]The entries for each industry under each regressor are the regression coefficients and t-values (in parentheses). The adjusted coefficient of determination (R^2), standard error of the estimate (SEE), and Durbin-Watson statistic (DW) are also given.

Table 8-2
Estimated Material Price Equations [a]

SIC Industry	Estimated Equation	R^2	SEE	DW
29	$PM29 = -4.248 + .734*AHENG(-4) + 4.42*CUAP(-3)$ $\quad\quad (3.1) \quad (2.6) \quad\quad\quad (2.5)$	.297	.551	1.34
	$PM29 = -2.906 + .705*AHENG(-4) + 2.836*CUAP(-3) + .358*PM29(-1)$ $\quad\quad (1.9) \quad (2.5) \quad\quad\quad (1.5) \quad\quad\quad (1.8)$	.330	.537	1.74
301	$PM30 = -.579 + .144*WCNMEF(-2) + .618*AHENG(-4) + .464*PM30(-1)$ $\quad\quad (2.2) \quad (2.8) \quad\quad\quad (2.1) \quad\quad\quad (4.1)$	.439	.599	1.90
331	$PM331 = -3.573 + .352*WCNMEF + .581*AHEDG(-4) + 3.907*CUPP$ $\quad\quad\quad (2.3) \quad (6.1) \quad\quad (1.8) \quad\quad\quad (2.2)$	.519	.662	1.67
35,3541	$PM35 = -4.701 + .133*WCNMEF + .934*AHEDG(-2) + 5.034*CUPP$ $\quad\quad (3.9) \quad (2.9) \quad\quad (4.1) \quad\quad\quad (3.6)$	.464	.537	.98
	$PM35 = -2.426 + .145*WCNMEF + .609*AHEDG(-2) + 2.46*CUPP + .661*PM35$ $\quad\quad (1.8) \quad (3.4) \quad\quad (2.6) \quad\quad\quad (1.6) \quad\quad (3.1) \quad (-1)$	.556	.489	1.02
371	$PM371 = -.978 + .126*WCNMEF + 5.782*URI(-1) + .531*PM371(-1)$ $\quad\quad\quad (2.7) \quad (3.1) \quad\quad (3.1) \quad\quad\quad (3.2)$	.536	.466	1.61

Notes:

PM equations are not estimated for SIC22 and SIC23, since their final industry price equations in Table 7-1 do not include a PM term. The output price for SIC24 is the input price into SIC25, so that the final industry price equation for SIC24 is used as the PM equation in the SIC25 model.

[a]The entries for each industry under each regressor are the regression coefficients and t-values (in parentheses). The adjusted coefficient of determination (R^2), standard error of the estimate (SEE), and Durbin-Watson statistic (DW) are also given.

no *PM* equation. Therefore, three two-equation industry models are formed and simulated.

(A221) $C22 = -1.213 + .121*P22(-1) + .207*AHERW(-1)$
$$+ 6.013*URI$$

(A222) $P22 = -.864 + .547*AHE22 + .235*Q22(-1)$

(A223) $P22 = -.680 + .564*AHE22 + .125*Q22(-1) + .419*P22(-1)$

(A224) $P22 = -.300 + .563*AHE22 - .002*FDI22$
$$- .0006*FDIN22 + .627*P22(-1) - .214*P22(-2)$$

The industry price is related to the retail price with a one-quarter lag. However, its coefficient in the retail equation is quite low. The final industry equations contain all exogenous regressors except for the lagged price terms in A223 and A224.

SIC 23: Apparel and Related Products

SIC 23, like SIC 22, has no *PM* equation in its price model, given by A231 and either A232 or A233 below. The retail and final wholesale prices are simultaneously related in the *C23* equation whereas the *P23* equations are in the reduced form, one having a lagged price adjustment.

(A231) $C23 = -1.685 + .278*P23 + .333*AHERW(-1)$
$$+ 8.377*URI(-1)$$

(A232) $P23 = .120 + .197*AHE23(-2) + .658*FDRLT(-3)$
$$- .034*SHP23$$

(A233) $P23 = .100 + .112*AHE23(-2) + .832*FDRLT(-3)$
$$- .039*SHP23 + .324*P23(-1)$$

SIC 25: Furniture and Fixtures

The industry price model for furniture contains price equations for all three stages of processing. It is also the best model overall in terms of the fit of each equation. The effect of final industry price on retail price is immediate. However, there is a two-quarter lag in the effect of *P24* on *P25*. Therefore, an examination of the model in F251, F252, and either F253 or F254 reveals that there is a five-quarter lag between a change in *AHE*24 and its effect on *C*25 (i.e., a wage settlement in SIC 24 in 1968:1 will affect *C*25 in 1969:2). Thus, the importance of lag structure in the formulation of policy measures and the timing of their implementation is aptly demonstrated by this industry model. Alternate lumber price (*P*24) equations, with and without lagged price adjustment, are tried.

(F251) $C25 = -1.472 + .496*P25 + .426*AHERW + 5.561*URI$

(F252) $P25 = -13.411 + .087*P24(-2) + .212*ULCN25$
$$+ .135*CUIN25$$

(F253) $P24 = -.038 + 1.097*AHE24(-3) - .687*INV24$

(F254) $P24 = -.173 + .671*AHE24(-3) - .786*INV24$
$$+ .394*P24(-1)$$

SIC 29: Petroleum and Coal Products

Two retail prices are considered when simulating the petroleum industry price models: one for gas (*CGAS*) and the other for motor oil (*CMOTOIL*). Also, two final industry and two material price equations are considered, one of each being autoregressive in structure. Thus, one autoregressive and one nonautoregressive price model (at the wholesale levels), combined with each of the retail price equations, are specified. Note, as in SIC 25, the long lags that exist between certain regressors in the *PM* equations O295 and O296, and the *CGAS* and *CMOTOIL* retail prices.

(O291) $CGAS = -1.779 + .321*P29 + 1.788*AHERW(-4)$

(O292) $CMOTOIL = .831 + .161*P29(-3) + .745*AHERW(-1)$
$$+ 3.186*URI(-4)$$

(O293) $P29 = .195 + 657*PM29(-2) - .453*INV29$

(O294) $P29 = .218 + .618*PM29(-2) - .513*INV29$
$$+ .303*P29(-1)$$

(O295) $PM29 = -4.248 + .734*AHENG(-4) + 4.42*CUAP(-3)$

(O296) $PM29 = -2.906 + .705*AHENG(-4) + 2.836*CUAP(-3)$
$$+ .358*PM29(-1)$$

SIC 301: Tires and Tubes

The price model for the tire industry has a structure similar to that for furniture, in that the final industry price ($P301$) influences $C301$ in the same quarter while at the same time being affected by $PM30$ from the four quarters before. There is a long lag structure on all cost variables in this model except for those in the retail price equation $T3011$.

(T3011) $C301 = -2.418 + .568*P301 + 2.328*AHERW$

(T3012) $P301 = 1.264 + .263*PM30(-4) + .052*DULC,N301(-2)$
$$- .481*INV30$$

(T3013) $PM30 = -.579 + .144*WCNMEF(-2) + .618*AHENG(-4)$
$$+ .464*PM30(-1)$$

SIC 331: Primary Ferrous Metals

The price model for primary ferrous metals contains equations for only the final industry and materials stages. The model, given in equations S3311 and S3312 below, contains a lengthy lag structure on most cost regressors whereas the excess demand regressors enter simultaneously with price at both stages of processing.

(S3311) $P331 = -.702 + .087*PM331(-1) + .127*ULCN331$
$$+ 4.333*URI$$

(S3312) $PM331 = -3.573 + .352*WCNMEF + .581*AHEDG(-4)$
$$+ 3.907*CUPP$$

SIC 35: Machinery, Except Electrical, and SIC 3541:
Machine Tools–Metal-Cutting Types

Two models can be formed for both SIC 35 and SIC 3541, combining each of their final industry price equations, E351 and E35411, respectively, with either E352 or E353. The lag structures in the SIC 35 and 3541 models are very similar, with each final price equation including a normalized *DED* regressor.

(E351) $P35 = -1.166 + .084*PM35(-1) + .217*AHE35(-1)$
$$+ .164*INVN35(-3) + .424*UNFSC$$

(E35411) P3541 $= -.340 + .479*PM35(-1) + .104*ULC3541$
$+ 17.571*PREQ35 + .268*QN3541$

(E352) PM35 $= -2.426 + .145*WCNMEF + .609*AHEDG(-2)$
$+ 2.46*CUPP + .661*PM35(-1)$

(E353) PM35 $= -4.701 + .133*WCNMEF + .934*AHEDG(-2)$
$+ 5.034*CUPP$

SIC 371: Motor Vehicles and Parts

The model for SIC 371 consists of equations at the retail and manufacturing stages of processing. The model is strongly autoregressive in structure, with both the retail equation (M3711) and the materials equation (M3713) including the lagged price as a regressor. Also, a lagged form of the *IED* measure *URI* is included in equations (M3711) and (M3713), with its presence in the latter equation in place of some form of *CUI* difficult to explain. *C371* is the retail price for new cars and not for all output of SIC 371 sold at retail.

(M3711) C371 $= -.735 + .385*P371 + 3.800*URI(-4)$
$+ .345*C371(-1)$

(M3712) P371 $= .297 + .211*PM\ 371(-1) + .028*DULC, N371(-4)$
$- .071*INV371(-2)$

(M3713) PM371 $= -.978 + .126*WCNMEF + 5.782*URI(-1)$
$+ .531*PM371(-1)$

Ex Post Simulations

The industry models described in the preceding section are simulated over the 1965:1 to 1969:2 period and their results are compared with the single-equation results at the retail and final industry stages. The identification of the models described in the preceding section in terms of the equations included is given in Table 8-3. Tables 8-4 and 8-5 contain the summary results of the ex post simulations for the consumer prices and final industry prices, respectively. The format of these tables is similar to that of Table 7-11. Note that there is no simulation analysis for the *PM* equations, since the results are the same when solved either as single equations or as part of the models.

Table 8-3
Model Identification

Model	Equations
SIC22I	A221,A222
SIC22II	A221,A223
SIC22III	A221,A224
SIC231	A231,A232
SIC23II	A231,A233
SIC25I	F251,F252,F253
SIC25II	F251,F252,F254
SIC29I	0291,0293,0295
SIC29II	0291,0294,0296
SIC29III	0292,0293,0295
SIC29IIII	0292,0294,0296
SIC301	T3011,T3012,T3013
SIC331	S3311,S3312
SIC351	E351,E352
SIC35II	E351,E353
SIC3541I	E35411,E352
SIC3541II	E35411,E353
SIC371	M3711,M3712,M3713

The results for the *CPI* equations in Table 8-4 are mixed with regard to the relative accuracy of single-equations versus models in simulating actual consumer price changes over the 1965:1 to 1969:2 period. Examining both the AARs and the correlations between fitted C and actual C, the single-equation results are best (i.e., lower AARs and higher correlations) for industries 22, 23, 25, and 29(*CGAS*). On the other hand, the model results are superior for industries 29(*CMOTOIL*), 301, and 371, with the most significant difference between single-equation and model results occurring in SIC 301. In general, the tracking of turning points and the frequency of over- and underpredictions of C are similar within a given industry based on either the single-equation or the model results. In only one industry, SIC 371, are actual *CPI* declines predicted, although the proportion of actual declines predicted is only two out of six. In only three industries (SICs 29[*CMOTOIL*], 25, and 23) is the AAP at least twice as large as the AAR. This result coupled with the poor turning-point tracking capability is indicative of the poor overall performance of the *CPI* equations.

The results from the ex post simulations of final industry prices, using both single equations and models, are superior to those from the consumer price simulations. The accuracy of single-equation compared with model simulations is

Table 8-4
Residual, Correlation, and Turning-Point Analysis of Consumer Price Equations, 1965:1–1969:2

Model or Single Equation	Average Absolute Price Change (AAP)	Average Absolute Residual (AAR)	Correlation of Predicted with C	Number of Positive Residuals	Number of Negative Residuals	Turning Points, Predicted-Actual	P Declines, Predicted-Actual	False P Declines
SIC22I	.710	.461	.455	9	9	4–9	0–3	0
SIC22II	.710	.472	.398	9	9	4–9	0–3	0
SIC22III	.710	.855	.264	10	8	2–9	0–3	3
A221	.710	.443	.505	9	9	4–9	0–3	0
SIC23I	1.014	.193	.877	8	10	4–10	0–1	0
SIC23II	1.014	.194	.873	9	9	4–10	0–1	0
A231	1.014	.175	.885	7	11	3–10	0–1	0
SIC25I	.973	.304	.691	11	7	4–8	0–1	0
SIC25II	.973	.305	.691	11	7	4–8	0–1	0
F251	.973	.301	.736	9	9	3–8	0–1	0
SIC29I	1.151	.940	.281	11	7	5–14	1–4	0
SIC29II	1.151	.934	.277	10	8	4–14	0–4	0
0291	1.151	.837	.338	10	8	8–14	1–4	0
SIC29III	.996	.376	.585	10	8	5–11	0–1	0
SIC29IIII	.996	.365	.596	9	9	4–11	0–1	0
0292	.996	.371	.555	10	8	4–11	0–1	0
SIC301	1.118	.652	.522	11	7	2–12	0–3	3
T3011	1.118	.819	.369	8	10	3–12	0–3	2
SIC371	.593	.520	.747	6	12	2–9	2–6	1
M3711	.593	.496	.735	8	10	4–9	4–6	1

Table 8-5
Residual, Correlation, and Turning-Point Analysis of Final Industry Price Equations, 1965:1–1969:2

Model or Single Equation	Average Absolute Price Change (AAP)	Average Absolute Residual (AAR)	Correlation of Predicted with P	Number of Positive Residuals	Number of Negative Residuals	Turning Points, Predicted-Actual	P Declines, Predicted-Actual	False P Declines
SIC25I	.793	.208	.775	9	9	7–10	0–0	0
SIC25II	.793	.192	.797	10	8	6–10	0–0	0
F252	.793	.196	.816	10	8	7–10	0–0	0
SIC29I	1.005	.684	.662	11	7	6–9	3–4	3
SIC29II	1.005	.699	.706	10	8	7–9	4–4	3
0293	1.005	.660	.723	12	6	5–9	3–4	3
SIC29III	1.005	.684	.662	11	7	6–9	3–4	3
SIC29IIII	1.005	.699	.706	10	8	7–9	3–4	3
0293	1.005	.660	.723	12	6	5–9	3–4	3
SIC301	1.058	.777	.741	12	6	7–12	3–4	3
T3012	1.058	.760	.772	14	4	7–12	3–4	3
SIC331	.521	.184	.679	10	8	5–7	0–0	0
S3311	.521	.193	.675	9	9	4–7	0–0	0
SIC35I	.785	.208	.562	8	10	5–7	0–0	0
SIC35II	.785	.214	.528	9	9	5–7	0–0	0
E351	.785	.212	.549	9	9	4–7	0–0	0
SIC3541I	1.233	.285	.791	4	14	5–9	0–0	0
SIC3541II	1.233	.249	.803	7	11	5–9	0–0	0
E35411	1.233	.251	.760	9	9	5–9	0–0	0
SIC371	.374	.357	.558	5	13	6–11	1–3	1
M3712	.374	.347	.529	7	11	6–11	1–3	1

again mixed. As Table 8-5 indicates, the single-equation simulations are best for SICs 29 and 301, as measured in terms of a lower AAR and a higher correlation of the simulated P with actual P. The models are superior to single equations for simulating final industry price movements in SIC 35 and SIC 3541. SICs 25, 331, and 371 present mixed results. For industries 331 and 25, the AARs and correlations from the models are lower than those from the single equations. The opposite is true for SIC 371, with the AAR and correlation from SIC 371 being higher than those from M3712. Turning-point prediction and the frequency of over- and underpredictions, on the basis of both the single-equation and the model results, is similar within each industry. No results are included for the final industry price equations in the SIC 22 and SIC 23 models, since these equations are in reduced form.

A comparison of results in Tables 8-4 and 8-5 indicates a superiority of the simulated price series from industry models for tracking actual industry price behavior in two thirds of the industries examined. This finding reflects the information that is gained for explaining price behavior when models that are structured so as to capture the endogenous behavior particular to each industry are examined. The policy simulations in the next section employ the "best" industry models developed, with best being measured in terms of the lowest AAR and highest correlation in cases where more than one industry model is simulated. In the multiple model cases the models chosen are SIC22I, SIC23I, SIC25II, SIC29II (for *CGAS*), SIC29IIII (for *COMOTOIL*), SIC35I, and SIC354III.

Policy Simulations

This section contains discussion of both the design and the results of the policy simulations that are performed. The intent of these simulations, run over the 1967:1 to 1969:2 period, is twofold. First, the relative effectiveness on price behavior of the same percentage modification on selected regressors (i.e., equal percentage change policies, or *EPCP*), both within an industry and across all industries, is determined. Second, industry-specific combinations of regressor modifications (i.e., industry-specific policies, or *ISP*) are designed in an attempt to reduce the quarterly percentage change, expressed at annual rates (*AAPC*), in each industry's price below 2.5 percent. This target level of *AAPC* is chosen in order that the 1967-69 period can be examined in retrospect with the same price goals as the current Economic Stabilization Program. Before discussing the design and results of the *EPCP* and *ISP* simulations, we describe the method of selecting regressors as policy variables.

Selection of Regressors as Policy Variables

Table 8-6 summarizes the regressors chosen as policy variables in each industry model, including the equation that contains the regressor and the prices that are

Table 8-6
Regressor Modifications for Policy Simulations

SIC Industry	Regressor Modified	Equation(s) Containing Regressor	Price(s) Affected	Simulation Identification Letter
22	URI	A221	C22	N
	AHERW	A221	C22	M
	AHE22	A222	P22,C22	R
	Q22	A222	P22,C22	S
23	URI	A231	C23	N
	AHERW	A231	C23	M
	SHP23	A232	P23,C23	U
	AHE23	A232	P23,C23	R
25	URI	F251	C25	N
	AHERW	F251	C25	M
	ULCN25	F252	P25,C25	T
	AHE24	F253	P24,P25,C25	R
	INV24	F253	P24,P25,C25	S
29	URI	0292	CMOTOIL	N
	AHERW	0291,0292	CGAS,CMOTOIL	M,MM[a]
	INV29	0294	P29,CGAS,CMOTOIL	R,RR[a]
	AHENG	0296	PM29,P29,CGAS,CMOTOIL	O,OO[a]
301	AHERW	T3011	C301	M
	AHENG	T3013	PM30,P301,C301	O
	WCNMEF	T3013	PM30,P301,C301	V
331	UR	S3311	P331	N
	ULCN331	S3311	P331	R
	AHEDG	S3312	PM331,P331	P
	CUPP	S3312	PM331,P331	Q
	WCNMEF	S3312	PM331,P331	V
35	AHE35	E351	P35	R
	INVN35	E351	P35	S
	UNFSC	E351	P35	T
	AHEDG	E352	PM35,P35	P
	CUPP	E352	PM35,P35	Q
	WCNMEF	E352	PM35,P35	V
3541	PREQ35	E35411	P3541	RR
	QN3541	E35411	P3541	SS
	AHEDG	E353	PM35,P3541	PP
	CUPP	E353	PM35,P3541	QQ

Table 8-6 (cont.)

SIC Industry	Regressor Modified	Equation(s) Containing Regressor	Price(s) Affected	Simulation Identification Letter
	WCNMEF	E353	PM35,P3541	VV
371	URI	M3711,M3713	PM371,P371,C371	N
	WCNMEF	M3713	PM371,P371,C371	V

[a]The single identification letters refer to SIC29 simulations that include CGAS; the double identification letters refer to those with CMOTOIL.

affected by its change. Two types of information are used as the basis for selecting the industry policy variables, both of which indicate the relative effect of the individual regressors on price change. The first is the regression coefficients and Beta coefficients given in Tables 7-1, 7-2, 7-11, 8-1, and 8-2, along with the specific industry discussions in Chapter 7. (Note that Beta coefficients are not calculated for the *CPI* and *PM* equations.) From this information can be determined for each industry the relative influence of each regressor on price at the *CPI, P,* and *PM* levels. However, these coefficients reflect structural relationships that apply to the period of estimation, generally from 1958:1 to 1969:2. Given the more rapid increase in prices during the latter part of this period, especially since 1967, the relative effects of the regressors on prices may have shifted or accentuated somewhat if the behavior of the regressor is different in the latter part of the period than it was in the earlier part. This can best be measured by examining each component contribution (*CC*), equal to the coefficient times the regressor, within each equation. These are given in Appendix E and represent the actual contribution of each regressor to the price change in each quarter of the period. Utilization of the above two types of information results in a variety of regressors representing different policy areas being chosen. *UR* is representative of Phillips curve analysis, with policies affecting it being influential on price change in SICs 22, 23, 25, and 29 at the retail stage, SIC 331 at the final industry stage, and SIC 371 at all three stages of processing. The effect of minimum wage laws on retail prices is tested by the use of *AHERW* as a policy variable in SICs 22, 23, 25, 29, and 301. The effect of reduced market pressures on price change is tested in industries 22, 25, 24, 29, 35, and 3541. The influence of unions and minimum wage on manufacturing prices is seen for all industries through policy simulations using the macro wage variables (*AHENG* and *AHEDG*), certain industry-specific wages, and unit labor costs. Finally, the effect of changes in crude prices on prices at other stages of processing is measured in industries 301, 331, 35, 3541, and 371. The policy variables representing market forces, union influence, and crude prices are present at the final industry and/or intermediate materials stages of processing, depending on the industry considered. Therefore, they normally affect price behavior at more than one stage of processing. Policy variables representative of macro policies and industry-specific policies are modified in the simulations for all industries except SIC 301 and SIC 371, both of whose prices are affected by only macro policies, given the models that represent them. The following comments concern the selection of the regressors contained in Table 8-6 as policy variables in each industry model.

SIC 22. The *URI* component is five times as influential as the *AHERW* component on *C22*, with the effect of the *P22* component being very slight. The contribution of the *AHE*22 component to *P22* is three times that of *Q22*(−1). The relative sizes of the regression coefficients on *AHE*22 and *Q22*(−1) reflect the same result as the component contributions for *P22*.

SIC 23. *C23* is most strongly affected by the *URI* component, with the latter's contribution being five times that of *AHERW* and ten times that of *P23*. The *AHE*23 component contribution to *P23* is substantially greater than that of either *FDRLT* or *SHP23*, with the *SHP23* component's contribution being either slightly positive or negative. These results pertaining to the relative effects of the regressors on *P23* differ slightly from those based on the Beta coefficients, where the *SHP23* influence is considerably greater than the *FDRLT* influence.

SIC 25. The contributions of the *P25* and *AHERW* components to *C25* are nearly equal, whereas that of *URI* is almost three times larger. Even though the *CUIN25* component is the largest contributor to *P25*, *CUIN25* has been decreasing since 1967:1, thus helping to dampen *P25* increases. The *P24* component contribution is generally one and one-half times that of the *ULCN25* component. The *INV*24 component fluctuates greatly relative to *AHE*24 in its contribution to *P24*. Both the *P25* and *P24* results based on component contributions are consistent with those from the Beta and regression coefficient analysis.

SIC 29. The *AHERW* component makes the largest contribution of all components to both *CGAS* and *CMOTOIL*, with its effect being slightly larger than that of *URI* on *CMOTOIL*. In both cases, the contribution of the *P29* component is small. The *PM29* component contribution to *P29* has been steady whereas the *INV29* component usually dampens any *P29* increase. The *CUAP* component contributes twice as much to *PM29* as does the *AHENG* component. However, *CUAP* has been decreasing over the simulation period and therefore has lessened the pressure on *P29*. Once again the component contribution and regression analysis results agree in signifying *PM29* as the most important factor affecting *P29*.

SIC 301. The *AHERW* component contribution to *C*301 has been usually about ten times as large as that of *P*301, with the *P*301 component actually being negative in three out of the last four quarters. None of the components have consistently made significant contributions to *P*301, with the *PM*30 component contribution being negative in 1968 and slightly positive in 1969:1 and 1969:2. The Beta coefficients indicate that *INV*30 is the most significant regressor in the *P*301 equation. However, this result is not supported by examination of its component contribution.

SIC 331. The contribution of the *URI* component is nearly ten times as large as any of the others (*PM*331(−1), *ULCN*331) to *P*331. *ULCN*331 in turn generally makes a larger contribution to *P*331 than does *PM*331(−1). These results are consistent with those from the Beta coefficient analysis.

SIC 35. Both Beta coefficient and component contribution analyses indicate that *UNFSC* exercises the most significant effect on *P*35. Its component contributes four to five times more than the other components to *P*35. The *AHE*35 component contributes over two times as much to *P*35 as does the *PM*35 component.

SIC 3541. The *PM*35 and *PREQ*35 components contribute nearly equal amounts to *P*3541, with the contributions being three times as large as those from the *ULC*3541 and *QN*3541 components. In the *PM*35 equation, the component contribution of *CUPP* is three times that of *AHEDG* and ten times that of *WCNMEF*. The Beta coefficient results indicate the long-run market measure *QN*3541 as the most important determinant in the *P*3541 equation. However, *QN*3541 provides the smallest component contribution to *P*3541.

SIC 371. The contribution of the *URI* component in the *C*371 equation is five times greater than that of either the *P*371 or *C*371(−1) components. Furthermore, the contribution of the *URI* component in the *PM*371 equation is more than double that of either the *PM*30(−1) or the *WCNMEF* component. Since the *PM*371 component provides the largest contribution to *P*371, policies affecting *UR* are felt at all three stages of SIC 371 pricing. The Beta coefficient analysis indicates *INV*371 to be the most important influence on *P*371. However, its component contribution is either negative or slightly positive in the time period examined.

Equal Percentage Change Policy
(EPCP) Simulations

Design: This type of policy simulation is designed to allow assessment to be made of the relative impacts on price change of an equal percentage adjustment in each policy variable, both within each industry and across all industries in which the policy variable appears. The regressors are modified one at a time so that their individual impacts on quarterly percentage price change, expressed at annual rates (AAPC) may be measured. For each price, the various AAPCs that result from each policy modification are then compared.

Table 8-6 contains a list of the regressors modified within each industry. Within-industry comparisons using alternative policy effects can be made since at least two regressors are modified within each industry. Further, most industries contain both macro and industry-specific policy variables present at various stages of processing, so that policy implications relating to these aspects may also be analyzed. Across-industry comparisons of alternative policy measures can be made for macro variables *UR, AHERW, AHEDG, AHENG, CUPP,* and *WCNMEF.* These variables appear in either the *CPI* or *PM* equation of each industry model. All industry models except those for SIC 301 and SIC 371 contain industry-specific policy variables in their final price equations, so that industry-specific policy comparisons across industries can also be made. Note that when exogenous policy measures in the *PM* equations are chosen, their modifications affect *P,* assuming that *PM* itself affects *P.* The same explanation is relevant when *P* is an important influence on *C.*

The magnitudes of the percentage change adjustments made to the regressors are given in column 4 of Table 8-7. These are determined on the basis of the mean values of each regressor over the 1960:1 to 1966:4 and 1967:1 to 1969:2 periods. The difference between the averages for those two periods is examined for each regressor, and as a result a 25 percent modification based on the 1967:1 to 1969:2 average is made to every quarterly observation of each regressor. Thus, for all policy regressors, the same constant percentage adjustment is made in all observations over the simulation period. These adjustments reflect a lessening of inflationary pressures and are downward in all cases except for *UR, INV*24, *INV*29 and *SHP*23.

Results: The results of the *EPCP* simulations are presented in Table 8-8. The particular policy variables for each industry under each regressor category are given in Table 8-6. Every AAPC except for the actual and ex post figures is the result of the appropriate constant percentage modification, from Table 8-7, to all observations over the 1967:1 to 1969:2 period for each regressor.

The results indicate that those policies which change *UR* and *AHERW* are relatively more effective at the retail level than those which modify *P.* In those industries for which *UR* and *AHERW* are both important policy variables (SICs 22, 23, 25, 29) the *EPCP* on *UR* reduces *C* considerably more than does the *EPCP* on *AHERW* in all cases except *CMOTOIL.* Generally, the *EPCP* on *UR* decreases the AAPC of *C* by 20 to 40 percent, with a 50 percent reduction apparent in *C*371. (For example, the phrase "decreases the AAPC by 30 percent" means that an AAPC or 3.0 prior to a policy simulation is reduced to

Table 8-7

Magnitude and Direction of Regressor Modifications (Quarterly, in same units as Regressors)

Regressor	Mean of Regressor		Change in Regressor	
	1960:1-1966:4	1967:1-1969:2	Equal Percentage Change Policy (EPCP) Simulations	Industry-Specific Policy (ISP) Simulations
UR	5.271	3.643	+.90	+1.50
AHERW	1.096	1.569	−.393	−.500
AHENG	.760	1.436	−.360	−.700
AHEDG	.691	1.452	−.363	−.750
CUPP	.850	.868	−.218	−.018
SHP23	2.227	4.007	+1.002	—[a]
WCNMEF	1.376	1.588	−.398	−.200
AHE23	.854	1.774	−.443	−.900
AHE22	.829	1.549	−.388	−.700
Q22	2.138	1.784	−.445	—[a]
ULCN25	.400	1.036	−.260	−.600
AHE24	.788	1.632	−.408	−.800
INV24	1.740	3.453	+.863	—[a]
INV29	1.570	2.139	+.535	—[a]
ULCN331	.972	.932	−.233	—[a]
AHE35	.792	1.297	−.325	−.500
INVN35	1.024	2.124	−.530	−1.100
UNFSC	2.890	3.105	.775	−.200
PREQ35	.0259	.0322	−.0075	−.006
QN3541	2.350	1.255	−.315	—[a]

[a]These regressors are not used as policy variables in the industry-specific simulations, since their 1967:1-1969:2 averages indicate less pressure on price than do the 1960:1-1966:4 averages.

2.1 percent after the policy modification. This terminology is used in order to discuss the results consistently with the 25 percent reduction in the policy variables. In all cases, the comparison is made between the ex post AAPC values with and without policy changes.) However, the same *EPCP* on *AHERW* reduces the AAPC of *C*301 by 90 percent and causes an average decline in *CGAS* (AAPC = −.268). All other policy variables present at the *P* and *PM* stages have less than a 20 percent effect on reducing the AAPC of *C* when the *EPCP* is applied to each one. These results indicate that the effect of policy variables is relatively stronger at the retail stage than the effect of those at the *P* and *PM* stages in reducing the AAPC of *C*. For those consumer prices with an AAPC greater than 2.5 percent, a reduction to less than 2.5 percent by appropriate *EPCP* is accomplished for *C*22,

Table 8-8
Equal Percentage Change Policy Simulation Results

Stage of Processing / Price	AAPC	Ex Post AAPC	UR	AHERW	ULCN	AHE	PREQ	Market	CUPP	WCNMEF
						Quarterly Price Change at Annual Rates (AAPC) Resulting from a Constant Modification in[a]				
Retail										
C22	3.084	2.992	1.648	2.640		2.872		2.920		
C23	5.368	4.908	3.098	4.385		4.811		4.870		
C25	4.680	4.560	3.389	3.935	4.495	4.547		4.463		
CGAS	2.636	2.500		−.268		2.228		2.060		
CMOTOIL	4.468	4.188	3.636	3.112		4.192		4.116		
C301	4.880	4.092		.408		3.940				4.036
C371	1.976	2.752	1.352							2.656
Final Industry										
P22	1.108	.776				.072		.360		
P23	2.612	2.104				1.762		1.975		
P25	3.736	3.840			3.713	3.818		3.647		
P29	.648	.368				−.484		−1.008		
P301	1.632	.912				.644				.808
P331	2.640	2.476	1.560		2.389	2.442			2.241	2.464
P35b	3.356	3.500				AHE35,AHEDG 3.256,3.384		INVN,UNFSC 3.192,2.224	3.160	3.496
P3541	3.560	4.092				3.588	3.644	3.836	2.280	4.080
P371	1.976	2.000	1.604							1.964

Intermediate Materials							
P24	12.212	10.728		9.171	6.674		
PM29	2.512	3.120		1.676			−.176
PM30	−.228	.380		−1.300			
PM331	2.352	2.424		1.582		−.981	1.865
PM35	3.972	4.972		2.864		−.144	4.420
PM35[b]	3.972	3.692		2.336		−.696	3.480
PM371	4.116	4.812	2.572				4.520

[a]See Table 8-7 for the magnitude of each modification and Table 8-6 for the specific cost and market policy regressors for each industry.

[b]These results are for the PM35 equation included in the SIC35411I model.

CGAS, and *C*301 but not for *C*23, *C*25, and *CMOTOIL*. However, the reduction in AAPC attained for these latter three prices is in all cases approximately 30 percent.

In contrast to the general effectiveness of macro policy variables *AHERW* and *UR* at the retail level, the final industry price equations do not appear to contain particular policy variables that are effective in all industries. However, in all cases except *P*25 in which the AAPC is greater than 2.5 percent, an *EPCP* is available which reduces the AAPC below that rate. Furthermore, the most effective *EPCP* for reducing *P* in SICs 29, 301, and 3541 is on regressors in the *PM* equations of those industries, indicating a stronger link between *P* and *PM* than that which is observed between *C* and *P*. There are generally four kinds of regressors to which *EPCP* are applied: wage rate (*AHE*), long-run cost (*ULCN* and *PREQ*), market (*UNFSC, Q, QN, INV, INVN, SHP, CUPP,* and *UR*), and *WCNMEF*. The *EPCP* on *AHE*22 causes a 90 percent decline in the AAPC of *P*22 while the *EPCP* on *AHE*23 results in a decline of less than 10 percent in the AAPC of *P*23. The *EPCP* applied to *AHE* variables at the *PM* stage of processing results in a 30 percent reduction in the AAPC of *P*301, a negative AAPC for *P*29, and only slight declines in the AAPC for all other industry prices. The effectiveness, in reducing the AAPC of *P*, of market policy variables contained in the final price equations is generally greater than that of those contained in the *PM* equation. Of course, the market measures in the *PM* equation affect *P* indirectly through the effect of *PM* on *P*. The *EPCP* on *Q*22 reduces the AAPC of *P*22 by over 50 percent whereas that on *INV*29 results in a negative AAPC of over 1 percent for *P*29. The AAPC for *P*35 is reduced by nearly 40 percent using the *EPCP* on *UNFSC*, with a similar reduction in the AAPC of *P*331 evident when *UR* is the policy variable. The *EPCP* applied to the *CUPP* variable in the *PM* equation of the SIC 3541 model reduces the AAPC of *P*3541 by over 40 percent. However, this same policy measure in the *PM* equations of SIC 331 and SIC 35 is ineffective in reducing the rate of increase of *P*331 and *P*35. Similarly, an *EPCP* applied to *UR* in the *PM*371 equation results in only a 20 percent reduction in the AAPC of *P*371. Finally, the effect of the *EPCP* applied to *WCNMEF* in the *PM* equations for SICs 301, 331, 3541, and 371 is negligible on the AAPCs of the final industry prices. This result reflects both the minor contribution of *WCNMEF* in the *PM* equations and the limited effect of *PM* on *P* in certain industries (SICs 331, 35, 371).

The effectiveness of *EPCP* in reducing inflation is greater at the intermediate stage of processing than at the final and retail stages. The AAPC for each of the *PM* variables over the 1967:1 to 1969:2 period is greater than 2.5 percent in all industries except SIC 301, for which *PM*30 has an AAPC of $-.228$ over the period. An *EPCP* on at least one regressor results in a reduction in the AAPC of *PM* below 2.5 percent in all cases except for *P*24. However, *P*24 is reduced nearly 40 percent by an *EPCP* applied to *INV*24, from an ex post AAPC of 10.728 to an ex post of 6.674. The two most effective policy variables at this stage are *AHE* and *CUPP*. The *EPCP* on *AHE* results in at least a 30 percent decline in the AAPC of all affected *PM* variables except *P24*. The same *EPCP* applied to *CUPP* results in a negative AAPC for *PM331* and *PM35*. However, this latter result has serious political and social implications, given the strong inverse relationship between *CUPP* and *UR*. Therefore, the *EPCP* reduction applied to *CUPP* will probably result in a sizeable increase in *UR*. The *EPCP* applied to the *WCNMEF* variables in the *PM* equations is not nearly as effective in reducing AAPC as those applied to *AHE* and *CUPP*.

The results discussed in this section reflect the great difference in reducing AAPC which results from applying an *EPCP* to different regressors at three main stages of processing within selected industries. In general, the results indicate the superiority of an *EPCP* applied to *AHERW* and *UR* at the retail level, *PM* and *AHE* at the final goods stage, and *AHE* and *CUPP* at the intermediate materials stage in reducing the AAPC below 2.5 percent.

Industry-Specific Policy (ISP) Simulations

Design: These policy simulations are designed to illustrate the effectiveness of alternate types of policies on each industry's price behavior. As in the *EPCP* simulations, the average percentage change in price(s) over the 1967:1 to 1969:2 period from each of the simulations is compared. These simulations are basically of five types and differ from the *EPCP* simulations in that they do not necessarily incorporate equal percentage modifications for all regressors either within or across industries. Thus, it is hoped that they are more realistic from a policy viewpoint.

The first type of *ISP* simulation is based on constant modifications in all policy regressors for each industry (see Table 8-6). Each modification is a constant adjustment applied to all time periods, with the magnitude of the modification for each regressor equal to the approximate difference between the two average values, given in Table 8-7. All adjustments are made in a direction that lessens inflationary pressures. Therefore, the movement of each policy variable over the 1967:1 to 1969:2 period is being constrained to its 1960:1 to 1966:4 average. These adjustments are given in the last column of Table 8-7. Note that adjustments to *INV24*, *INV29*, *Q22*, *ULCN331*, *SHP23*, and *QN3541* are not made, since the average values of these regressors already indicate a lessening of inflationary pressures in 1967:1 to 1969:2 as compared with the 1960:1 to 1966:4 period.

The second type of *ISP* simulation is based on constant modifications to only the key policy regressors in each industry. The key regressors are determined on the basis of the relative size of the component contribution made to the relevant price by each policy regressor within the industry models. These key regressors are as follows:

SIC 22:	*AHE22, UR*
SIC 23:	*AHE23, UR*
SIC 25:	*AHE24, UR*
SIC 29:	*AHENG, AHERW*
SIC 301:	*AHENG, AHERW*
SIC 331:	*AHEDG, UR*
SIC 35:	*UNFSC*
SIC 3541:	*CUPP*
SIC 371:	*URI*

All of the key regressors are macro in nature except for *AHE22* and *UNFSC.* However, the presence of *AHE24, AHENG, CUPP,* and *AHEDG* in SICs 25, 29, 301, 3541, and 331 indicates important contributions of *P24, PM29, PM30, PM35,* and *PM331,* respectively.

The third *ISP* simulation also involves the key regressors. However, instead of constant adjustments being made to each, new variables are formed. These series are given in Appendix E and in general reflect dampened movement in the series when contrasted to the actual series, with the average value for each falling between the two averages given in Table 8-7. In the case of wage variables, the average values reflect basically average productivity increase plus a 1 percent annual cost of living adjustment. Two series are constructed for *UR*, with one having *UR* decline to 2.5 percent by the end of the period ($\overline{UR} = 3.0$) and the other having *UR* increase to 5.0 by the end of the period ($\overline{UR} = 4.53$).

These three types of simulations are performed both with and without modification to *UR*. The policies without increasing *UR* are certainly more politically appealing, leaving *UR* at an average value of 3.71 percent over the 1967:1 to 1969:2 period as opposed to 5.20 percent in the constant adjustment simulation and 4.50 percent in the modified series simulation (*UR* increasing).

The fourth and fifth types of *ISP* simulations involve modifications to only *UR*. In the fourth type, the other regressors in the industry models follow their actual behavior while the different *UR* series are tried. This simulation results in the values of AAPC for each price at various unemployment rates given in Table 8-10. The implicit assumption being made is that control of industry-specific measures (wages, quantities, capacity) is not feasible, so that only policy measures directed at *UR* will decrease the AAPC of industry prices. The fifth *ISP* simulation utilizes a long-run equilibrium consumer; price model in order to generate two long-run Phillips curves. The first assumes that all regressors other than *UR* remain constant at their 1960-66 average values. The second assumes tha all regressors except *UR* remain constant at their 1967-69 values. These results are given in Table 8-11.

Results: The results of the first three industry-specific policy simulations are given in Table 8-9. They will be discussed in relation to a goal of reducing each

AAPC below 2.5 percent. The simulation results for certain industry prices that have an AAPC less than 2.5 percent over the 1967:1 to 1969:2 period are discussed only in relation to the effect a further reduction in their AAPC has on other prices. The results will be discussed with regard to reducing the AAPC of each industry both without and with policies directed at modifying the unemployment rate. The results from simulations four and five, given in Tables 8-10 and 8-11, will then be discussed.

The results from the first simulation, which uses constant modifications on all policy variables within an industry, are substantially better than those from the second and third simulations for all industries except SIC 22. This result is to be expected, since multiple policy measures are being used as opposed to one (or at most two) policy measures in the key regressor simulations. $C22$ is best reduced in the simulation in which the $AHE22$ variable alone is modified. Nine of the 15 AAPC values that are greater than 2.5 are reduced below that level by the appropriate industry policies. The reduction in the AAPC values for the prices in the consumer goods industries is considerably less than that in the producer and mixed goods industries. Furthermore, the six that are not reduced below 2.5 ($C23$, $C25$, $P25$, $P24$, $CMOTOIL$, and $PM371$) are all prices at various stages of processing in consumer goods industries. (SIC 371 will be considered a consumer goods industry, since the retail price used is that for new cars and a substantial proportion of the output is consumer goods.) The consumer prices $CGAS$ and $C301$ and the materials price $PM35$ have a negative AAPC as a result of this simulation, compared with ex post AAPC values without policy measures of 2.500, 4.092, and 4.972, respectively. Both macro and industry-specific policy variables are in all industry price models except those for SIC 301 and SIC 371. However, in these two industries macro regressors affect material prices that are specific to each industry.

In all cases except that of $PM371$, a reduction in labor cost is an important contributor, either directly or indirectly (through a lower stage of processing price), in reducing the AAPC of each price. The magnitude of reductions in both the macro and industry-specific wage variables ranges from 2.0 percent annually ($AHERW, AHE35$) to 3.6 percent annually ($AHE23$). The unit labor cost variable $ULCN25$ is a significant policy variable in SIC 25, with its 2.4 percent annual reduction possible through wage decreases and/or productivity increases. These modifications represent from 35 to 50 percent of their average annual increase over the 1960 to 1966 period. This percentage modification is substantially higher than the 25 percent adjustment in the $EPCP$ simulations.

No other exogenous policy variable has the wide industry coverage of labor cost. Long-run cost and the target return concept are reflected in policy variables for only SICs 25 and 3541. The modification of market pressures as a policy variable is important in SICs 331, 35, and 3541. Even though $WCNMEF$ is treated as a policy variable in several industries, its effect compared with that of the measures mentioned above is slight. Most of these exogenous policy variables

Table 8-9
Industry-Specific Policy Simulation Results

Price	AAPC	Ex Post AAPC	Quarterly Price Change at Annual Rates (AAPC) Resulting from Constant Modification in[a]				AAPC Resulting from Modified Policy Variables for	
			All Policy Regressors	All Policy Regressors Except UR[b]	Key Policy Regressors	Key Policy Regressors Except UR[b]	Key Policy Regressors (UR = 4.5)	Key Policy Regressors Except UR[b]
C22	3.084	2.992	.448	2.384	.864	2.796	1.312	2.376
P22	1.108	.776	−.752		−.752		−.804	
C23	5.368	4.908	1.380	4.045	2.046	4.711	2.809	4.710
P23	2.612	2.104	1.402		1.402		1.396	
C25	4.680	4.560	1.599	3.388	2.703	4.492	3.146	4.521
P25	3.736	3.840	3.198		3.707		3.765	
P24	12.212	10.728	7.548		7.548		7.988	
CGAS	2.636	2.500	−1.648		−1.648		−.648	
CMOTOIL	4.468	4.188	1.660	2.616	1.660		2.708	
P29	.648	.368	−1.416		−1.416		−.348	
PM29	2.512	3.120	.264		.264		1.404	
C301	4.880	4.092	−.852		−.836		−.640	
P301	1.632	.912	.400		.432		.692	
PM30	−.228	.380	−2.928		−2.732		−1.532	

P331	2.640	2.476	.933	2.327	.977	2.371	1.379	2.809
PM331	2.352	2.424	.120		.683		1.672	
P35	3.356	3.500	1.672		3.200		3.384	
PM35	3.972	4.972	-.084		4.972		4.972	
P3541	3.560	4.092	2.340		4.016		4.020	
PM35	3.972	3.692	.424		3.332		3.304	
C371	1.976	2.752	.688	2.676	.708		1.744	
P371	1.976	2.000	1.364	1.996	.140		1.636	
PM371	4.116	4.812	1.280	4.708	1.472		2.588	

aSee Table 8-7 for the magnitude of each modification.

bThese simulations apply only where UR is a policy varaible for an industry, as given in Table 8-4, and only at the retail stage except for SIC 371.

(i.e., exogenous in the models constructed) enter at various stages and therefore both directly and indirectly affect more than one price. Therefore, the importance of the links between the prices at different stages of processing is apparent, with policies being addressed not directly at those prices but instead at the factors that influence them.

Including policies that affect *UR* along with the other policies has a substantial influence on behavior of the retail prices *C*22, *C*23, *C*25, and *CMOTOIL*, the final industry price *P*331, and the prices at all stages of SIC 371 (see Table 8-9). The simulation with constant adjustments on all policy regressors, including *UR*, results in the reduction of each affected AAPC to approximately 1.5 percent or less. The key regressor policy change simulation, which includes for certain industries the constant adjustment on *UR*, is not as effective as the previously discussed simulation in reducing AAPC of all prices except for *P*371. A similar result holds for the key regressor simulation with a modified *UR*, in which the average *UR* is increased only to 4.5 percent. In this case only *C*22 and *P*331 have their AAPCs reduced below 2.5 percent.

Examination of the price-unemployment rate relationship without modification to the other policy regressors is the intent of the fourth simulation. Table 8-10 includes the AAPC for affected prices at four different unemployment rates, ranging from 3.0 to 5.2, over the 1967:1 to 1969:2 period. The behavior of all prices over that range is similar, with the most pronounced relationship existing for *C*371 (*CPI* for new cars). The least pronounced relationship exists for *C*25, with an AAPC greater than 2.5 percent still present at an unemployment rate of 5.2 percent.

The Phillips curves for the consumer goods industries analyzed are given below. Definitions of variables can be found in Appendix F. The results in Table 8-11 are based on the 1967-1969:2 averages of all regressors except *UR*.

Table 8-10
Effect of Change in Unemployment Rate (UR) on Quarterly Percentage Change (at annual rates) of Selected Prices, 1967:1–1969:2

Price Affected	Modified Series (UR=3.0)	Ex Post (UR=3.71)	Modified Series (UR=4.5)	Constant Change (UR=5.2)
C22	5.624	2.992	1.476	1.028
C23	8.602	4.908	3.008	2.243
C25	7.065	4.560	3.230	2.815
C371	5.548	2.752	1.744	.708
P371	2.980	2.000	1.636	1.400
PM371	9.836	4.812	2.588	1.472
P331	4.424	2.476	1.436	1.113

Table 8-11
Long-Run Phillips Curves (Annual Rates)

CAVG[a]	C22	C23	C25	C371	UR
1.66	5.50	1.41	4.44	−.10	6.
1.72	5.67	1.41	4.61	.11	5.75
1.95	5.86	1.65	4.78	.35	5.5
2.20	6.07	1.91	4.97	.60	5.25
2.48	6.30	2.20	5.19	.88	5.
2.79	6.55	2.52	5.42	1.19	4.75
3.12	6.83	2.88	5.68	1.53	4.5
3.50	7.15	3.27	5.97	1.91	4.25
3.92	7.50	3.71	6.30	2.34	4.
4.40	7.90	4.20	6.67	2.83	3.75
4.94	8.36	4.76	7.09	3.39	3.5
5.56	8.89	5.40	7.58	4.04	3.25
6.27	9.51	6.13	8.15	4.79	3.

[a]CAVG is a weighted average, normalized to sum to 1.0, of C22, C23, C25, and C371, using their December 1971 CPI weights, which are .55, 9.03, 1.40, and 2.12, respectively.

$$C22 = -.1045 + .066*AHE22 + .028*Q22 + .207*AHERW$$
$$+ 6.013*(1/UR)$$

$$C23 = -1.652 + .055*AHE23 + .183*FDRLT - .099*SHP23$$
$$+ .333*AHERW + 8.377*(1/UR(-1))$$

$$C25 = -8.135 + .483*AHE24 - .057*INV24 + .105*ULCN25$$
$$+ .067*CUIN25 + .426*AHERW + 5.561*(1/UR)$$

$$C371 = -1.206 + .033*WCNMEF + .016*DULCN371$$
$$-.042*INV371 + 7.331*(1/UR)$$

$$CAVG = .042*C22 + .689*C23 + .107*C25 + .162*C371$$

The most pronounced nonlinear relationships between C and UR exist in SIC 23 and SIC 371. Furthermore, only in these two industries does the AAPC of C fall below 2.5 percent. For $C371$ it occurs at a UR slightly less than 4 percent whereas for $C23$ it occurs at a UR of slightly less than 5 percent. The AAPCs of $C25$ and $C22$ never go below 4.4 and 5.5 percent, respectively. A new series $CAVG$ is formed by constructing a normalized weighted average of $C22$, $C23$, $C25$, and $C371$. These four retail prices represent approximately 13 percent of the *CPI* and 25 percent of the *CPI* less food and services. The results for *CAVG* indicate that policy measures that adversely affect the unemployment rate have serious implications for price behavior, especially at low unemployment rates. An increase in $\overline{UR}$ from 3.0 percent to 5.0 percent is accompanied by a corresponding *CAVG* decrease from an AAPC of 6.3 to an AAPC of 2.5. The AAPC of *CAVG* is greater than 2.5 percent at all *UR* less than 5.0 percent. The tradeoffs are consistent with findings of much Phillips curve analysis. Given that services and food prices have been rising at more rapid rates than *CAVG* over the period, the AAPC for the overall *CPI* is probably higher. If so, this relationship reflects the current policy goals of a *UR* about 5.0 percent and an AAPC of the *CPI* equal to approximately 2.5 percent. However, traditional Phillips curve analysis hypothesizes the inverse *P,UR* relationship to be viable in a free market economy. In contrast, the present policy constrains prices through controls while attempting to reduce the unemployment rate through fiscal policies.

The results based on the 1960-66 averages of the regressors differ from the results given in Table 8-11 by a constant value. The AAPC of *CAVG* declines from 5.3 at a *UR* of 3.00 percent to 1.5 at a *UR* of 5.00 percent. Therefore, the constant adjustment in AAPC is a negative 1 percent at all *UR* values as compared with the results based on the 1967:-1969:2 regressor averages. Even in this case, the AAPC for *C22* never falls below 2.5 percent. The tradeoffs of *CAVG* equal to 1.5 at a *UR* of 5.00 percent or of *CAVG* equal to 2.5 at a *UR* of 4.25 percent seem unattainable within the institutional framework of today's U.S. economy.

An important result emerges from these industry-specific policy simulations. There are no effective policy variables representing direct market pressures at any stage of the consumer goods industry price models (SICs 22, 23, 25, 301, and 371). Policies relating to labor cost are most effective in these industries at wholesale levels whereas strong Phillips curve relationships exist in many cases at the retail level. This indicates the importance of *UR*, which is an indirect market measure, as a target for policies. In contrast to the consumer goods industries, the producer and mixed goods industries (SIC 35 and SIC 3541) have direct market pressure policy variables, along with those relating to costs, in their models. Note however that *CUPP* is a policy variable at the intermediate materials stage in all three industries. Recalling the preceding discussion concerning the strong link between *UR* and *CUPP*, it seems apparent in the industries analyzed that with regard to market pressures the most effective policy measure for reducing AAPC is a macro measure relating to either capacity or employment, dependent on the type of goods being produced. However, *UR* affects only the retail stage in the consumer goods industries (except SIC 371) whereas *CUPP* enters at the material stage in the producer goods industries. Thus, the filtering upward through stages of processing of the effects of policy measures addressed at market pressures appears to be absent generally in the consumer goods industries and quite significant in the producer and mixed goods industries. Note that both *UR* and *CUPP* are present in the SIC 331 model.

General Conclusions and Suggested Areas for Further Research

Specific conclusions relating to the best reestimated price equations, the final industry price equations, and the *EPCP* and *ISP* simulations on the industry price models are given in Chapters 6, 7, and 8, respectively. In this chapter these specific conclusions will not be repeated but instead will be synthesized into general conclusions relating to industrial price behavior. It is hoped that future research can be built upon these general conclusions in order to provide additional insights into industrial price formation processes.

General Conclusions

Eight conclusions with selected comments on each are presented in this section. The first two draw comparisons of the final industry price equations with past results. The next two relate to structural characteristics of the final industry price equations. The fifth conclusion concerns the structure of stage of processing price models, and the following two state preferred policy choices on the basis of simulations using these models. The final conclusion is addressed to the price data available for this and future analyses.

The final industry price equations provide sounder structural explanations of industry price behavior than do the best reestimated equations from past studies. Based on the overall regression results, this conclusion applies to the 22 industries examined. The most notable improvements over past work are in the development of long-run, industry-specific *PM* and *DED* regressors and the refinement of lag structures. Furthermore, macro regressors are contained in only two final industry price equations (*UR* in *P331* equation and *FDRLT* in *P23* equation). This result is not inconsistent with the importance of *CUPP*, *AHEDG, AHENG,* and *WCNMEF* as policy regressors in the *EPCP* and *ISP* simulations inasmuch as these regressors directly affect *PM*, which is an industry-specific regressor in the price equation. A further advantage of the final industry price equations over the best reestimated equations is the absence of $P(-1)$ as a regressor, which makes the final equations more appealing because of their lack of autoregressivity.

The classes of industries delineated by Eckstein and Wyss are not substantiated by present results. Of the common industries analyzed, the Eckstein and Wyss

167

classification, based on price formation, has SICs 21, 333, and 371 as target return; SICs 30, 331, and 36 as utilization-sensitive; and SICs 22, 23, 24, 25, and 35 as competitive. On the basis of the results shown in Tables 7-1, 7-2, and 7-11, along with the industry discussions, SIC 21 is possibly target return; SIC 25 is utilization-sensitive; SICs 22, 23, and 36 are short-run, cost-based; and SICs 333, 371, 30, 24, 331, and 35 are competitive (market-based). The only agreement between the two industry classifications is for SICs 21, 24, and 35. This disparity in results does not reflect on the correctness of either classification scheme. However, it does indicate problems inherent in classifying results that are dependent on different forms of data. A preferred alternative to the division of industries into specific price formation groups is the careful examination of each industry's price formation process, utilizing pertinent industry information.

Final industry prices are best explained by relationships based on hybrid hypotheses, although the regressors representing those hypotheses vary greatly across industries. The final industry price equations of Tables 7-1 and 7-2 reflect short- and/or long-run variants of both the cost and the market hypotheses in all cases except for that of the SIC 36 equation. However, a wide variety of both cost regressors (*AHE*, forms of *ULC*, forms of *PM, FDRLT,* and *PREQ*) and *DED* regressors (forms of *SHP, INV, Q, CUI,* and *UNF*) are represented. The *DED* regressors have a greater effect on price change than do the cost regressors in the price equations for two thirds of the industries examined. This result does not conflict with that of the component contribution analysis, since the behavior of certain *DED* regressors is considerably different over the simulation period than over the estimation period, lessening their influence on price during the simulations. However, comparing the coefficients of the labor cost and material cost regressors with the census data ratios for payroll over shipments and materials over shipments does little to support the coefficients that were estimated in this analysis. In only one half of the industries are the coefficients reasonably close to the census ratios. This result further supports the need for extensive study of industry-specific behavior so that the estimated results impart the same structural characteristics as do known descriptive statistics.

The lag structure on cost regressors is more pronounced than on excess demand regressors. The longest lag present on a *SR-DED* regressor is two quarters, a majority of these regressors being most significant when simultaneously related to price. However, many short-run cost variables enter the price equations with a one- to four-quarter lag. The lag structure does not seem to be dependent on any particular industry characteristics. This finding is contrary to those of several studies (e.g., Eckstein and Wyss[159], and Fromm and Eckstein[81]) which found the price equations for durable goods to be characterized by longer lag structures than those for nondurable goods.

The price linkage is strongest between the final industry and intermediate materials stages of processing. The regression results in Tables 8-1 and 8-2 show the significance of *PM* in the *P* equations to be considerably greater than that of *P* in the *C* equations. Furthermore, the component analysis in Chapter 8 concludes that *UR* and *AHERW* are the most important contributors to the AAPC of *C* whereas *PM* or regressors in its equation are key contributors to change in many final price variables. The widening gap between *C* and *P* over recent periods reflects the importance of variables other than *P* on the AAPC of *C*.

The most effective policy measures for controlling inflation, given a desire to achieve or maintain full employment, are those directed at controlling wages. Both the *EPCP* and the *ISP* simulations indicate the effectiveness of *AHE* as a policy measure at all stages of processing. *AHERW* is the key policy variable at the retail stage in three industries and nearly as important as *UR* in the others, with its upward movement in recent years being in part a function of changes in minimum wage laws. This result reflects the need to investigate the influence of minimum wage legislation on consumer goods prices. The importance of *AHEDG*, *AHENG*, and industry-specific wage variables is indicative of both the strong union pressures exerted at the manufacturing stages of processing and the minimum wage law changes. The simulations in Table 8-9, with *UR* unaltered and averaging 3.7 percent, result in reduction of the AAPC of most prices to near or below 2.5 percent. Even though other policy variables as well as wages are altered, the wage variables are of primary importance in a majority of cases.

The unemployment rate is the key market policy variable in consumer goods industries, whereas the capacity utilization index is the key market policy variable in producer and mixed goods industries. The unemployment rate generally affects only the retail price of consumer goods, whereas capacity utilization affects the prices of producer and mixed goods at both manufacturing stages. Thus, the filtering upward through stages of processing of the effects of policy measures directed at market pressures appears to be absent generally in the consumer goods industries (except SICs 29 and 371) and quite significant in the producer and mixed goods industries. Even though policies that result in an increased *UR* and/or reduced *CUI* are extremely effective in reducing AAPC in most prices, they are accompanied by highly undesirable social consequences.

The Eckstein and Wyss price data should be updated so that current policy simulations and future projections of industry price movements can be made. These prices are advantageous over others (e.g., commodity groupings), since they are directly compatible with the SIC industry data available for wages, employment, financial behavior, and market behavior (shipments, inventories, orders). Given the importance of industry-specific regressors in this analysis, it is essential that the industry-specific prices be refined and continuously updated so that additional research into industry price formation processes can be pursued.

Areas for Further Research

This research has provided many insights into industry price behavior as well as affirmation of certain past findings across a representative sample of industries. It has also exposed areas ripe for further research. Three key areas are explored in this section.

Although a wide variety of cost and excess demand regressors are tested for each industry, representation of certain influences on price behavior is still weak. The industry-specific *DED* measures can be improved through use of regressors that reflect characteristics peculiar to each industry. This can be accomplished only through extensive research into the behavior of each industry. Price behavior at the company level should be examined where possible and the aggregation between these units carefully studied. Events peculiar to one or more industries should be accounted for by dummy variables whenever possible. The fixed-cost influence on price is another variable that needs further experimentation. The depreciation-output ratio used in this research (adopted from Schultze and Tryon[51]) is based on accounting data and may be biased because of methods of writing off capital costs. The *CUI* is felt by some to reflect fixed costs. However, the measurement of capacity is tenuous at best and may include equipment and facilities which are obsolete, totally paid for, and/or not used in production. Any one of these occurrences in the capital series results in a *CUI* that does not accurately represent *CUI*. A unit capital cost variable based on capital stock, output, and the physical cost of capital should be constructed and tested. This in itself is difficult because of the lack of reliable industry physical cost of capital series. A final area of concern regarding the regressors used is the length of the moving average adopted in constructing *LRC* and *LR-DED* measures. Each industry's lag structure is probably different because of a variance in decision-making considerations. Again, specific industry behavior should be carefully investigated in order to select the proper time span over which to construct *LRC* and *LR-DED* measures.

A second area for further research is in the estimation and simulation of these and other industry price models over an extended time period. In order that the Eckstein and Wyss prices may be used, it has been recommended that these series be updated. However, most data for the three- and four-digit industries of this research (exceptions: SICs 331, 333, and 371) are available currently. Also, for most other three- and four-digit industries, the major data series are available. In order to study price behavior in these industries, a careful mapping between BLS commodity codes and SIC classifications must be undertaken to ensure that the coverage of the BLS prices (or a weighted average of them) is adequate to use in conjunction with SIC wage and quantity data. Analysis along these lines will permit structural models of price behavior at disaggregate levels to be built. Analysis below the two-digit level of aggregation is not necessary in all cases. For example, SIC 2111 comprises nearly 90 percent of the shipments of SIC 21. Therefore, analyzing either SIC 21 or SIC 2111 would suffice, the choice being dependent on the data available for each.

The third major area suggested for further research is in simulation design and analysis. Industry models can be built for those final price equations not simulated in Chapter 8 and similar simulation analysis can be performed. These results can then be compared with those of Chapter 8 to determine whether the general conclusions remain valid. The types of policy simulations performed can be tailored more to industry-specific characteristics. However, the usefulness of this extension is limited unless current data are available. An important extension to the industry models constructed is to increase their endogeneity by developing behavioral relations for various cost (especially *AHE*) and *DED* regressors. This will increase the usefulness and accuracy of the models as policy-making instruments. An important link to make explicit is that between *UR* and *CUI*. Since *UR* and *CUI* as a rule do not influence the same industry prices, industry models should be combined into a general model with a linking equation between industries which relates *CUI* to *UR*. In this way any policy addressed at adjusting *UR* will also be influential on price behavior in the producer and mixed goods industries through a corresponding *CUI* effect. Further experimentation at the retail and materials stages of the industry model with regard to industry-specific *DED* measures is also necessary.

Other areas also are conducive to further research, including the testing of selected models on monthly data, experimentation using unadjusted data, and the use of techniques such as covariance analysis to compare industry models. It is felt that the areas expounded in this section, however, are the most critical to research at this time in an endeavor to thoroughly develop sound structural explanations of industry price behavior.

Appendixes

Appendix A:
Sources of Data, Variable
Construction, and Time
Periods of Data
Availability

The sources for the variables used in the analysis in Chapters 6, 7, and 8 are given in this appendix, along with the procedures followed to construct certain of these variables and the general time period of availability for each industry's data.

Sources of Data

Final Industry Price

The quarterly, seasonally adjusted prices contained in appendix to the Eckstein and Wyss study for the two-digit industries and SICs 331, 333, and 371 are used in the analysis. For all other industries, Bureau of Labor Statistics (BLS) Commodity Price Indexes are used. In all these latter industries except SIC 251 and SIC 341, an exact equivalence can be made between the price for a SIC industry and the BLS commodity price index. These equivalences are based on the *WPI* Weight Diagram at BLS which shows mappings, based on percentage of industry shipments covered, of SIC into BLS commodity classification and vice versa. For SICs 251 and 341, weighted averages of selected BLS commodity prices had to be used in order to get reasonable industry coverage. The tabulation below contains the mappings used. These prices are available monthly, not seasonally adjusted.

Industry	Commodity	SIC to BLS(%)	BLS to SIC(%)
SIC 227	123100	100	95
SIC 301	071201	100	99
SIC 2111	152101	100	100
SIC 3141	0431	100	95
SIC 251	120000, 121501, 121400	97.5	100
SIC 341	101300, 103101	86	100
SIC3263	12610111	100	100
SIC 3541	113101	99.9	100
SIC 3562	114905	100	100

All prices are rebased to 1967 = 100 and seasonally adjusted.

PM *Material Price*

The quarterly, seasonally adjusted material prices for most two-digit industries and SICs 331, 333, and 371 are taken from the appendix to the Eckstein and Wyss study. For SIC 25, the output price of SIC 24 is used as *PM*25. For SIC 23, the output price of SIC 22 is used as *PM*23. For other three- and four-digit industries, the appropriate two-digit *PM* is tried as the *PM* regressor. For all industries, one of the following stage of processing price indexes is also tried as the material price regressor, depending on both type of product (FP, IP, or MP) and durability of good (DG or NG).

WMDM: materials for durables manufacturing
WMNM: materials for nondurables manufacturing
WCNMEFM: crude nonfood materials, except fuel, for manufacturing

The historical series for these prices were obtained from BLS and the updates from the BLS monthly publication *Wholesale Prices and Price Indexes*. These series are available monthly, not seasonally adjusted. The Eckstein and Wyss material input prices prove superior in all but SICs 21, 227, 2111, and 3141, in which *WMNM* is best, and SICs 24 and 333, in which *WCNMEFM* is best. Note that Eckstein and Wyss *PM* variables are not available for SICs 21, 24, and 333. All *PM* variables are rebased to 1967 = 100 and seasonally adjusted.

AHE   *Average Hourly Earnings for Production Workers*
AWH   *Average Weekly Hours for Production Workers*
NPW   *Number of Production Workers*
UR   *Civilian Worker Unemployment Rate*

The two-, three-, and four-digit data for the *AHE*, *AWH*, and *NPW* variables, as well as updates for *UR*, are from the BLS monthly publication *Employment and Earnings*. The historical series for *UR* was provided by BLS. The *AHERW*, *AHEDG*, and *AHENG* indexes used in the *C* and *PM* equations were obtained from the Division of Trends in Employee Compensation at BLS. *AHEDG* and *AHENG* were extrapolated backward beginning in 1958:4 whereas *AHERW* was extrapolated backward beginning in 1963:4. These extrapolations are based on regression results of each series run as a function of the appropriate BLS wage rate series for those sectors. All of the above series are available monthly in seasonally adjusted form.

SHP   *Shipments*
INV   *Inventories*
UNF   *Unfilled Orders*

These variables are published monthly, not seasonally adjusted, for several industries, by the Bureau of the Census in *Manufacturer's Shipments, Inven-*

tories, and Orders. The best reestimated and final industry price equations include only two-digit *INV, SHP,* and *UNF* variables even in the three- and four-digit industries because of the greater reliability of those data (exceptions: SICs 331, 333, and 371). All data in current dollar form had to be deflated by the appropriate industry price variables before they were used as *DED* measures in the analysis. Unpublished data were obtained from the Bureau of the Census for the following industries:

SHP: SICs 23, 24, 25, 31, 227, 251
INV: SICs 23, 24, 25, 31, 227, 251
UNF: SICs 22, 24, 25, 31, 32, 333, 371.

SC	*Corporate Sales*
PFT	*Provision for Taxes (Federal)*
PRAT	*Net Profit after Taxes*
DD	*Depreciation and Depletion*
STEQ	*Total Stockholders' Equity*

The above variables are all published quarterly, not seasonally adjusted, in the *Quarterly Financial Reports for Manufacturing Corporations* by the Federal Trade Commission and Securities Exchange Commission. They are not available for any of the four-digit industries and are available only for SICs 331, 333, and 371 of the three-digit industries. Therefore, two-digit data were used for all industries except these three-digit industries. None of these variables is available for any industry prior to 1958.

IPI = Q	*Industrial Production Index*
RST	*Treasury Three-Month Bill Rate*
RLT	*Moody's Triple-A Bond Rate*
CUM	*Capacity Utilization Index for Manufacturing*

These variables are from the *Federal Reserve Bulletin*, with *IPI, RST*, and *RLT* available monthly, seasonally adjusted. The *IPI* is available for all industries in the analysis and is on a 1967 = 100 base. Alternative output measures were constructed on the basis of $Q_t = SHP_t + (INV - INV(-1))$ for each industry. However, these are not used in the final analysis because superior fits are obtained when the *IPI*s are used.

CAP	*Capacity*
CUIFRB	*Capacity Utilization Indexes, Two-Digit Industries*
CUPP	*Capacity Utilization Index for Primary Processing Industries*
CUAP	*Capacity Utilization Index for Advanced Processing Industries*

All of these variables are unpublished and were obtained from the Federal Reserve Board. All series are quarterly and all but *CAP* are seasonally adjusted.

The *CUIFRB*, or *CAP* in combination with an industry-specific *IPI*, were not considered further after initial testing because of their questionable reliability and the superior quality of the Wharton capacity utilization indexes.

CUIWH = CUI   *Wharton Capacity Utilization Index*

This variable is available quarterly, seasonally adjusted, for all two-digit industries with the exception of SICs 31 and 32. It is also available for SICs 331, 333, and 371. In all other three- and four-digit industries, the appropriate two-digit *CUIWH* is used in the analysis.

GNP   *Gross National Product*
DY   *Disposable Income*

The historical series through 1965 is available for each of these variables in the *National Income and Product Accounts of the United States*. The updates since 1965 are contained in the *Survey of Current Business*. Both variables are available quarterly, seasonally adjusted. Both of these sources are from the Bureau of Economic Analysis (BEA).

K   *Capital Stock*

This variable is derived for each of the industries analyzed from 1958 thru 1969 on a quarterly, seasonally adjusted basis. The procedure is as follows:
    1. 1958 benchmark capital stock figures for each industry were found in the 1958 *Census of Manufacturing*. These capital stock figures pertain to only the manufacturing activities of these industries. Annual capital stock figures for each industry were then found in the Bureau of the Census' *Annual Surveys of Manufacturing*.
    2. Industry-specific depreciation rates were obtained from the Bureau of Economic Analysis.
    3. Quarterly new plant and equipment expenditures series (from BEA-SEC) for each industry were used along with the industry depreciation rate in order to interpolate each annual capital stock series into a quarterly series. The expenditures series for other nondurables or other durables was used as the interpolative device in those industries where a specific expenditures series was not available. Note that the BEA-SEC series used to interpolate includes capital expenditures in manufacturing and nonmanufacturing establishments of an industry, thereby reflecting larger expenditure figures than the census data. However, the pattern of the BEA-SEC series was felt to be similar to that in only manufacturing

establishments, which is the relevant consideration because it is being used to interpolate several quarterly series between annual observations.

CPI or C *Consumer Price Indexes*

All of the consumer price data were obtained from the Bureau of Labor Statistics. However, only the *CPI* for new cars, used as *C*371 in the analysis, and the *CPI* for apparel, representing *C*23, are available over the entire time period. These monthly indexes are seasonally adjusted and converted to quarterly indexes with a 1967 = 100 base. The other *CPIs*, namely those for textiles (*C*22), gasoline (*CGAS*), premium motor oil (*CMOTOIL*), new tires (*C*301), and furniture and bedding (*C*25) are in general available monthly only since 1969. Prior to 1969, the only data available for these series are three-month observations (March, June, September, and December). Therefore, the following procedure was followed to construct quarterly, seasonally adjusted series for these variables beginning in 1956. (a) Two unadjusted monthly *CPIs*, one for durable consumer goods (*CPIDCG*) and the other for nondurable consumer goods less food (*CPINCGEF*), are used as the basic interpolation series in order to distribute the three-month *CPI* series into monthly series. *CPIDCG* was used for *C*25, with *CPINCGEF* being used for the others. (b) Each new monthly series was combined with its existing monthly data from 1969-71 in order to form new *CPIs* over the 1956-71 period. (c) The monthly *CPIs* were seasonally adjusted using the BLS seasonal adjustment method and then converted to quarterly indexes, with a 1967 = 100 base.

Derived Variables

$$ULC = \frac{13*NPW*AWH*AHE}{Q}$$ unit labor costs

$$ULCN = (\sum_{1}^{12} ULC)/12$$ normal (standard) unit labor costs

$$DULC,N = ULC - ULCN$$ difference between actual and standard unit labor costs

$$AWE = AHE*AWH$$ average weekly earnings

$$PMN = (\sum_{1}^{12} PM)/12$$ normal (standard) material price index

$$4TMAP = (\sum_{1}^{4} P)/4$$ four-term moving average of P

$TAX = PFT/SC$ corporate tax per dollar of sales

$PREQ = PRAT/STEQ$ profit-equity ratio

$URI = 1/UR$ inverse of the unemployment rate

$4TMAUR = (\sum_{1}^{4} UR)/4$ four-term moving average of UR

$PP = \dfrac{Q}{13*NPW*AWH}$ productivity (output per man-hour)

$FDQ = Q - Q(-1)$ change in output

$QN = (\sum_{1}^{12} Q)/12$ normal (standard) output

$CUIN = (\sum_{1}^{12} CUI)/12$ normal (standard) capacity utilization

$UNFSC = UNF/SC$ unfilled orders-sales ratio

$IS = INV/SHP$ inventory-shipment ratio

$FDINV = INV - INV(-1)$ change in inventories

$INVN = (\sum_{1}^{12} INV)/12$ normal (standard) inventory level

$FDIVN = INVN - INVN(-1)$ change in standard inventories

$FDI,IN = (INV - INVN) - (INV(-1) - INVN(-1))$ change in the difference between actual and standard inventories

$FDIQT = (\dfrac{INV}{Q}) - (\dfrac{INV}{Q})^{TR}$ inventory-output ratio minus trend inventory-output ratio (note: SHP or SC can be used in place of Q).

$FDIQN = (INV/Q) - \sum_{1}^{12} (INV/Q)/12$ deviation of normal inventory-output ratio from current inventory-output ratio (note: SHP or SC can be used in place of Q).

Availability of Industry Data

The limits imposed on the time period of analysis because of the absence of *FTC-SEC* variables prior to 1958 and the lack of most price data beyond 1969:2

was noted in Chapter 5. Allowing for varying lag structures, it should be possible to examine most industries over at least the 1959:1 to 1969:2 period. However, certain industries lack one or more variables (either original or derived) beyond 1958 and therefore have shorter time periods for analysis. These cases are noted below. The exact time periods of analysis for each industry are given in Tables 7-1 and 7-2.

SICs 333, 227, 3541, 3562: One or more of the variables necessary to construct ULC for each of these industries is not available until 1958. Therefore, $ULCN$ and $DULC,N$ are not available until 1961.

SICs 22, 23, 24, 25, 251, 3141: The SHP, INV, and UNF data for these industries are not available until 1961. Therefore, DED hypotheses incorporating these variables as regressors cannot be tested on data prior to 1961. Furthermore, analysis including $INVN$, FDI,IN and/or $FDINQN$ cannot be performed on data prior to 1964.

Appendix B:
Industry Classification

The 1967 Standard Industrial Classification (SIC) system, including its market classification codes, is the basis for the organization of the industries into the appropriate cells of Table 5-1. Each two-digit industry, and the three- and four-digit industries that compose it, are considered to be either durable goods (DG) producers or nondurable goods (NG) producers, as indicated in Table 5-1. The classification of an industry as either a final (FP), intermediate (IP), or mixed (MP) product industry is based on the market classification codes, as is the breakdown of industries into consumer (CG), producer (PG), and mixed (MG) goods types. The market classification codes are as follows:

Code	Market Category	Type of good	Type of product
1	Home Goods and Apparel	CG	FP
2	Consumer Staples	CG	FP
3	Equipment and Defense Products, except Automotive	PG	FP
4	Automotive Equipment	MG	FP
5	Construction Materials, Supplies, and Intermediate Products	MG	IP
6	Other Materials and Supplies, and Intermediate Products	PG or NMGEF	IP

Referring to Appendix B of the *Manufacturer's Shipments, Inventories, and Orders, 1961-68*, Series M3-1.1, pp. 76-79, the industries of this analysis may be classified by market codes as follows:

Code		SICs
1	–	227, 23, 3141, 22, 251, 3263, 25, 34, 36
2	–	21, 2111
3	–	3541, 25, 35, 36, 371
4	–	301, 30, 371
5	–	29, 24, 34
6	–	29, 22, 30, 331, 341, 3562, 333, 24, 35, 34, 36, 371.

Appendix C:
Means, Standard Deviations, and Coefficients of Variation of Price Variables[a]

SIC Industry	Mean[b]	Standard Deviation	Coefficient of Variation	R^{2} [c]	SEE[c]
333	.909	1.888	2.08	.793	.873
22	.129	.832	6.45	.601	.534
29	.105	1.650	15.71	.453	1.234
251	.561	.471	.84	.699	.263
3141	.711	1.082	1.52	.430	.830
227	−.247	1.181	−4.79	.549	.805
34	.397	.444	1.12	.518	.312
35	.487	.367	.75	.670	.213
23	.337	.350	1.04	.529	.245
24	1.215	2.855	2.35	.708	1.566
301	−.100	2.083	−20.83	.640	1.263
30	.042	1.255	29.88	.441	.949
3562	−.188	1.115	−5.93	.532	.776
25	.503	.446	.89	.741	.231
3541	.923	.615	.67	.750	.312
331	.248	.418	1.69	.447	.314
3263	.497	.962	1.94	.346	.787
341	.406	.805	1.98	.229	.715
21	.355	.626	1.76	.311	.525
371	.158	.597	3.78	.385	.474
36	.037	.698	18.86	.371	.560
2111	.373	.754	2.02	.368	.606

[a]Time periods used for those given in Tables 7-1 and 7-2.

[b]Average percent change per quarter.

[c]R^{2} and SEE for each industry are those for final industry equations, taken from Tables 7-1 and 7-2.

Appendix D:
Tables and Plots Related to
Final Industry Price
Equations

This appendix contains the fitted and actual series for each of the final industry price equations over the 1965:1 to 1969:2 period. Tables are of the actual, fitted, and residuals (*RES*) whereas plots are of the actual versus predicted. Furthermore, for those industries used in the simulations, the simulated series are included. The plotted series are identified by the following characters:

$$A = \text{actual}$$
$$F = \text{fitted}$$
$$S,R = \text{simulated}$$

The tables include *P* and *RES* series with tags attached to the fitted and simulated series. The identification of these tagged *P* terms as either actual, fitted, or simulated is given for each industry.

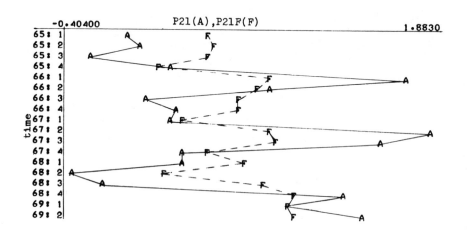

SIC 21

DATE	P21	P21F	RES21
65: 1	-.190000E-01	0.472000	-0.491000
65: 2	.570000E-01	0.506000	-0.449000
65: 3	-0.257000	0.457000	-0.714000
65: 4	0.229000	0.146000	.830000E-01
66: 1	1.69500	0.865000	0.830000
66: 2	0.854000	0.778000	.760000E-01
66: 3	.640000E-01	0.646000	-0.582000
66: 4	0.285000	0.679000	-0.394000
67: 1	0.220000	0.323000	-0.103000
67: 2	1.88300	0.875000	1.00800
67: 3	1.56100	0.901000	0.660000
67: 4	0.300000	0.456000	-0.156000
68: 1	0.308000	0.703000	-0.395000
68: 2	-0.404000	0.183000	-0.587000
68: 3	-0.185000	0.811000	-0.996000
68: 4	1.30700	0.999000	0.308000
69: 1	0.959000	0.969000	-.100000E-01
69: 2	1.45100	1.01300	0.438000

SERIES	CHARACTER
P21#	A
P21F#	F

-0.40400   P21(A),P21F(F)   1.8830

SIC 2111

DATE	P2111	P2111F	RES2111
65: 1	0.369000	0.530000	-0.161000
65: 2	0.188000	0.500000	-0.312000
65: 3	-1.14700	0.177000	-1.32400
65: 4	0.571000	0.369000	0.202000
66: 1	1.73100	0.898000	0.833000
66: 2	2.19500	1.21500	0.980000
66: 3	-0.537000	0.536000	-1.07300
66: 4	0.732000	0.843000	-0.111000
67: 1	0.636000	0.435000	0.201000
67: 2	0.975000	0.451000	0.524000
67: 3	2.34200	1.05900	1.28300
67: 4	0.969000	0.844000	0.125000
68: 1	0.735000	0.789000	-.540000E-01
68: 2	-0.713000	0.208000	-0.921000
68: 3	0.553000	1.16700	-0.614000
68: 4	0.465000	0.997000	-0.532000
69: 1	1.29300	1.22400	.690000E-01
69: 2	1.44500	1.46000	-.150000E-01

SERIES	CHARACTER
P2111#	A
P2111F#	F

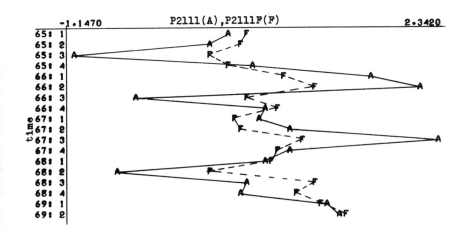

SIC 22

DATE	P22	P22B	RES22B
65: 1	0.166487	0.115503	.509841E-01
65: 2	0.273758	0.134496	0.139262
65: 3	0.253510	0.680044	-0.426534
65: 4	-0.398755	-0.367837	-.309181E-01
66: 1	-0.322234	0.401481	-0.723715
66: 2	0.646552	0.881466	-0.234914
66: 3	.973331E-01	0.129160	-.318269E-01
66: 4	-1.16686	-0.564970	-0.601891
67: 1	-1.36757	-0.863225	-0.504347
67: 2	-1.12718	-0.492184	-0.634998
67: 3	-0.605327	-0.802770	0.197443
67: 4	2.18230	1.34123	0.841068
68: 1	2.56283	1.59299	0.969835
68: 2	0.164649	.818200E-02	0.156467
68: 3	1.01528	0.529375	0.485903
68: 4	0.325452	0.432364	-0.106912
69: 1	-0.400725	-0.244545	-0.156180
69: 2	.191589E-01	0.443238	-0.424079

SERIES	CHARACTER
P22∅	A
P22B∅	F

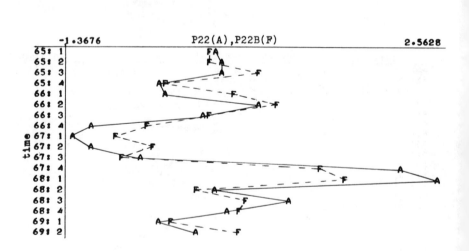

P22(A),P22B(F)

SIC 227

DATE	P227	P227F	RES227
65: 1	-1.25500	-0.625000	-0.630000
65: 2	-0.431000	.370000E-01	-0.468000
65: 3	-0.570000	-1.75200	1.18200
65: 4	-0.870000	-1.60700	0.737000
66: 1	0.717000	0.790000	-.730000E-01
66: 2	.530000E-01	-0.677000	0.730000
66: 3	-.320000E-01	0.235000	-0.267000
66: 4	-0.871000	-0.412000	-0.459000
67: 1	-3.70800	-1.91500	-1.79300
67: 2	-0.568000	.850000E-01	-0.653000
67: 3	-0.549000	-0.122000	-0.427000
67: 4	1.24900	1.16000	.890000E-01
68: 1	0.178000	-0.994000	1.17200
68: 2	0.100000	-0.595000	0.695000
68: 3	.550000E-01	-0.208000	0.263000
68: 4	-0.598000	-0.498000	-0.100000
69: 1	1.19300	1.45500	-0.262000
69: 2	-0.782000	0.294000	-1.07600

SERIES	CHARACTER
P227#	A
P227F#	F

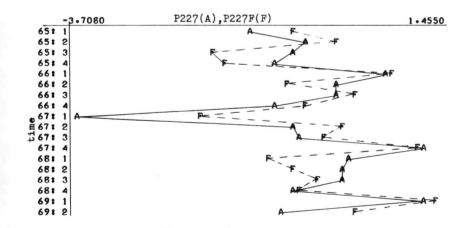

SIC 23

DATE	P23	P23A	RES23A
65: 1	0.135423	.614900E-01	.739327E-01
65: 2	0.164219	0.147345	.168745E-01
65: 3	0.327900	0.199364	0.128536
65: 4	.480631E-01	0.128188	-.801249E-01
66: 1	0.269024	0.308131	-.391072E-01
66: 2	0.364124	0.501201	-0.137077
66: 3	.954745E-02	0.124998	-0.115451
66: 4	0.133652	0.327651	-0.193999
67: 1	-.953380E-01	.841880E-01	-0.179526
67: 2	0.381716	0.837904	-0.456188
67: 3	1.31191	0.774563	0.537349
67: 4	0.337806	0.431292	-.934859E-01
68: 1	0.495651	0.302701	0.192950
68: 2	0.986414	0.459358	0.527056
68: 3	1.10579	1.18918	-.833920E-01
68: 4	1.10281	0.729814	0.372993
69: 1	0.450735	0.221066	0.229669
69: 2	0.448712	0.247375	0.201337

SERIES	CHARACTER
P23#	A
P23A#	F

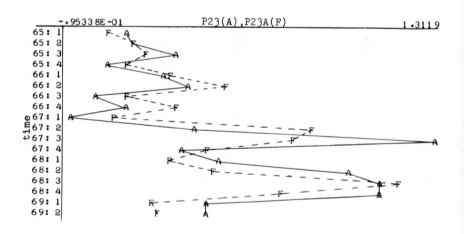

SIC 24

DATE	P24	P24B	RES24B
65: 1	0.569168	1.20818	-0.639009
65: 2	-1.53477	-0.361374	-1.17340
65: 3	1.32489	2.95045	-1.62556
65: 4	2.00942	3.13214	-1.12271
66: 1	1.44204	2.10345	-0.661419
66: 2	3.83722	2.87898	0.958245
66: 3	-2.09377	-3.39247	1.29870
66: 4	-1.17894	-1.78597	0.607024
67: 1	-1.31323	-0.198999	-1.11423
67: 2	0.609128	-1.56164	2.17077
67: 3	2.30999	1.25965	1.05034
67: 4	2.59468	3.12418	-0.529495
68: 1	2.83077	3.13107	-0.300297
68: 2	4.43562	4.74815	-0.312530
68: 3	5.56106	6.37705	-0.815990
68: 4	6.52838	5.57811	0.950262
69: 1	11.4116	8.50486	2.90671
69: 2	-4.43873	-4.20515	-0.233582

SERIES	CHARACTER
P24#	A
P24B#	F

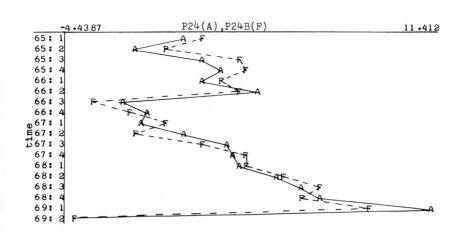

SIC 25

DATE	P25	P25B	RES25B
65: 1	0.314495	0.206601	0.107895
65: 2	0.114003	0.223908	-0.109905
65: 3	.948947E-01	0.454010	-0.359115
65: 4	0.331816	0.211157	0.120660
66: 1	0.245677	0.575335	-0.329658
66: 2	1.44217	0.860572	0.581600
66: 3	0.873444	0.781131	.923125E-01
66: 4	1.51990	1.04430	0.475595
67: 1	0.771255	0.774020	-.276493E-02
67: 2	0.738340	0.780390	-.420503E-01
67: 3	0.625670	0.746783	-0.121112
67: 4	0.710606	0.965402	-0.254796
68: 1	1.23479	1.05435	0.180431
68: 2	1.15874	1.04119	0.117549
68: 3	0.921540	0.876209	.453305E-01
68: 4	0.921659	1.17018	-0.248522
69: 1	1.26839	1.22961	.387771E-01
69: 2	0.985304	1.25595	-0.270651

DATE	P25D	RES25D
65: 1	0.206601	0.107895
65: 2	0.223908	-0.109905
65: 3	0.509603	-0.414709
65: 4	0.313242	.185740E-01
66: 1	0.716759	-0.471082
66: 2	0.958248	0.483924
66: 3	0.838675	.347691E-01
66: 4	0.960935	0.558962
67: 1	0.661033	0.110222
67: 2	0.727579	.107608E-01
67: 3	0.843721	-0.218051
67: 4	0.776546	-.659397E-01
68: 1	0.962976	0.271810
68: 2	1.08726	.714830E-01
68: 3	0.902335	.192046E-01
68: 4	1.19737	-0.275712
69: 1	1.30061	-.322141E-01
69: 2	1.17328	-0.187978

SIC 25

SERIES	CHARACTER
P25#	A
P25B#	F
P25D#	S

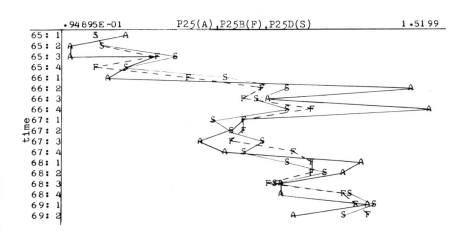

.94895E-01   P25(A),P25B(F),P25D(S)   1.51 99

SIC 251

DATE	P251	P251F	RES251
65: 1	0.211000	.930000E-01	0.118000
65: 2	-.180000E-01	0.311000	-0.329000
65: 3	0.300000	0.357000	-.570000E-01
65: 4	0.315000	0.107000	0.208000
66: 1	0.402000	0.478000	-.760000E-01
66: 2	1.48000	0.749000	0.731000
66: 3	0.873000	0.878000	-.500000E-02
66: 4	1.49300	1.01900	0.474000
67: 1	0.557000	0.590000	-.330000E-01
67: 2	0.314000	0.703000	-0.389000
67: 3	0.630000	0.671000	-.410000E-01
67: 4	0.859000	0.903000	-.440000E-01
68: 1	1.21200	1.10700	0.105000
68: 2	1.09800	1.01000	.880000E-01
68: 3	0.869000	1.08000	-0.211000
68: 4	1.21800	1.27400	-.560000E-01
69: 1	1.49900	1.25100	0.248000
69: 2	0.770000	1.13400	-0.364000

SERIES	CHARACTER
P251#	A
P251F#	F

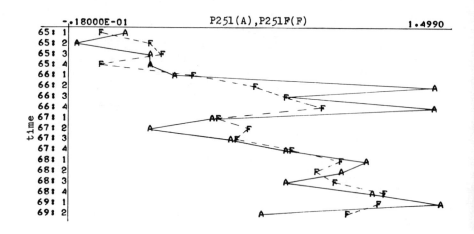

P251(A),P251F(F)

SIC 29

DATE	P29	P29B	RES29B
65: 1	0.907100	-0.189455	1.16875
65: 2	1.47758	1.15269	0.300434
65: 3	1.52734	1.80143	-0.328691
65: 4	0.812356	0.268155	0.568449
66: 1	0.179069	.343896E-01	0.130429
66: 2	1.16187	0.935688	0.276496
66: 3	1.46265	.743867E-01	1.41130
66: 4	0.309598	0.401567	-.910017E-01
67: 1	0.781250	-0.108819	0.825747
67: 2	1.10058	-0.563690	1.60969
67: 3	0.747823	.337381E-01	0.757547
67: 4	-3.01607	-1.72535	-1.25527
68: 1	-0.125945	.174500E-01	-0.148062
68: 2	0.766321	0.401498	0.354408
68: 3	-0.125144	-1.23230	1.16277
68: 4	-1.05060	-0.607427	-0.485620
69: 1	1.16891	2.26129	-1.06613
69: 2	1.37685	1.29793	.561665E-01

DATE	P29A	RES29A	P29C	RES29C
65: 1	-0.189455	1.09656	0.301623	0.605477
65: 2	1.15269	0.324889	1.39262	.849533E-01
65: 3	1.76988	-0.242543	2.41944	-0.892105
65: 4	0.169787	0.642568	0.918968	-0.106612
66: 1	.281470E-01	0.150922	0.264347	-.852779E-01
66: 2	0.864919	0.296948	1.01896	0.142910
66: 3	.723292E-01	1.39032	0.330403	1.13225
66: 4	0.363796	-.541981E-01	0.453970	-0.144373
67: 1	-0.138285	0.919535	-0.103944	0.885194
67: 2	-0.708566	1.80915	-0.871881	1.97246
67: 3	.868202E-01	0.661003	-0.215524	0.963347
67: 4	-1.39870	-1.61737	-1.77791	-1.23816
68: 1	.425352E-01	-0.168480	-0.519814	0.393870
68: 2	0.682399	.839219E-01	0.588419	0.177901
68: 3	-0.829959	0.704815	-0.779859	0.654715
68: 4	-0.321177	-0.729425	-0.541381	-0.509222
69: 1	2.34025	-1.17134	2.54810	-1.37919
69: 2	1.62907	-0.252218	2.59100	-1.21415

198

SIC 29

SERIES	CHARACTER
P29#	A
P29B#	F
P29A#	S
P29C#	R

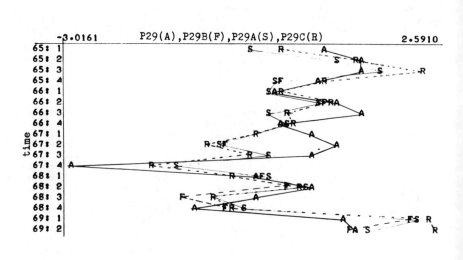

SIC 30

DATE	P30	P30F	RES30
65: 1	0.420000	.340000E-01	0.386000
65: 2	1.22200	0.351000	0.871000
65: 3	0.837000	0.384000	0.453000
65: 4	-0.248000	0.334000	-0.582000
66: 1	0.422000	0.570000	-0.148000
66: 2	2.69200	0.956000	1.73600
66: 3	-0.723000	-0.206000	-0.517000
66: 4	0.106000	0.135000	-.290000E-01
67: 1	1.05500	.290000E-01	1.02600
67: 2	0.605000	0.641000	-.360000E-01
67: 3	1.75400	1.72100	.330000E-01
67: 4	2.26400	1.19500	1.06900
68: 1	0.658000	0.864000	-0.206000
68: 2	0.446000	-0.656000	1.10200
68: 3	0.207000	-0.204000	0.411000
68: 4	0.187000	-0.445000	0.632000
69: 1	-0.973000	-0.544000	-0.429000
69: 2	0.853000	0.477000	0.376000

SERIES	CHARACTER
P30#	A
P30F#	F

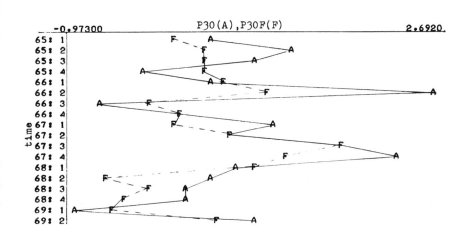

SIC 301

DATE	P301	P301B	RES301B
65: 1	0.850322	.880579E-01	0.762264
65: 2	1.26473	0.150358	1.10069
65: 3	0.661827	.921470E-01	0.588853
65: 4	0.296925	0.206719	.956951E-01
66: 1	0.644957	0.624509	-.422730E-02
66: 2	4.02353	1.86750	2.17807
66: 3	-1.71682	-1.83188	0.104088
66: 4	-.411015E-01	-0.508427	0.478342
67: 1	1.94285	0.384884	1.55516
67: 2	-0.383180	0.386170	-0.780284
67: 3	1.84229	2.69157	-0.841037
67: 4	0.824968	1.23476	-0.423467
68: 1	0.916798	0.730634	0.191594
68: 2	0.439582	-0.917337	1.36240
68: 3	0.165337	-0.671964	0.851158
68: 4	0.184484	-0.982235	1.14728
69: 1	-2.35511	-1.31619	-1.02199
69: 2	0.506203	0.321576	0.161940

DATE	P301A	RES301A
65: 1	.880579E-01	0.762264
65: 2	0.150358	1.11437
65: 3	.921470E-01	0.569681
65: 4	0.206719	.902057E-01
66: 1	0.651959	-.700283E-02
66: 2	1.79286	2.23067
66: 3	-1.82479	0.107969
66: 4	-0.546887	0.505785
67: 1	0.169866	1.77298
67: 2	0.430971	-0.814151
67: 3	2.73774	-0.895448
67: 4	1.36056	-0.535596
68: 1	0.707107	0.209691
68: 2	-0.989865	1.42945
68: 3	-0.593661	0.758998
68: 4	-0.817705	1.00219
69: 1	-1.20226	-1.15285
69: 2	0.476869	.293340E-01

SIC 301

SERIES	CHARACTER
P301#	A
P301B#	F
P301A#	S

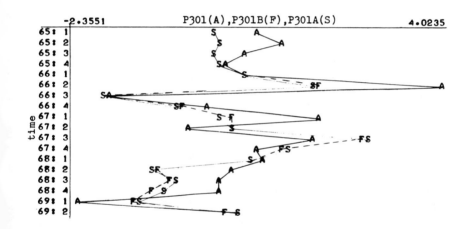

DATE	P3141	P3141F	RES3141
65: 1	0.371000	0.964000	-0.593000
65: 2	0.749000	1.06100	-0.312000
65: 3	0.833000	0.509000	0.324000
65: 4	3.12500	1.62100	1.50400
66: 1	0.852000	1.35900	-0.507000
66: 2	5.17300	2.31200	2.86100
66: 3	1.03100	1.92300	-0.892000
66: 4	0.193000	1.07500	-0.882000
67: 1	1.40300	1.61200	-0.209000
67: 2	-0.775000	0.308000	-1.08300
67: 3	0.574000	0.704000	-0.130000
67: 4	0.333000	1.55800	-1.22500
68: 1	1.26400	1.57600	-0.312000
68: 2	1.22400	1.53500	-0.311000
68: 3	1.04000	1.44100	-0.401000
68: 4	2.19600	1.56200	0.634000
69: 1	0.604000	0.559000	.450000E-01
69: 2	-0.185000	-0.268000	.830000E-01

SIC 3141

SERIES	CHARACTER
P3141#	A
P3141F#	F

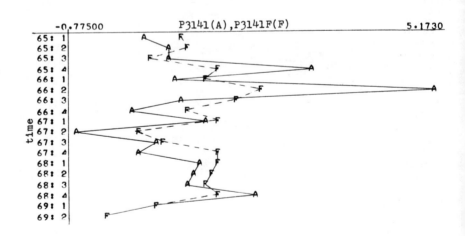

SIC 3263

DATE	P3263	P3263F	RES3263
65: 1	-0.501000	-0.148000	-0.353000
65: 2	-0.201000	0.292000	-0.493000
65: 3	0.303000	.130000E-01	0.290000
65: 4	0.466000	0.318000	0.148000
66: 1	2.99300	1.17300	1.82000
66: 2	-0.398000	0.624000	-1.02200
66: 3	0.302000	0.883000	-0.581000
66: 4	0.601000	1.09900	-0.498000
67: 1	0.202000	1.01300	-0.811000
67: 2	4.14900	1.61800	2.53100
67: 3	0.194000	0.182000	.120000E-01
67: 4	0.773000	1.17500	-0.402000
68: 1	2.36900	1.25400	1.11500
68: 2	-0.562000	0.800000	-1.36200
68: 3	0.238000	0.901000	-0.663000
68: 4	0.834000	0.660000	0.174000
69: 1	-0.438000	0.444000	-0.882000
69: 2	2.49200	1.37800	1.11400

SERIES	CHARACTER
P3263#	A
P3263F#	F

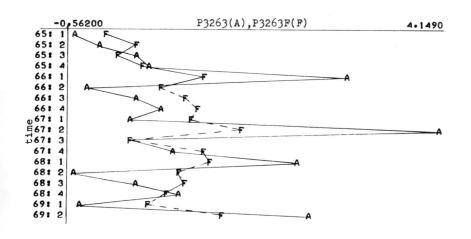

SIC 331

DATE	P331	P331A	RES331A
65: 1	0.574428	0.216787	0.357641
65: 2	0.137863	.470530E-01	.908101E-01
65: 3	0.226178	0.257560	-.313822E-01
65: 4	0.235479	0.367234	-0.131755
66: 1	0.323023	0.570028	-0.247006
66: 2	0.380525	0.637161	-0.256636
66: 3	0.495723	0.472374	.233495E-01
66: 4	0.415901	0.232744	0.183157
67: 1	0.327490	0.371065	-.435751E-01
67: 2	0.163210	0.361305	-0.198094
67: 3	0.297134	0.535903	-0.238769
67: 4	0.707187	0.578846	0.128341
68: 1	0.673752	0.630882	.428697E-01
68: 2	0.574984	0.781062	-0.206079
68: 3	0.824742	0.430662	0.394081
68: 4	0.920245	0.729271	0.190975
69: 1	0.681588	0.866314	-0.184726
69: 2	1.42713	0.903995	0.523139

DATE	P331B	RES331B
65: 1	0.216787	0.357641
65: 2	.835039E-01	.543593E-01
65: 3	0.245369	-.191917E-01
65: 4	0.381990	-0.146512
66: 1	0.558348	-0.235325
66: 2	0.673372	-0.292847
66: 3	0.446743	.489797E-01
66: 4	0.202511	0.213390
67: 1	0.290715	.367751E-01
67: 2	0.369201	-0.205991
67: 3	0.530490	-0.233356
67: 4	0.548626	0.158561
68: 1	0.670755	.299753E-02
68: 2	0.778538	-0.203555
68: 3	0.531250	0.293492
68: 4	0.828337	.919081E-01
69: 1	0.803239	-0.121651
69: 2	0.837538	0.589596

SIC 331

SERIES	CHARACTER
P331#	A
P331A#	F
P331B#	S

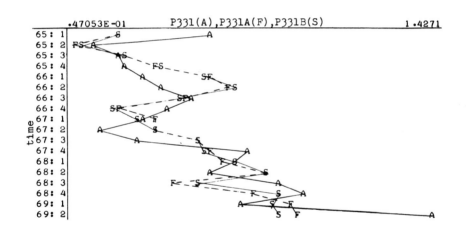

SIC 333

DATE	P333	P333F	RES333
65: 1	0.694000	0.578000	0.116000
65: 2	1.63900	1.82700	-0.188000
65: 3	1.10700	-0.141000	1.24800
65: 4	0.594000	0.223000	0.371000
66: 1	0.169000	-0.362000	0.531000
66: 2	2.69500	1.25000	1.44500
66: 3	0.640000	-0.286000	0.926000
66: 4	-0.196000	-1.27000	1.07400
67: 1	0.931000	0.514000	0.417000
67: 2	-0.679000	-1.58000	0.901000
67: 3	0.122000	0.885000	-0.763000
67: 4	3.57900	3.97200	-0.393000
68: 1	4.06000	4.04200	.180000E-01
68: 2	-2.01500	-.270000E-01	-1.98800
68: 3	-2.49600	-2.08600	-0.410000
68: 4	-.240000E-01	-.400000E-01	.160000E-01
69: 1	0.379000	1.02400	-0.645000
69: 2	6.51000	6.17200	0.338000

SERIES	CHARACTER
P333#	A
P333F#	F

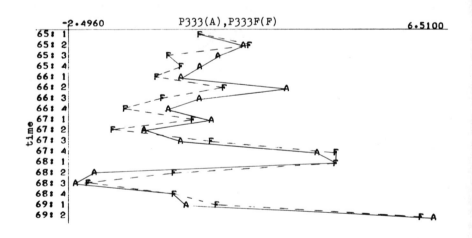

SIC 34

DATE	P34	P34F	RES34
65: 1	0.827000	0.455000	0.372000
65: 2	0.821000	0.488000	0.333000
65: 3	0.426000	0.541000	-0.115000
65: 4	0.302000	0.395000	-.930000E-01
66: 1	0.582000	0.469000	0.113000
66: 2	0.925000	0.994000	-.690000E-01
66: 3	0.814000	0.689000	0.125000
66: 4	0.716000	0.631000	.850000E-01
67: 1	0.283000	0.474000	-0.191000
67: 2	0.227000	0.517000	-0.290000
67: 3	0.580000	0.682000	-0.102000
67: 4	0.685000	1.14800	-0.463000
68: 1	1.07500	1.13900	-.640000E-01
68: 2	1.05400	0.530000	0.524000
68: 3	0.149000	0.469000	-0.320000
68: 4	1.20800	0.660000	0.548000
69: 1	1.34100	1.02600	0.315000

SERIES	CHARACTER
P34#	A
P34F#	F

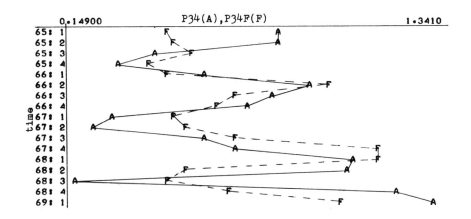

208

SIC 341

DATE	P341	P341F	RES341
65: 1	-0.600000	-0.411000	-0.189000
65: 2	1.58400	1.57100	.130000E-01
65: 3	1.32700	0.478000	0.849000
65: 4	0.861000	0.411000	0.450000
66: 1	0.563000	0.562000	.100000E-02
66: 2	-0.397000	0.671000	-1.06800
66: 3	0.562000	0.688000	-0.126000
66: 4	0.370000	-0.138000	0.508000
67: 1	0.871000	1.05500	-0.184000
67: 2	-0.258000	0.194000	-0.452000
67: 3	0.670000	0.784000	-0.114000
67: 4	1.19700	0.334000	0.863000
68: 1	-0.184000	0.348000	-0.532000
68: 2	3.19600	0.942000	2.25400
68: 3	0.562000	0.531000	.310000E-01
68: 4	0.322000	0.581000	-0.259000
69: 1	0.835000	0.599000	0.236000

SERIES	CHARACTER
P341#	A
P341F#	F

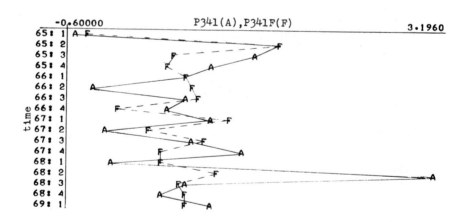

SIC 35

DATE	P35	P35B	RES35B
65: 1	0.493299	0.357575	0.205252
65: 2	0.527924	0.585621	-0.121841
65: 3	0.552792	0.439705	0.114107
65: 4	0.577240	0.689144	-.516496E-01
66: 1	0.737907	0.775906	-.448602E-01
66: 2	1.12136	0.829564	0.253793
66: 3	0.608120	0.991268	-0.364339
66: 4	1.12000	0.900482	0.256675
67: 1	0.606540	0.838446	-0.316809
67: 2	0.567934	0.775640	-0.156595
67: 3	0.590791	0.811540	-0.204170
67: 4	1.15737	0.996826	0.119480
68: 1	1.10997	0.830472	0.285993
68: 2	0.954231	1.05036	-.384360E-01
68: 3	0.836470	0.805132	.325159E-01
68: 4	0.141020	0.665544	-0.588740
69: 1	1.45792	0.834151	-7.62709
69: 2	0.971587	0.885821	9.07510

DATE	P35A	RES35A
65: 1	0.357575	0.135724
65: 2	0.579650	-.517259E-01
65: 3	0.453859	.989325E-01
65: 4	0.690380	-0.113140
66: 1	0.819209	-.813021E-01
66: 2	0.900453	0.220907
66: 3	1.02181	-0.413690
66: 4	0.904992	0.215008
67: 1	0.804388	-0.197848
67: 2	0.746925	-0.178991
67: 3	0.816433	-0.225642
67: 4	0.986899	0.170468
68: 1	0.812922	0.297051
68: 2	1.05286	-.986321E-01
68: 3	0.879649	-.431791E-01
68: 4	0.783923	-0.642903
69: 1	0.952305	0.505614
69: 2	0.910695	.608921E-01

210

SIC 35

SERIES   CHARACTER

P35#   A
P35B#   F
P35A#   S

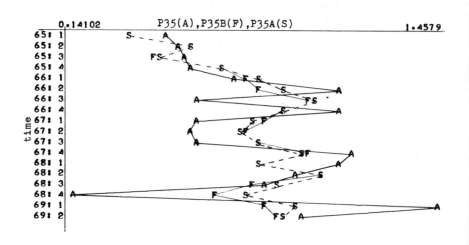

SIC 3541

DATE	P3541	P3541D	RES3541D
65: 1	2.08211	1.33681	0.745294
65: 2	1.00254	1.36415	-0.361615
65: 3	1.19795	1.35630	-0.158351
65: 4	1.46561	1.46467	.946333E-03
66: 1	1.47778	1.73983	-0.262054
66: 2	2.05847	2.06335	-.487588E-02
66: 3	1.90967	2.00851	-.988446E-01
66: 4	2.08443	1.73413	0.350301
67: 1	1.21687	1.30526	-.883935E-01
67: 2	1.59959	1.11831	0.481284
67: 3	0.952667	0.988091	-.354237E-01
67: 4	0.774809	0.952821	-0.178012
68: 1	0.532282	1.14671	-0.614426
68: 2	0.627513	1.10385	-0.476334
68: 3	0.672318	0.870665	-0.198347
68: 4	0.687185	1.04753	-0.360344
69: 1	0.538306	1.00200	-0.463698
69: 2	1.30032	1.54642	-0.246106

DATE	P3541F	RES3541F
65: 1	1.33681	0.745294
65: 2	1.33795	-0.335419
65: 3	1.21466	-.167183E-01
65: 4	1.51209	-.464804E-01
66: 1	1.69799	-0.220210
66: 2	1.96811	.903562E-01
66: 3	1.80172	0.107942
66: 4	1.47915	0.605284
67: 1	1.30238	-.855076E-01
67: 2	1.20227	0.397326
67: 3	1.06928	-0.116610
67: 4	0.989313	-0.214504
68: 1	1.16590	-0.633620
68: 2	0.968764	-0.341252
68: 3	0.608002	.643161E-01
68: 4	0.973708	-0.286523
69: 1	0.681222	-0.142915
69: 2	1.27288	.274371E-01

SIC 3541

SERIES	CHARACTER
P3541#	A
P3541D#	F
P3541F#	S

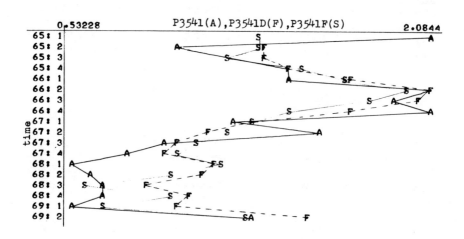

P3541(A),P3541D(F),P3541F(S)

SIC 3562

DATE	P3562	P3562F	RES3562
65: 1	-2.20700	-1.40700	-0.800000
65: 2	-1.38700	-1.07300	-0.314000
65: 3	-.360000E-01	-0.958000	0.922000
65: 4	-0.274000	-0.966000	0.692000
66: 1	-0.502000	-0.581000	.790000E-01
66: 2	-0.192000	-0.340000	0.148000
66: 3	0.325000	-0.718000	1.04300
66: 4	0.228000	-0.449000	0.677000
67: 1	.240000E-01	-0.305000	0.329000
67: 2	-0.670000	-.490000E-01	-0.621000
67: 3	0.169000	0.770000	-0.601000
67: 4	-0.168000	0.307000	-0.475000
68: 1	0.494000	1.63200	-1.13800
68: 2	0.863000	0.752000	0.111000
68: 3	1.37900	1.24100	0.138000
68: 4	0.446000	0.952000	-0.506000
69: 1	-0.502000	-0.550000	.480000E-01
69: 2	0.728000	-.180000E-01	0.746000

SERIES	CHARACTER
P3562#	A
P3562F#	F

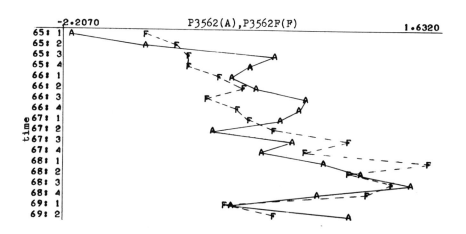

SIC 36

DATE	P36	P36F	RES36
65: 1	-0.147000	0.258000	-0.405000
65: 2	-0.922000	-.560000E-01	-0.866000
65: 3	0.624000	0.551000	.730000E-01
65: 4	-0.210000	0.401000	-0.611000
66: 1	0.601000	0.127000	0.474000
66: 2	0.670000	0.229000	0.441000
66: 3	0.208000	0.384000	-0.176000
66: 4	1.17300	0.199000	0.974000
67: 1	0.790000	0.667000	0.123000
67: 2	0.224000	0.567000	-0.343000
67: 3	0.295000	0.314000	-.190000E-01
67: 4	0.537000	0.664000	-0.127000
68: 1	1.17900	0.493000	0.686000
68: 2	0.388000	0.888000	-0.500000
68: 3	0.466000	0.610000	-0.144000
68: 4	0.227000	0.454000	-0.227000
69: 1	-0.896000	-0.196000	-0.700000
69: 2	0.974000	1.27400	-0.300000

SERIES	CHARACTER
P36#	A
P36F#	F

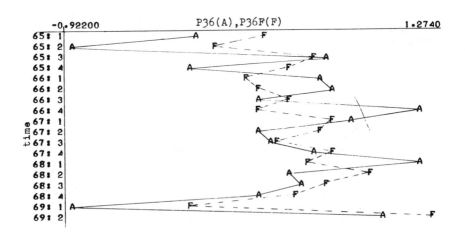

215

SIC 371

DATE	P371	P371B	RES371B
65: 1	.996016E-01	0.114640	-.191973E-01
65: 2	.0	-0.282649	0.276446
65: 3	-0.199005	0.217548	-0.416553
65: 4	-.997009E-01	-0.263767	0.172173
66: 1	-0.199601	.901879E-02	-0.220753
66: 2	0.300000	0.401643	-0.103641
66: 3	.997009E-01	0.576003	-0.474238
66: 4	0.796813	0.303315	0.507431
67: 1	.0	0.206023	-0.208063
67: 2	.0	0.285651	-0.301391
67: 3	0.197628	0.413766	-0.208305
67: 4	1.97239	0.894571	1.07392
68: 1	0.290135	0.559446	-0.273144
68: 2	0.385728	0.752273	-0.356876
68: 3	0.576369	0.211700	0.355180
68: 4	0.859599	.396183E-01	0.825666
69: 1	0.189394	0.118534	.689779E-01
69: 2	0.472590	0.883204	-0.412396

DATE	P371A	RES371A
65: 1	0.114640	-.150380E-01
65: 2	-0.373104	0.373104
65: 3	0.232087	-0.431092
65: 4	-0.237946	0.138245
66: 1	0.119508	-0.319109
66: 2	0.581731	-0.281731
66: 3	0.652160	-0.552459
66: 4	0.343976	0.452837
67: 1	0.165432	-0.165432
67: 2	0.316746	-0.316746
67: 3	0.482801	-0.285173
67: 4	0.934771	1.03762
68: 1	0.624618	-0.334482
68: 2	0.819530	-0.433802
68: 3	0.342660	0.233709
68: 4	0.225754	0.633845
69: 1	0.423450	-0.234056
69: 2	0.660888	-0.188298

SIC 371

SERIES	CHARACTER
P371#	A
P371B#	F
P371A#	S

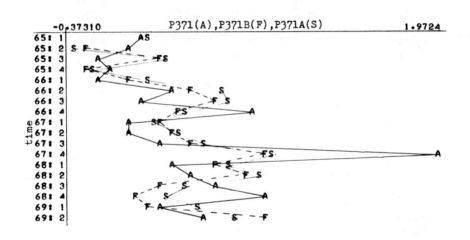

P371(A),P371B(F),P371A(S)

Appendix E:
Component Contributions
and Modified Regressors
for Industry Models

Component contributions, each equal to a regression coefficient times its regressor, are given for each of the regressors in the equations of the industry models. These are followed by the actual and modified regressors used in certain policy simulations of Chapter 8.

217

SIC221

COMPONENT CONTRIBUTIONS

A221: C22=-1.213+.121*P22(-1)+.207*AHERW(-1)+6.013*URI

A222: P22=-.864+.547*AHE22+.235*Q22(-1)

WHERE   C3=.121*P22A(-1)
        C4=.207*AHERW(-1)
        C5=6.013*URI
        C1=.547*AHE22
        C2=.235*Q22(-1)

DATE	C3	C4	C5
65: 1	.559524E-01	0.206379	1.22714
65: 2	.139759E-01	0.292698	1.28850
65: 3	.162740E-01	0.247986	1.37702
65: 4	.822853E-01	0.331407	1.46659
66: 1	-.445083E-01	0.204102	1.55509
66: 2	.485792E-01	0.245088	1.56861
66: 3	0.106657	0.244260	1.59637
66: 4	.156284E-01	0.243432	1.62514
67: 1	-.683614E-01	0.282555	1.59637
67: 2	-0.104450	0.241569	1.55509
67: 3	-.595543E-01	0.279657	1.56861
67: 4	-.971352E-01	0.278001	1.52873
68: 1	0.162289	0.314226	1.61063
68: 2	0.192752	0.348588	1.68589
68: 3	.990022E-03	0.271791	1.68589
68: 4	.640544E-01	0.342171	1.78604
69: 1	.523160E-01	0.338238	1.78604
69: 2	-.295899E-01	0.265995	1.73452

DATE	C1	C2
65: 1	0.601153	0.378350
65: 2	0.297021	0.701475
65: 3	1.18261	0.361430
65: 4	0.289363	0.206800
66: 1	0.575991	0.689490
66: 2	1.13940	0.606065
66: 3	0.557940	0.435220
66: 4	0.276235	.227950E-01
67: 1	0.549735	-0.548960
67: 2	0.816671	-0.444855
67: 3	0.268030	-0.206800
67: 4	1.86800	0.337225
68: 1	1.03219	1.42481
68: 2	0.506522	0.365660
68: 3	1.00375	0.389630
68: 4	0.985694	0.310670
69: 1	0.484095	0.135360
69: 2	0.959438	0.347800

S IC23

A231: $C23 = -1.685 + .278*P23C + .333*AHERW(-1) + 8.377*URI(-1)$

A232: $P23 = .120 + .197*AHE23(-2) + .658*FDRLT(-3) - .034*SHP23$

WHERE $D4 = .278*P23C$
$D6 = .333*AHERW(-1)$
$D5 = 8.377*URI(-1)$
$D1 = .197*AHE23(-2)$
$D2 = .658*FDRLT(-3)$
$D3 = -.034*SHP23$

DATE	D4	D5	D6
65: 1	.170942E-01	1.68664	0.332001
65: 2	.409619E-01	1.70959	0.470862
65: 3	.554232E-01	1.79507	0.398934
65: 4	.356363E-01	1.91840	0.533133
66: 1	.856604E-01	2.04317	0.328338
66: 2	0.139334	2.16647	0.394272
66: 3	.347494E-01	2.18530	0.392940
66: 4	.910870E-01	2.22398	0.391608
67: 1	.234043E-01	2.26405	0.454545
67: 2	0.232937	2.22398	0.388611
67: 3	0.215329	2.16647	0.449883
67: 4	0.119899	2.18530	0.447219
68: 1	.841509E-01	2.12975	0.505494
68: 2	0.127702	2.24384	0.560772
68: 3	0.330592	2.34869	0.437229
68: 4	0.202888	2.34869	0.550449
69: 1	.614563E-01	2.48822	0.544122
69: 2	.687703E-01	2.48822	0.427905

DATE	D1	D2	D3
65: 1	.0	.263200E-01	-.848300E-01
65: 2	0.110123	-.217140E-01	-.610640E-01
65: 3	0.109532	.125020E-01	-.426700E-01
65: 4	.0	.164500E-01	-.826200E-02
66: 1	0.326429	.138180E-01	-0.152116
66: 2	0.214139	.197400E-01	0.147322
66: 3	.0	.671160E-01	-.621180E-01
66: 4	0.211775	0.157920	-0.162044
67: 1	0.104804	0.119756	-0.260372
67: 2	0.416852	0.205954	.950980E-01
67: 3	0.408381	.217140E-01	0.224468
67: 4	0.499986	-0.150682	-.380120E-01
68: 1	0.292545	.881720E-01	-0.198016
68: 2	0.192272	0.248066	-0.100980
68: 3	0.761405	0.240828	.669460E-01
68: 4	0.458222	.756700E-01	.759220E-01
69: 1	0.268708	.789600E-01	-0.246602
69: 2	0.264965	-.815920E-01	-.559980E-01

S IC25

F251 : C25 =-1 .472 +.4 96 *P25D +.426 *A HERW +5 .561 *UR I

F252 : P25 =-13 .411 +.0 87 *P24D (-2) +.212 *U LC N25 +.1 35 *CU IN25

F253 : P24 =-.173 +.671 *A HE24 (-3) -.7 86 *INV24 +.3 94 *P24D (-1)

WHERE   B4 =.4 96 *P25D
         B5 =5 .561 *UR I
         B 9 =.426 *A HERW
         B1 =.0 87 *P24D (-2)
         B2 =.212 *U LC N25
         B3 =.1 35 *CU IN25
         B6 =.671 *A HE24 (-3)
         B7 =-.7 86 * INV24
         B 8 =.3 94 *P24D (-1)

DATE	B4	B9	B5
65: 1	0. 102474	0. 602364	1. 13490
65: 2	0. 111058	0. 510348	1. 19164
65: 3	0. 252763	0. 682026	1. 27351
65: 4	0. 155368	0. 420036	1. 35634
66: 1	0. 355512	0. 504384	1. 43819
66: 2	0. 475291	0. 502680	1. 45070
66: 3	0. 415983	0. 500976	1. 47637
66: 4	0. 476624	0. 581490	1. 50297
67: 1	0. 327872	0. 497142	1. 47637
67: 2	0. 360879	0. 575526	1. 43819
67: 3	0. 418486	0. 572118	1. 45070
67: 4	0. 385167	0. 646668	1. 41381
68: 1	0. 477636	0. 717384	1. 48955
68: 2	0. 539279	0. 559338	1. 55916
68: 3	0. 447558	0. 704178	1. 55916
68: 4	0. 593896	0. 696084	1. 65178
69: 1	0. 645100	0. 547410	1. 65178
69: 2	0. 581948	0. 544428	1. 60413

DATE	B1	B2	B3
65: 1	-.502213E-01	0.117872	13.5499
65: 2	.269402E-01	.188680E-01	13.5891
65: 3	0.105111	0.204792	13.6107
65: 4	-.314396E-01	.977320E-01	13.6579
66: 1	0.256689	0.124020	13.7470
66: 2	0.272496	0.237652	13.8591
66: 3	0.183001	0.111724	13.9549
66: 4	0.250471	.841640E-01	14.0373
67: 1	-0.295145	0.263728	14.1034
67: 2	-0.155379	0.166208	14.1277
67: 3	-.173129E-01	0.160484	14.1115
67: 4	-0.135862	0.251008	14.0724
68: 1	0.109590	0.233836	14.0305
68: 2	0.271803	0.232352	13.9941
68: 3	0.272403	.765320E-01	13.9644
68: 4	0.413089	0.267332	13.9279
69: 1	0.554804	0.274752	13.8820
69: 2	0.485296	0.270936	13.8280

DATE	B6	B7	B8
65: 1	.0	1.25917	0.122005
65: 2	0.638792	-1.30319	0.476022
65: 3	.0	3.26583	-0.142381
65: 4	0.632753	1.50991	1.16248
66: 1	0.627385	0.415008	1.23406
66: 2	0.621346	1.60187	0.828761
66: 3	0.615307	-4.96909	1.13432
66: 4	0.305305	-0.581640	-1.33663
67: 1	1.21451	-0.536838	-0.703671
67: 2	0.297924	-1.60816	-.784057E-01
67: 3	0.593835	1.45410	-0.615285
67: 4	0.883036	1.91784	0.496302
68: 1	1.16217	0.910974	1.23093
68: 2	0.571021	3.11649	1.23364
68: 3	1.41581	3.26347	1.87077
68: 4	2.21833	1.02023	2.51256
69: 1	1.34200	5.13808	2.19778
69: 2	0.789767	-8.17283	3.35091

SIC29II,SIC29IIII

0291: CGAS=-1.779+.321*P29C+1.788*AHERW(-4)

0292: CMOTOIL=-.831+.161*P29G(-3)+.745*AHERW(-1)+3.186*URI(-4)

0294: P29=.218+.619*PM29C(-2)-.513*INV29+.303*P29C(-1)

0296: PM29=-2.906+.705*AHENG(-4)+2.836*CUAP(-3)+.358*PM29C(-1)

```
        WHERE    J1=.321*P29C
                 J2=1.788*AHERW(-4)
                 J3=.161*P29G(-3)
                 J4=.745*AHERW(-1)
                 J5=3.186*URI(-4)
                 J6=.619*PM29C(-2)
                 J7=-.513*INV29
                 J8=.303*P29C(-1)
                 J9=.705*AHENG(-4)
                 J10=2.836*CUAP(-3)
                 J11=.358*PM29C(-1)
```

DATE	J1	J2
65: 1	.968210E-01	1.79336
65: 2	0.447033	2.17421
65: 3	0.776642	2.16527
65: 4	0.294989	1.78264
66: 1	.848553E-01	2.52823
66: 2	0.327085	2.14202
66: 3	0.106059	2.86259
66: 4	0.145724	1.76297
67: 1	-.333659E-01	2.11699
67: 2	-0.279874	2.10984
67: 3	-.691831E-01	2.10269
67: 4	-0.570709	2.44062
68: 1	-0.166860	2.08660
68: 2	0.188883	2.41559
68: 3	-0.250335	2.40128
68: 4	-0.173783	2.71418
69: 1	0.817941	3.01099
69: 2	0.831712	2.34764

DATE	J3	J4	J5
65: 1	-0.389529	0.742765	0.582805
65: 2	-.594535E-01	1.05343	0.612692
65: 3	0.252335	0.892510	0.637200
65: 4	.485613E-01	1.19275	0.641477
66: 1	0.224213	0.734570	0.650204
66: 2	0.389531	0.882080	0.682714
66: 3	0.147954	0.879100	0.729618
66: 4	.425598E-01	0.876120	0.777073
67: 1	0.164052	1.01693	0.823966
67: 2	.531948E-01	0.869415	0.831130
67: 3	.730892E-01	1.00650	0.845841
67: 4	-.167349E-01	1.00054	0.861081
68: 1	-0.140373	1.13091	0.845841
68: 2	-.346993E-01	1.25458	0.823966
68: 3	-0.286244	0.978185	0.831130
68: 4	-.836901E-01	1.23149	0.810000
69: 1	.947355E-01	1.21733	0.853393
69: 2	-0.125557	0.957325	0.893271

DATE	J6	J7	J8
65: 1	-0.218387	-0.172881	0.474891
65: 2	.644590E-02	1.07679	.913918E-01
65: 3	-.242289E-01	1.80371	0.421965
65: 4	-.762415E-01	.441180E-01	0.733092
66: 1	-.115106E-01	-0.220590	0.278447
66: 2	-.173476E-01	0.738207	.800971E-01
66: 3	.329698E-01	-0.229311	0.308744
66: 4	.794283E-01	.564300E-01	0.100112
67: 1	0.207916	-0.667413	0.137553
67: 2	0.176405	-1.23479	-.314950E-01
67: 3	0.127683	-0.297027	-0.264180
67: 4	0.350704	-2.28131	-.653037E-01
68: 1	0.344159	-0.543267	-0.538707
68: 2	0.422758	0.105165	-0.157504
68: 3	0.545991	-1.72214	0.178291
68: 4	0.498812	-1.02190	-0.236297
69: 1	0.410334	2.08381	-0.164038
69: 2	0.584677	1.01625	0.772075

DATE	J9	J10	J11
65: 1	0.466710	2.39642	.372800E-02
65: 2	0.403260	2.39358	-.140128E-01
65: 3	0.537915	2.39358	-.440944E-01
65: 4	0.425820	2.45881	-.665717E-02
66: 1	0.499140	2.47016	-.100330E-01
66: 2	0.522405	2.49284	.190682E-01
66: 3	0.663405	2.53255	.459375E-01
66: 4	0.489975	2.58076	0.120249
67: 1	0.403965	2.60628	0.102024
67: 2	0.789600	2.60912	.738458E-01
67: 3	0.644370	2.61479	0.202831
67: 4	0.840360	2.54956	0.199045
68: 1	1.00533	2.53822	0.244503
68: 2	0.883365	2.51270	0.315775
68: 3	0.773385	2.50702	0.288489
68: 4	1.09486	2.51837	0.237318
69: 1	1.38180	2.50419	0.338149
69: 2	1.10897	2.50135	0.471893

SIC301

T3011: C301=-2.418+.568*P301A+2.328*AHERW
T3012: P301=1.264+.263*PM30A(-4)+.052*DULCN301(-2)-.481*INV30
T3013: PM30=-.579+.144*WCNMEF(-2)+.618*AHENG(-4)+.464*PM30A(-1)

WHERE   E4=.568*P301A
         E5=2.328*AHERW
         E1=.263*PM30A(-4)
         E2=.052*DULCN301(-2)
         E3=-.481*INV30
         E6=.144*WCNMEF(-2)
         E7=.618*AHENG(-4)
         E8=.464*PM30A(-1)

DATE	E4	E5
65: 1	.500169E-01	3.29179
65: 2	.854034E-01	2.78894
65: 3	.523395E-01	3.72713
65: 4	0.117416	2.29541
66: 1	0.370313	2.75635
66: 2	1.01834	2.74704
66: 3	-1.03648	2.73773
66: 4	-0.310632	3.17772
67: 1	.964836E-01	2.71678
67: 2	0.244791	3.14513
67: 3	1.55504	3.12650
67: 4	0.772800	3.53390
68: 1	0.401637	3.92035
68: 2	-0.562243	3.05666
68: 3	-0.337199	3.84818
68: 4	-0.464457	3.80395
69: 1	-0.682883	2.99148
69: 2	0.270862	2.97518

DATE	E6	E7	E8
65: 1	0.222048	0.409116	-.386989E-01
65: 2	-.720000E-01	0.353496	-.919717E-01
65: 3	0.205200	0.471534	-.442785E-01
65: 4	-.100800E-01	0.373272	-0.103817
66: 1	0.134496	0.437544	-.484163E-01
66: 2	0.449712	0.457938	-.927779E-01
66: 3	0.174960	0.581538	-.368156E-01
66: 4	-0.466560	0.429510	0.192762
67: 1	-0.618336	0.354114	0.101259
67: 2	-0.222336	0.692160	-0.273847
67: 3	-0.285984	0.564852	-0.361466
67: 4	-.460800E-01	0.736656	-0.277449
68: 1	0.277344	0.881268	-0.188281
68: 2	0.367344	0.774354	.315091E-01
68: 3	-0.260928	0.677946	0.233952
68: 4	.360000E-01	0.959754	0.324912
69: 1	-.658080E-01	1.21128	0.206359
69: 2	0.236160	0.972114	0.405832

DATE	E1	E2	E3
65: 1	0.109927	-0.669708	-0.616161
65: 2	-.410510E-01	-0.461240	-0.611351
65: 3	-.822303E-02	-0.302640	-0.860990
65: 4	-.219349E-01	-0.197444	-0.837902
66: 1	-.521305E-01	-.741000E-01	-0.485810
66: 2	-.250975E-01	-0.113672	0.667628
66: 3	-.588448E-01	-0.201188	-2.82876
66: 4	-.274428E-01	-.884000E-01	-1.69504
67: 1	-.525874E-01	-.665600E-01	-0.974987
67: 2	-.208674E-01	-.743080E-01	-0.737854
67: 3	0.109259	0.113880	1.25060
67: 4	.573949E-01	0.323440	-0.284271
68: 1	-0.155219	-0.431496	.298220E-01
68: 2	-0.204883	-0.335660	-1.71332
68: 3	-0.157261	-0.615264	-1.08514
68: 4	-0.106719	-0.444444	-1.53054
69: 1	.178597E-01	-0.222456	-2.26166
69: 2	0.132606	-0.215072	-0.704665

S IC331

S3311: $P331 = -.702 + .087*PM331B(-1) + .127*ULCN331 + 4.333*URI$

S3312: $PM331 = -3.573 + .352*WCNMEF + .581*AHEDG(-4) + 3.907*CUPP$

WHERE $A1 = .087*PM331B(-1)$
$A2 = .127*ULCN331$
$A3 = 4.333*URI$
$A9 = .352*WCNMEF$
$A10 = .581*AHEDG(-4)$
$A11 = 3.907*CUPP$

DATE	A1	A2	A3
65: 1	0.154643	-0.120142	0.884286
65: 2	.572086E-02	-0.148717	0.928500
65: 3	.709033E-01	-0.115824	0.992290
65: 4	.342730E-01	-.711200E-02	1.05683
66: 1	.255716E-01	0.114173	1.12060
66: 2	0.138217	0.106807	1.13035
66: 3	.785265E-01	-.801370E-01	1.15035
66: 4	-.590521E-01	-0.207518	1.17108
67: 1	-.927422E-01	-.648970E-01	1.15035
67: 2	-.309873E-01	-.184150E-01	1.12060
67: 3	-.361609E-01	0.138303	1.13035
67: 4	.173165E-01	0.131699	1.10161
68: 1	0.102910	0.109220	1.16063
68: 2	0.109469	0.156210	1.21486
68: 3	-.132324E-01	.316230E-01	1.21486
68: 4	.529346E-01	0.190373	1.28703
69: 1	.288521E-01	0.189357	1.28703
69: 2	0.135964	0.153670	1.24990

DATE	A9	A10	A11
65: 1	-0.176000	0.251573	3.56318
65: 2	0.501600	0.327103	3.55928
65: 3	-.246400E-01	0.404957	3.58663
65: 4	0.328768	.232400E-02	3.53584
66: 1	1.09930	0.460152	3.60225
66: 2	0.427680	0.418320	3.62960
66: 3	-1.14048	0.409024	3.62570
66: 4	-1.51149	0.478744	3.53974
67: 1	-0.543488	0.357315	3.40300
67: 2	-0.699072	0.558922	3.29751
67: 3	-0.112640	0.567637	3.31704
67: 4	0.677952	0.698362	3.37956
68: 1	0.897952	0.569380	3.36393
68: 2	-0.637824	0.636195	3.42253
68: 3	.880000E-01	0.709982	3.38346
68: 4	-0.160864	0.666407	3.39909
69: 1	0.577280	1.09693	3.46160
69: 2	1.19398	0.758205	3.46551

SIC35I

E351: P35=-1.166+.084*PM35A(-1)+.217*AHE35(-1)+.164*INVN35(-3)+.424*UNFSC

E352: PM35=-2.426+.145*WCNMEF+.609*AHED6(-2)+2.460*CUPP+.661*PM35A(-1)

WHERE H1=.084*PM35A(-1)
       H2=.217*AHE35(-1)
       H3=.164*INVN35(-3)
       H4=.424*UNFSC
       H5=.145*WCNMEF
       H6=.609*AHED6(-2)
       H7=2.460*CUPP
       H8=.661*PM35A(-1)

DATE	H1	H2	H3	H4
65: 1	.457109E-01	.0	0.219432	1.25843
65: 2	.444523E-01	0.225246	0.250592	1.22536
65: 3	.314091E-01	.742140E-01	0.284212	1.23002
65: 4	.463359E-01	0.222208	0.299300	1.28854
66: 1	.620617E-01	0.293167	0.294380	1.33560
66: 2	0.101813	0.217000	0.303072	1.44457
66: 3	0.112434	0.286440	0.315536	1.47340
66: 4	.542946E-01	0.212009	0.321112	1.48358
67: 1	.162317E-01	0.210056	0.334724	1.40938
67: 2	.181021E-01	0.138663	0.373920	1.38224
67: 3	.198857E-01	0.137795	0.426400	1.39835
67: 4	.310331E-01	0.273854	0.467892	1.38012
68: 1	.749470E-01	0.135191	0.478552	1.29023
68: 2	0.117257	0.403186	0.453132	1.24529
68: 3	.913452E-01	0.329840	0.403768	1.22070
68: 4	0.135173	0.259966	0.343416	1.21137
69: 1	0.126534	0.385175	0.306188	1.30041
69: 2	0.151974	0.315301	0.280604	1.32882

DATE	H5	H6	H7	H8
65: 1	-.725000E-01	0.424473	2.24352	0.359701
65: 2	0.206625	.243600E-02	2.24106	0.349797
65: 3	-.101500E-01	0.482328	2.25828	0.247160
65: 4	0.135430	0.438480	2.22630	0.364620
66: 1	0.452835	0.428736	2.26812	0.488366
66: 2	0.176175	0.501816	2.28534	0.801170
66: 3	-0.469800	0.374535	2.28288	0.884749
66: 4	-0.622630	0.585858	2.22876	0.427247
67: 1	-0.223880	0.594993	2.14266	0.127728
67: 2	-0.287970	0.732018	2.07624	0.142446
67: 3	-.464000E-01	0.596820	2.08854	0.156481
67: 4	0.279270	0.666855	2.12790	0.244201
68: 1	0.369895	0.744198	2.11806	0.589761
68: 2	-0.262740	0.698523	2.15496	0.922699
68: 3	.362500E-01	1.14979	2.13036	0.718799
68: 4	-.662650E-01	0.794745	2.14020	1.06368
69: 1	0.237800	0.822150	2.17956	0.995705
69: 2	0.491840	1.08341	2.18202	1.19589

SIC35411I

E35411: P3541=-.340+.479*PM35F(-1)+.104*ULC3541+17.571*PREQ35+.268*ON3541
E353:   PM35=-4.701+.133*WCNMEF+.934*AHEDG(-2)+5.034*CUPP

WHERE   I1=.479*PM35F(-1)
        I2=.104*ULC3541
        I3=17.571*PREQ35
        I4=.268*ON3541
        I5=.133*WCNMEF
        I6=.934*AHEDG(-2)
        I7=5.034*CUPP

DATE	I1	I2	I3	I4
65: 1	0.260661	0.252512	0.579843	0.785776
65: 2	0.227288	-0.220896	0.632556	0.767820
65: 3	.374746E-01	0.178152	0.667698	0.799444
65: 4	0.311652	0.175344	0.667698	0.842860
66: 1	0.312055	-0.186680	0.773124	0.913076
66: 2	0.485343	0.167232	0.755553	0.958368
66: 3	0.434356	0.296296	0.702840	0.945772
66: 4	.546261E-01	0.178984	0.790695	0.925136
67: 1	.896736E-01	0.219232	0.650127	0.854116
67: 2	0.187184	0.215072	0.632556	0.703232
67: 3	0.194582	.462800E-01	0.614985	0.561192
67: 4	0.213455	-.641680E-01	0.544701	0.436840
68: 1	0.446571	.707200E-01	0.579843	0.337412
68: 2	0.533560	-0.211016	0.535916	0.229944
68: 3	0.258222	.334880E-01	0.549972	0.121136
68: 4	0.696986	0.105352	0.509559	.605680E-01
69: 1	0.400764	.276640E-01	0.502531	-.268000E-02
69: 2	0.593071	0.188136	0.544701	-.568160E-01

DATE	I5	I6	I7
65: 1	-.665000E-01	0.650998	4.59101
65: 2	0.189525	.373600E-02	4.58597
65: 3	-.931000E-02	0.739728	4.62121
65: 4	0.124222	0.672480	4.55577
66: 1	0.415359	0.657536	4.64135
66: 2	0.161595	0.769616	4.67659
66: 3	-0.430920	0.574410	4.67155
66: 4	-0.571102	0.898508	4.56080
67: 1	-0.205352	0.912518	4.38461
67: 2	-0.264138	1.12267	4.24870
67: 3	-.425600E-01	0.915320	4.27387
67: 4	0.256158	1.02273	4.35441
68: 1	0.339283	1.14135	4.33427
68: 2	-0.240996	1.07130	4.40978
68: 3	.332500E-01	1.76339	4.35944
68: 4	-.607810E-01	1.21887	4.37958
69: 1	0.218120	1.26090	4.46012
69: 2	0.451136	1.66159	4.46516

SIC371

M3711: C371=-.735+.354*P371A+3.800*URI(-4)+.345*C371A(-1)

M3712: P371=.297+.211*PM371A(-1)+.028*DULCN371(-4)-.071*INV371(-2)

M3713: PM371=-.978+.126*WCNMEF+5.782*URI(-1)+.531*PM371A(-1)

        WHERE   F4=.354*P371A
                F5=3.800*URI(-4)
                F6=.345*C371A(-1)
                F1=.211*PM371A(-1)
                F2=.028*DULCN371(-4)
                F3=-.071*INV371(-2)
                F7=.126*WCNMEF
                F8=5.782*URI(-1)
                F9=.531*PM371A(-1)

DATE	F4	F5	F6
65: 1	.440216E-01	0.695122	-0.187355
65: 2	-0.143272	0.730769	-.632078E-01
65: 3	.891215E-01	0.760000	-.726951E-01
65: 4	-.913712E-01	0.765101	.142921E-01
66: 1	.458912E-01	0.775510	-.162076E-01
66: 2	0.223385	0.814286	.242169E-01
66: 3	0.250429	0.870229	0.112776
66: 4	0.132087	0.926829	0.171960
67: 1	.635260E-01	0.982759	0.171077
67: 2	0.121630	0.991304	0.166415
67: 3	0.185396	1.00885	0.187801
67: 4	0.358952	1.02703	0.223231
68: 1	0.239853	1.00885	0.301602
68: 2	0.314700	0.982759	0.281280
68: 3	0.131581	0.991304	0.291090
68: 4	.866895E-01	0.966102	0.234247
69: 1	0.162605	1.01786	0.190453
69: 2	0.253781	1.06542	0.219391

DATE	F1	F2	F3
65: 1	.782626E-01	-.728280E-01	-0.187795
65: 2	.675444E-01	-0.102340	-0.635308
65: 3	0.116373	-.510720E-01	-0.130214
65: 4	0.115004	-.823760E-01	-0.567574
66: 1	0.158930	-.826000E-02	-0.328162
66: 2	0.258624	-.412720E-01	.673790E-01
66: 3	0.278791	-.607320E-01	0.137101
66: 4	0.173803	-.591640E-01	-.676630E-01
67: 1	.956653E-01	-.205520E-01	-0.206681
67: 2	0.133122	.320320E-01	-0.145408
67: 3	0.135424	0.104692	-.543150E-01
67: 4	0.172562	-.320040E-01	0.497213
68: 1	0.254739	0.187544	-0.114665
68: 2	0.306899	.454440E-01	0.170187
68: 3	0.235218	.448840E-01	-0.234442
68: 4	0.267246	-.402920E-01	-0.298200
69: 1	0.265456	.568120E-01	-0.195818
69: 2	0.340577	-.443520E-01	.676630E-01

DATE	F7	F8	F9
65: 1	-.630000E-01	1.16416	0.196955
65: 2	0.179550	1.18000	0.169981
65: 3	-.882000E-02	1.23900	0.292863
65: 4	0.117684	1.32412	0.289418
66: 1	0.393498	1.41024	0.399962
66: 2	0.153090	1.49534	0.650849
66: 3	-0.408240	1.50835	0.701602
66: 4	-0.541044	1.53504	0.437390
67: 1	-0.194544	1.56270	0.240750
67: 2	-0.250236	1.53504	0.335013
67: 3	-.403200E-01	1.49534	0.340807
67: 4	0.242676	1.50835	0.434269
68: 1	0.321426	1.47000	0.641072
68: 2	-0.228312	1.54875	0.772339
68: 3	.315000E-01	1.62112	0.591946
68: 4	-.575820E-01	1.62112	0.672548
69: 1	0.206640	1.71743	0.668044
69: 2	0.427392	1.71743	0.857092

MODIFIED REGRESSORS

DATE	Actual UR ($\overline{UR}=3.7$)	Modified UR ($\overline{UR}=4.5$)	Modified UR ($\overline{UR}=3.0$)
65: 4	4.20000	4.20000	3.4
66: 1	4.11000	4.11000	3.25
66: 2	4.06000	4.06000	2.95
66: 3	4.04000	4.10000	2.85
66: 4	3.90000	4.22000	2.7
67: 1	3.77000	4.40000	2.6
67: 2	3.77000	4.35000	2.55
67: 3	3.75000	4.50000	2.5
67: 4	3.70000	4.62000	2.6
68: 1	3.68000	4.68000	2.5
68: 2	3.61000	4.80000	2.7
68: 3	3.54000	4.85000	2.7
68: 4	3.52000	4.90000	2.65
69: 1	3.45000	5.00000	2.6
69: 2	3.50000	4.90000	2.55

DATE	Actual AHERW	Modified AHERW
65: 1	1.41400	0.950000
65: 2	1.19800	0.850000
65: 3	1.60100	1.00000
65: 4	0.986000	0.986000
66: 1	1.18400	1.10000
66: 2	1.18000	0.800000
66: 3	1.17600	0.850000
66: 4	1.36500	0.900000
67: 1	1.16700	0.950000
67: 2	1.35100	1.20000
67: 3	1.34300	0.750000
67: 4	1.51800	0.750000
68: 1	1.68400	1.10000
68: 2	1.31300	0.800000
68: 3	1.65300	0.825000
68: 4	1.63400	0.950000
69: 1	1.28500	1.00000
69: 2	1.27800	0.950000

	Actual	Modified
DATE	A HEDG	A HEDG
65: 1	0.792000	.800
65: 2	0.720000	.700
65: 3	0.704000	.700
65: 4	0.824000	.800
66: 1	0.615000	.650
66: 2	0.962000	.800
66: 3	0.977000	.800
66: 4	1.20200	.800
67: 1	0.980000	.850
67: 2	1.09500	.750
67: 3	1.22200	.900
67: 4	1.14700	.850
68: 1	1.88800	.850
68: 2	1.30500	.900
68: 3	1.35000	.950
68: 4	1.77900	1.000
69: 1	1.40100	.900
69: 2	1.35400	.900

	Actual	Modified
DATE	AHENG	AHENG
65: 1	0.708000	0.708000
65: 2	0.741000	0.741000
65: 3	0.941000	0.941000
65: 4	0.695000	0.695000
66: 1	0.573000	0.573000
66: 2	1.12000	0.750000
66: 3	0.914000	0.914000
66: 4	1.19200	0.800000
67: 1	1.42600	0.850000
67: 2	1.25300	0.750000
67: 3	1.09700	0.900000
67: 4	1.55300	0.950000
68: 1	1.96000	0.875000
68: 2	1.57300	0.850000
68: 3	1.41000	1.00000
68: 4	1.52400	0.900000
69: 1	1.16400	1.16400
69: 2	1.40200	0.850000

	Actual	Modified
DATE	A HE23	A HE23
65 : 1	0 .556000	.600
65 : 2	.0	.750
65 : 3	1 .65700	.800
65 : 4	1 .0 8700	.800
66 : 1	.0	.600
66 : 2	1 .07500	.800
66 : 3	0 .532000	.700
66 : 4	2 .11600	.950
67 : 1	2 .07300	1 .000
67 : 2	2 .53800	1 .200
67 : 3	1 .4 8500	.800
67 : 4	0 .976000	.900
6 8 : 1	3 .86500	1 .300
6 8 : 2	2 .32600	1 .100
6 8 : 3	1 .36400	.800
6 8 : 4	1 .34500	.800
69 : 1	0 .442000	.700
69 : 2	1 .32200	.900

	Actual	Modified
DATE	A HE24	A HE24
65 : 1	0 .943000	.940
65 : 2	0 .935000	.940
65 : 3	0 .926000	.930
65 : 4	0 .917000	.920
66 : 1	0 .455000	.460
66 : 2	1 .81000	.700
66 : 3	0 .444000	.700
66 : 4	0 .885000	.900
67 : 1	1 .31600	.900
67 : 2	1 .73200	1 .000
67 : 3	0 .851000	.900
67 : 4	2 .11000	.900
6 8 : 1	3 .30600	.950
6 8 : 2	2 .00000	.900
6 8 : 3	1 .17700	.800
6 8 : 4	1 .55000	.850
69 : 1	1 .14500	.800
69 : 2	1 .13200	.800

234

DATE	Actual AHE22	Modified AHE22
67: 1	1.00500	0.800000
67: 2	1.49300	0.700000
67: 3	0.490000	0.700000
67: 4	3.41500	0.900000
68: 1	1.88700	0.800000
68: 2	0.926000	0.926000
68: 3	1.83500	0.900000
68: 4	1.80200	0.850000
69: 1	0.885000	0.885000
69: 2	1.75400	0.800000

Date	Actual UNFSC	Modidied UNFSC
67: 1	3.32400	3.32400
67: 2	3.26000	3.26000
67: 3	3.29800	3.22000
67: 4	3.25500	3.22500
68: 1	3.04300	3.04300
68: 2	2.93700	2.93700
68: 3	2.87900	2.87900
68: 4	2.85700	2.85700
69: 1	3.06700	2.77500
69: 2	3.13400	2.61500

DATE	Actual CUPP	Modified CUPP
66: 4	0.906000	0.906000
67: 1	0.871000	0.871000
67: 2	0.844000	0.844000
67: 3	0.849000	0.845000
67: 4	0.865000	0.852000
68: 1	0.861000	0.849000
68: 2	0.876000	0.845000
68: 3	0.866000	0.840000
68: 4	0.870000	0.840000
69: 9	0.886000	0.845000
69: 2	0.887000	0.850000

Appendix F:
Alphabetical Listing of Variables

Notes

1. In the text, the SIC number is attached to each appropriate industry-specific variable symbol given in this appendix.

2. The form of the data which each variable symbol is representing is given in conjunction with the discussion containing the symbol. It differs throughout the text, being level in Chapter 2, several forms in Chapters 3 and 4, and in general percentage change from Chapter 5 to 9. The exact form of each variable in the models estimated in Chapters 6 and 7 is given in Table 5-5.

3. Lagged (or lead) values of the different variables are indicated by a minus (or plus) number in parentheses following the variable symbol.

Symbol	Definition
A	age of nonfarm equipment
AHE	average hourly earnings
$AHEDG$	average hourly earnings for durable goods workers (index)
$AHENG$	average hourly earnings for nondurable goods workers (index)
$AHEP$	peak average hourly earnings
$AHERW$	average hourly earnings for wholesale and retail workers (index)
AWE	weekly earnings index
AWH	average weekly hours
C	cost
CAP	capacity in manufacturing
$CAVG$	weighted average of $C22$, $C23$, $C25$, $C371$
$CGAS$	CPI for gasoline
$CMOTOIL$	CPI for motor oil
CPI (or C)	consumer price index
CS	steel industry ingot capacity
$CUAP$	Federal Reserve CUI for advanced product industries
CUI	capacity utilization index
$+CUI$	positive deviations from $CUIN$

$-CUI$	negative deviations from $CUIN$
$CUID$	desired CUI
$CUIE$	equilibrium CUI
$CUIN$	normal CUI (12-term moving average)
$CUIS$	CUI of principal supplying industry
$CUISN$	$CUIN$ of principal supplying industry
$CUIWH$	Wharton capacity utilization index
$CUPP$	Federal Reserve CUI for primary product industries
D	real consumption or real investment
$D1,D2,D3,D4$	quarterly seasonal dummies
DED	direct excess demand measure
DR	Kuh demand rachet: $(Q)/(QP)(.0375)^{t-p}$
$DULC,N$	difference between ULC minus $ULCN$
$DUM1$	Korean War dummy (1950:3-1951:1 = 1, all others = 0)
$DUM2$	wage-price guidepost dummy (1963:2 = 1, all others = 0)
$DUMMY$	excise tax dummy (1965:3 = 1, all others = 0)
DY	disposable income
$DY58$	disposable income in constant dollars
ED	excess demand (demand minus supply)
ER	employment rate in man-hours
F	political factor (1948-51 = 0, 1952-56 = 1)
FDI,IN	change in $(INV-INVN)$
$FDINV$	change in INV
$FDINVN$	change in $INVN$
$FDIQN$	change in $[(INV/Q)-$ normal $(INV/Q)]$
$FDIST$	change in $[(INV/S)-$ trend $(INV/S)]$
f_H	marginal productivity of labor
f_{MATO}	marginal productivity of materials
FDQ	change in output
$FDRLT$	change in RLT
$FDUNF$	change in unfilled orders
g	growth rate in capacity
GNP	gross national product

$GNP58$	gross national product in constant dollars
$(GNP-GNP*)/GNP*$	ratio of actual minus trend GNP to trend GNP
H	labor in man-hours
IED	indirect excess demand measure
INV	inventories
$INVD$	desired inventories
$INVE$	equilibrium inventories
$INVF$	farm inventories
$INVMAT$	materials inventory
$INVN(IN)$	normal inventories
$(INV/Q)^T$	trend of inventory-output ratio
K	capital stock
K/QN	capital-normal output ratio
LA	liquid assets
$MATO$	materials produced outside the manufacturing sector
M/Q	material per unit of output
$(M/Q)N$	normal material per unit of output
MS	money supply
N	total employees
NOR	new orders
NR	employment rate
P	price
PA	price anticipations
PE	price expectations
PFM	WPI for farm products
PI	import price index
PK	price of physical capital
PM	material price index
PMN	normal PM
POG	price index for other final goods and services
PP	productivity
PPN	normal productivity
PR	profit per unit of output

$PREQ$	profit-equity ratio (π/EQ)
PUS	United States price index
PWM	world price index of exports of raw materials
$Q\,(IPI)$	output, industrial production index
QN	normal output
QP	peak output
$(Q-MA\,)/MA$	relative deviation of Q from moving average of Q
$(Q-Q^*)/Q^*$	relative deviation of Q from trend of Q
r (or RLT)	long-term interest rate (Moody's AAA)
rr	short-term real rate of interest
r^*	target rate of return
$S\,(SC)$	corporate sales
$(\Sigma\,\Delta S\,)^*\,CUI$	sales change adjusted for CUI
SHP	shipments
$(SHP/INV\,)-MA$	sales-inventory ratio minus its two-year moving average
t	time trend
T (or TAX)	ratio of indirect taxes less subsidies to consumer expenditures
$4\,TMAP$	four-term moving average of P
$4\,TMAUR$	four-term moving average of UR
$(TOT\,COMP\,)/W$	ratio of total compensation per man-hour to the wage index
tx	corporate income tax-profits ratio
$UCCAN$	normal unit capital consumption allowances
$UI\,(U)$	unemployment rate index
UK	stockholders' equity per unit of output
UKC	unit capital cost
ULC	unit labor cost
$ULCN$	normal ULC
$ULCO$	nonproduction workers ULC
$ULCP$	peak ULC
$ULCPR$	production workers ULC
UMC	unit material cost

$+UMC$	positive deviations of UMC from $UMCN$
$-UMC$	negative deviations of UMC from $UMCN$
$UMCN$	normal UMC
UNF	unfilled orders
$UNFPD/EPD$	UNF/SHP for producer durable equipment
$UNF/Q*$	unfilled orders-capacity output ratio
$UNFSC$	unfilled orders-sales ratio
$(UNF/SHP)MAT$	UNF/SHP of materials
UPI	unit price of imported materials
UR	unemployment rate
URI	inverse of unemployment rate
USP	United States wholesale price
UT	unit tax
W	wage per person
$WAGE$	wages, salaries, and supplements–private nonfarm economy
WB	total wage bill
$WCNMEF$	nonfood, nonfuel crude materials for manufacturing
$WMNM$	intermediate nondurable materials excluding food
$WMNMN$	normal $WMNM$
WO	wage per person in organized labor force
WPI	wholesale price index
WS	total hourly employment cost in the steel industry
WU	wage per person in unorganized labor force
$W-W_{COMM}$	sector wage index minus private, nonfarm economy wage index
X	output per person
Y	income of purchasers of manufactured goods
YS	weighted product of steel-using industries
$\Delta Y-(Q-QCAP(-1))$	change in spending minus deviation of Q from capacity Q

Bibliography

Bibliography

Books

1. Arrow, Kenneth J. "Prices in Markets with Rising Demand." *Mathematical Models in the Social Sciences, 1959*. Edited by Kenneth Arrow, Samuel Karlin, and Patrick Suppes. Stanford: Stanford University Press, 1960.

2. Backman, Jules. *Price Practices and Price Policies*. New York: Ronald Press Co., 1953.

3. Bain, J.S. *Industrial Organization*. New York: John Wiley & Sons, 1959.

4. Ball, R.J., and Doyle, Peter. *Inflation*. Penguin Books, Manchester, Great Britain: C. Nicholls & Co., 1969.

5. Barback, R.H. *The Pricing of Manufactures*. London: MacMillan Co., 1964.

6. Baumol, W.J. *Business Behavior, Value, and Growth*. New York: MacMillan Co., 1959.

7. Bodkin, R.G. *The Wage-Price-Productivity Nexus*. Philadelphia: University of Pennsylvania Press, 1966.

8. Bowen, William G. *The Wage-Price Issue: A Theoretical Analysis*. New York: Greenwood Press, 1960.

9. Bronfenbrenner, Martin, and Holzman, F.D. "A Survey of Inflation Theory." Prepared for the American Economic Association and the Royal Economic Society. *Surveys of Economic Theory, Vol. I*. New York: St. Martin's Press, 1966.

10. Cagan, Phillip. "Theories of Mild, Continuing Inflation: A Critique and Extension." *Symposium on Inflation: Its Causes, Consequences, and Control*. New York: Kazanjian Foundation, 1968.

11. Central Planning Bureau. *Scope and Methods of the Central Planning Bureau*. The Hague: Central Planning Bureau, 1956.

12. Charles River Associates, Inc. *An Economic Analysis of the Copper Industry*. Cambridge, Mass., 1968.

13. Christ, Carl F. *Econometric Models and Methods*. New York: John Wiley & Sons, 1966.

14. Clark, John M. *The Wage-Price Problem*. New York: American Bankers Association, 1960.

15. Cyert, Richard M., and March, James G. *A Behavioral Theory of the Firm*. Englewood Cliffs, N.J.: Prentice Hall, 1963.

16. Eiteman, Wilford J. *Price Determination: Business Practice vs Economic Theory*. Ann Arbor: University of Michigan, 1949.

17. Evans, Michael K. *Macroeconomic Activity*. New York: Harper & Row, 1969.

18. _____ , and Klein, L.R. *The Wharton Econometric Forecasting Model*. Philadelphia: University of Pennsylvania Press, 1967.

243

19. Fitzpatrick, Albert. *Pricing Methods of Industry*. Boulder, Colo.: Pruett Press, 1964.

20. Friend, I., and Jones, Robert C. "Short Run Forecasting Models Incorporating Anticipatory Data." *Models of Income Determination, Studies in Income and Wealth*. Vol. XXVIII. New York: National Bureau of Economic Research, 1964.

21. Fromm, Gary, and Taubman, Paul. *Policy Simulations with an Econometric Model*. Washington, D.C.: Brookings Institution, 1968.

22. Hagger, A.J. *The Theory of Inflation: A Review*. Melbourne: Melbourne University Press, 1964.

23. Hague, D.C. *Pricing in Business*. London: George Allen & Unwin, 1971.

24. _____, ed. *Inflation*. Proceedings of International Economic Association. New York: MacMillan Co., 1962.

25. _____, ed. *Price Formation in Various Economies*. Proceedings of IEA Conference. London: MacMillan Co., 1967.

26. Hansen, B. *A Study in the Theory of Inflation*. London: Allen & Unwin, 1951.

27. Haynes, W.W. *Pricing Decisions in Small Businesses*. Lexington: University of Kentucky Press, 1962.

28. Hultgren, Thor. *Cost, Prices, & Profits: Their Cyclical Relations*. New York: Columbia University Press, 1965.

29. Johnston, J. *Statistical Cost Analysis*. New York: McGraw-Hill Book Co., 1960.

30. Kaplan, A.D.H.; Dirlam, Joel B.; and Lanzillotti, Robert F. *Pricing in Big Business*. Washington, D.C.: Brookings Institution, 1958.

31. Klein, Lawrence R. "A Postwar Quarterly Model: Description and Applications." *Models of Income Determination, Studies in Income and Wealth*. Vol. XXVIII. New York: National Bureau of Economic Research, 1964.

32. _____. *An Introduction to Econometrics*. Englewood Cliffs, N.J.: Prentice Hall, 1962.

33. _____. *The Keynesian Revolution*. New York: MacMillan Co., 1966.

34. _____, and Goldberger, A.S. *An Econometric Model of the United States, 1929-1952*. Amsterdam: North Holland Publishing Co., 1955.

35. _____; Ball, R.J.; Hazlewood, A.; and Vandome, P. *An Econometric Model of the United Kingdom*. Oxford: Basil Blackwell, 1961.

36. Langholm, Odd. *Full Cost and Optimal Price*. Bergen, Oslo: Scandinavian University Books, 1969.

37. Mills, E.S. *Price, Output, and Inventory Policy*. New York: John Wiley & Sons, 1962.

38. Mills, F.C. *Prices in Recession and Recovery*. New York: National Bureau of Economic Research, 1936.

39. _____. *The Behavior of Prices*. New York: National Bureau of Economic Research, 1927.

40. Myers, Charles A., ed. *Wages, Prices, Profits, and Productivity*. New York: American Assembly, Columbia University, 1959.

41. Naylor, Thomas H.; Balintfy, J.L.; Burdick, D.S.; and Chu, K. *Computer Simulation Techniques*. New York: John Wiley & Sons, 1966.

42. _____, and Vernon, John M. *Microeconomics and Decision Models of the Firm*. New York: Harcourt, Brace, and World, 1969.

43. Needham, Douglas. *Economic Analysis and Industrial Structure*. New York: Holt, Rinehart, & Winston, 1969.

44. Neild, R.R. *Pricing and Employment in the Trade Cycle*. Cambridge: Cambridge University Press, 1963.

45. Nelson, P.E., and Preston, L.E. *Price Merchandising in Food Retailing: A Case Study*. Berkeley, Calif.: Institute of Business and Economic Research, University of California, 1966.

46. Nourse, E.G., and Drury, H.B. *Industrial Price Policies and Economic Progress*. Washington, D.C.: Brookings Institution, 1934.

47. Oxenfeldt, A.R., ed. *Models of Markets*. New York: Columbia University Press, 1963.

48. Perry, G.L. *Unemployment, Money Wage Rates, and Inflation*. Cambridge, Mass.: M.I.T. Press, 1966.

49. Phelps, Edmund S., et al. *Microeconomic Foundations of Employment and Inflation Theory*. New York: Norton, 1970.

50. Phillips, Almarin, and Williamson, Oliver E. *Prices: Issues in Theory, Practice, and Public Policy*. Philadelphia: University of Pennsylvania Press, 1967.

51. Schultze, C.L., and Tryon, J.L. "Prices and Wages." *Brookings Quarterly Econometric Model of the United States*. Chicago: Rand McNally & Co., 1965.

52. Solow, Robert M. "Recent Controversy on the Theory of Inflation: An Eclectic View." *Inflation: Its Causes, Consequences, and Controls*. Edited by Stephen W. Rousseas. New York: Kazanjian Foundation, 1968.

53. Steckler, Herman O. *Economic Forecasting*. New York: Praeger, 1970.

54. Stigler, George. *The Price Statistics of the Federal Government*. New York: National Bureau of Economic Research, 1961.

55. _____, and Kindahl, James. *The Behavior of Industrial Prices*. New York: National Bureau of Economic Research, 1970.

56. *The Structure of American Industry, Part I, Basic Characteristics*. Washington, D.C.: National Resources Committee, 1939.

57. Troxel, C. Emery. "Comparison of Movements of Payrolls in Flexible and Inflexible Price Industries." *Papers on Price Policy*. New York: Rinehart and Co., 1939.

Articles

58. Ackley, Gardner. "Administered Prices and the Inflationary Process." *American Economic Review* XLIX (May 1959), 419-30.

59. Adelman, Irma, and Adelman, Frank L. "The Dynamic Properties of the Klein-Goldberger Model." *Econometrica* XXVII (October 1959), 596-625.

60. Adelman, Morris A.; Kahn, Alfred E.; and Lanzillotti, Robert F. "Pricing Objectives in Large Companies: Comment." *American Economic Review* XLIX (September 1959), 669-87.

61. Akerlof, George. "Relative Wages and the Rate of Inflation." *Quarterly Journal of Economics* LXXXIII (August 1969), 353-74.

62. Allen, R.G.D. "Movements in Retail Prices Since 1953." *Economica* XXV (February 1958), 14-25.

63. Anderson, Leonall C., and Carlson, Keith M. "A Monetarist Model for Economic Stabilization." *Review – Federal Reserve Bank of St. Louis* LII (April 1970), 7-25.

64. Barger, H., and Klein, Lawrence R. "A Quarterly Model of the United States Economy." *Journal of the American Statistical Association* XLIX (September 1954), 413-37.

65. Blair, John. "Administered Prices: A Phenomenon in Search of a Theory." *American Economic Review* XLIX (May 1959), 431-50.

66. Boger, L.L. "Discussion: Research Methods in Price Analysis." *Journal of Farm Economics* XXXVIII (December 1956), 1440-45.

67. Brittain, John. "A Bias in the Seasonally Adjusted Unemployment Series and a Suggested Alternative." *Review of Economics and Statistics* XLI (November 1959), 405-11.

68. Burger, Albert E. "The Effects of Inflation, 1960-68." *Review – Federal Reserve Bank of St. Louis* LI (November 1969), 25-36.

69. Christ, Carl F. "Aggregate Econometric Models." *American Economic Review* XLVI (June 1956), 385-408.

70. Clague, E. "Interrelationship of Prices, Wages, and Productivity, 1946-57." *Monthly Labor Review* LXXXI (January 1958), 14-22.

71. Clower, R.G., and Bushaw, D.W. "Price Determination in a Stockflow Economy." *Econometrica* XXII (July 1954), 328-43.

72. Cornwall, John. "Economic Implications of the Klein-Goldberger Model." *Review of Economics and Statistics* XLI (May 1959), 154-71.

73. Courchene, Thomas J. "An Analysis of the Price-Inventory Nexus with Empirical Application to the Canadian Manufacturing Sector." *International Economic Review* X (October 1969), 315-36.

74. Dean, J. "Cost Forecasting and Price Policy." *Journal of Marketing* XIII (January 1949), 279-88.

75. _____ , "Problems of Product-Line Pricing." *Journal of Marketing* XIV (January 1950), 518-28.

76. Dhrymes, Phoebus J. "On the Measurement of Price and Quality Changes in Some Consumer Capital Goods." *American Economic Review* LVII (May 1967), 501-21.

77. Dicks-Mireaux, L.A. "A Study of Inflation in Post-War Britain." *Oxford Economic Papers* XIII (October 1961), 267-92.

78. Doblin, Ernest M. "Some Aspects of Price Flexibility." *Review of Economics and Statistics* XXII (November 1940), 183-89.

79. Dow, J.C.R. "Analysis of the Generation of Price Inflation." *Oxford Economic Papers* VIII (October 1956), 252-301.

80. Eckstein, Otto. "A Theory of the Wage Price Process in Modern Industry." *Review of Economic Studies* XXXI (October 1964), 267-87.

81. _____ , and Fromm, Gary. "The Price Equation." *American Economic Review* LVIII (December 1968), 1159-83.

82. Edward, John B., and Orcutt, Guy H. "Should Aggregation Prior to Estimation be the Rule?" *Review of Economics and Statistics* LI (November 1969), 409-21.

83. Edwards, Ronald S. "The Pricing of Manufactured Products." *Economica* XIX (August 1952), 298-307.

84. Fair, Ray C. "Aggregate Price Changes and Price Expectations." *Review – Federal Reserve Bank of St. Louis* LII (November 1970), 18-28.

85. Friend, Irwin, and Taubman, P. "A Short-Term Forecasting Model." *Review of Economics and Statistics* XLVI (August 1964), 229-36.

86. Gordon, R.A. "Short-Term Price Determination in Theory and Practice." *American Economic Review* XXXVIII (June 1948), 265-88.

87. Gordon, Robert J. "The Recent Acceleration of Inflation and Its Lessons for the Future." *Brookings Papers on Economic Activity*, (1:1970), 8-47.

88. _____ . "Inflation in Recession and Recovery." *Brookings Papers on Economic Activity*, (1:1971), 105-66.

89. Hall, R.L., and Hitch, C.J. "Price Theory and Business Behavior." *Oxford Economic Papers,*, no. 2 (May 1939), 12-45.

90. Hay, G.A. "Production, Price, and Inventory Theory." *American Economic Review* LX (September 1970), 531-46.

91. Heflebower, R.B. "An Economic Appraisal of Price Measures," *Journal of the American Statistical Association* XLVI (December 1951), 461-79.

92. Holzman, Franklyn D. "Inflation: Cost-Push and Demand-Pull." *American Economic Review* L (March 1960), 20-42.

93. Hopp, Henry, and Foote, Richard J. "A Statistical Analysis of Factors that Affect Prices of Coffee." *Journal of Farm Economics* XXXVII (August 1955), 429-38.

94. Hotson, John H. "Monetary and Wage Markup Theories of the Price Level: Some Data." *International Economic Review* XI (February 1970), 53-76.

95. Johnson, Jack D. "Pricing of Cattle at Southern Auctions with Emphasis upon Factors Affecting Price and Farmer Price Uncertainty." *Journal of Farm Economics* XXXIX (December 1957), 1657-65.

96. Johnston, J. "An Econometric Model of the United Kingdom." *Review of Economic Studies* XXIX (October 1961), 29-40.

97. Kindahl, James K. "The Construction of Industrial Price Indices." *American Economic Review* LVII (May 1967), 492-500.

98. Klein, Lawrence R. "Estimation of Interdependent Systems in Macroeconomics." *Econometrica* XXXVII (April 1969), 171-93.

99. Klein, Lawrence R. "Single Equation vs Equation System Methods of Estimation in Econometrics." *Econometrica* XXVIII (October 1960), 866-71.

100. _____ , and Ball, R.J. "Some Econometrics of the Determination of Absolute Prices and Wages." *Economic Journal* LXIX (September 1959), 465-82.

101. Klein, L.R., and Shinkai, Y. "An Econometric Model of Japan." *International Economic Review* IV (January 1963), 1-28.

102. Kravis, I.B., and Lipsey, R.E. "The Measurement of Price Change." *American Economic Review* LVII (May 1967), 482-91.

103. Laden, Ben E. "Perfect Competition, Average Cost Pricing, and the Price Equation." *Review of Economics and Statistics* LIV (February 1972), 84-88.

104. Langholm, Odd. "Industrial Pricing: The Theoretical Basis." *Swedish Journal of Economics* LXX (June 1968), 65-93.

105. Lanzillotti, Robert F. "Competitive Price Leadership—A Critique of Price Leadership Models." *Review of Economics and Statistics* XXXIX (February 1957), 55-64.

106. _____ . "Pricing Objectives in Large Companies." *American Economic Review* XLVIII (December 1958), 921-40.

107. Leibenberg, M.; Hirsh, A.A.; and Popkin, J. "A Quarterly Econometric Model of the United States: A Progress Report." *Survey of Current Business* XLVI (May 1966), 13-39.

108. Leontief, Wassily. "Wages, Profits, and Prices." *Quarterly Journal of Economics* LXI (November 1946), 26-39.

109. Leser, C.E.V. "The Role of Macroeconomic Models in Short-Term Forecasting." *Econometrica* XXXIV (October 1966), 862-73.

110. Levitt, Theodore, and Livingston, S. Morris. "Competition and Retail Gasoline Prices." *Review of Economics and Statistics* XLI (May 1959), 119-32.

111. Liu, Ta-Chung. "An Exploratory Quarterly Econometric Model of Effective Demand in the Postwar United States Economy." *Econometrica* XXXI (July 1963), 301-48.

112. Lovell, Michael. "Seasonal Adjustment of Economic Time Series and Multiple Regression Analysis." *Journal of the American Statistical Association* LVIII (December 1963), 993-1110.

113. Machlup, F. "Marginal Analysis and Empirical Research." *American Economic Review* XXVI (September 1946), 519-54.

114. Malanos, George J., and Thomassen, Henry. "An Econometric Model of the United States, 1947-1958." *Southern Economic Journal* XXVII (July 1960), 18-27.

115. Massy, W., and Frank, R.E. "Short Term Price and Dealing Effects in Selected Market Segments." *Journal of Marketing Research* II (May 1965), 171-85.

116. McCallum, B.T. "The Effect of Demand on Prices in British Manufac-

turing: Another View." *Review of Economic Studies* XXXVII (January 1970), 147-56.

117. Means, Gardiner C. "The Administered–Price Thesis Reconfirmed." *American Economic Review* LXII (June 1972), 292-306.

118. Moffat, William R. "Taxes in the Price Equation: Textiles and Rubber." *Review of Economics and Statistics* LII (August 1970), 253-61.

119. Morgan, E.V. "Is Inflation Inevitable." *Economic Journal* LXXVI, (March 1966), 1-15.

120. Morkre, Morris E. "Short-Term Price Change in the Steel Industry." *Review of Economics and Statistics* LII (February 1970), 26-34.

121. Moss, R.B. "Industry and Sector Price Indices." *Monthly Labor Review* LXXXVIII (August 1965), 974-82.

122. Naylor, Thomas L.; Burdick, Donald S.; and Sasser, W. Earl. "Computer Simulation Experiments with Economic Systems: The Problem of Experimental Design." *Journal of the American Statistical Association* LXII (December 1967), 1315-37.

123. _____ ; Wallace, William H.; and Sasser, W. Earl. "A Computer Simulation Model of the Textile Industry." *Journal of the American Statistical Association* LXII (December 1967), 1338-64.

124. _____ ; Wertz, Kenneth; and Wonnacott, Thomas H. "Spectral Analysis of Data Generated by Simulation Experiments with Econometric Models." *Econometrica* XXXVI (April 1969), 333-53.

125. Nerlove, Marc. "A Quarterly Econometric Model for the United Kingdom." *American Economic Review* LII (March 1962), 154-76.

126. _____ . "Spectral Analysis of Seasonal Adjustment Procedures." *Econometrica* XXXII (July 1964), 241-86.

127. Nourse, E.G. "The Meaning of Price Policy." *Quarterly Journal of Economics* LV (February 1941), 175-209.

128. Oliver, H.M. "Marginal Theory and Business Behavior." *American Economic Review* XXXVII (June 1947), 375-82.

129. Pearce, I.F. "A Study in Price Policy." *Economica* XXIII (May 1956), 114-27.

130. Perry, George L. "The Determinants of Wage Rate Changes and the Inflation-Unemployment Trade-off for the United States." *Review of Economic Studies* XXXI (October 1964), 287-308.

131. Pitchford, J.D. "Cost and Demand Elements in the Inflationary Process." *Review of Economic Studies* XXIV (February 1957), 139-48.

132. Popkin, Joel. "Price Changes in the First Quarter of 1969 in Perspective." *Monthly Labor Review* XCII (July 1969), 26-30.

133. Popkin, Joel, and Earl, Paul H. "Relationship Between the Behavior of Consumer and Wholesale Prices." *Proceedings of the Business & Economic Statistics Section–American Statistical Association* (August 1971), 40-45.

134. "Price Movements in Perspective." *Review – Federal Reserve Bank of St. Louis* XLIII (July 1961), 5-11.

135. Rippe, Richard D. "Wages, Prices, and Imports in the American Steel Industry." *Review of Economics and Statistics* LII (February 1970), 34-46.

136. Rushdy, F., and Lund P.J. "The Effect of Demand on Prices in British Manufacturing Industry." *Review of Economic Studies* XXXIV (October 1967), 361-73.

137. Schultze, Charles L. "Uses of Capacity Measures for Short Run Economic Analysis." *American Economic Review* LIII (May 1963), 293-308.

138. Shepherd, Geoffrey. "Discussion: Research Methods in Price Analysis." *Journal of Farm Economics* XXXVIII (December 1956), 1436-40.

139. Stevens, W.H.S. "Effects of Cost Analysis on Prices." *Journal of Marketing* III (July 1938), 62-70.

140. Strotz, R.H., and Wold, H.O.A. "Recursive vs Nonrecursive Systems: An Attempt at Synthesis." *Econometrica* XXIX (April 1960), 417-27.

141. Suits, Daniel B. "Forecasting and Analysis with an Econometric Model." *American Economic Review* LII (March 1962), 104-32.

142. Vanderkamp, John. "Wage and Price Level Determination: An Empirical Model for Canada." *Economica* XXXIII (May 1966), 194-218.

143. Vickrey, W. "Some Objections to Marginal Cost Pricing." *Journal of Political Economy* LVI (June 1948), 218-38.

144. Wilson, T.A., and Eckstein, Otto. "Short-Run Productivity Behavior in U.S. Manufacturing." *Review of Economics and Statistics* XLVI (February 1964), 41-54.

145. Wood, Harleston R. "The Measurement of Employment, Cost and Prices in the Steel Industry." *Review of Economics and Statistics* XLI (November 1959), 412-18.

146. Working, Holbrook. "New Ideas and Methods for Price Research." *Journal of Farm Economics* XXVIII (December 1956), 1427-38.

147. Yance, J.V. "A Model of Price Flexibility." *American Economic Review* L (June 1960), 401-18.

148. _____ "A Model of Price Flexibility—Reply." *American Economic Review* LI (June 1961), 392-94.

149. Yordon, W.J., Jr. "A Model of Price Flexibility—Comment." *American Economic Review* LI (June 1961), 390-92.

150. _____ . "Industrial Concentration and Price Flexibility in Inflation: Price Response Rates in Fourteen Industries, 1947-1958." *Review of Economics and Statistics* XLIII (August 1961), 287-94.

151. Zarnowitz, Victor. "Unfilled Orders, Price Changes and Business Fluctuations." *Review of Economics and Statistics* XLIV (November 1962), 367-94.

**Unpublished Manuscripts and
Government Publications**

152. Attiyeh, Yossef. "Wage-Price Spiral vs Demand Inflation: U.S. 1949-1957." Ph.D. dissertation, University of Chicago, 1959.

153. Backman, Jules, and Gainsbrugh, Martin R. "Inflation and the Price Indices." Subcommittee on Economic Statistics, Joint Economic Committee. Washington, D.C.: Government Printing Office, 1966.

154. Bailey, M.J. "Administered Prices in the American Economy." *The Relationship of Prices to Economic Stability and Growth.* Joint Economic Committee. Washington, D.C.: Government Printing Office, 1958.

155. "Cost Behavior and Price Policy." New York: Conference on Price Research, 1943.

156. de Menil, George. "Putty-Clay Capital and Price Determination." Manuscript, April 1970.

157. _____. "The Determinants of the Price Level." Presented at the 1968 meetings of the Econometric Society, Evanston, Illinois.

158. _____ and Enzler, Jared J. "Prices and Wages in the FRB-MIT-PENN Econometric Model." Presented at Federal Reserve Board Conference, Washington, D.C., October 1970.

159. Eckstein, Otto, and Wyss, David. "An Econometric Analysis of the Behavior of Industrial Prices." Presented at the Federal Reserve Board–Social Science Research Council Conference, Washington, D.C., October 1971.

160. _____ and Fromm, Gary. "Steel and the Postwar Inflation." Study Paper No. 2, Joint Economic Committee. Washington, D.C.: Government Printing Office, November 1959.

161. _____ and Brinner, Roger. "The Inflation Process in the United States." Joint Economic Committee. Washington, D.C.: Government Printing Office, February 1972.

162. *Economic Report of the President.* Washington, D.C.: Government Printing Office, 1968, 1969, 1970, 1971.

163. Eiteman, W.J. "Price Determination in Oligopolistic and Monopolistic Situations." Michigan Business Report #33. Ann Arbor: Bureau of Business Research, 1960.

164. Fromm, Gary. "Inventories, Business Cycles, and Economic Stabilization." *Inventory Fluctuations and Economic Stabilization, Part IV.* Joint Economic Committee. Washington, D.C.: Government Printing Office, 1962.

165. _____. "Prices, Profits, and Productivity." Ph.D. dissertation, Harvard University, 1960.

166. Halfter, Faith (Ando). "The Cyclical Behavior of Materials Prices in United States Industry." Ph.D. dissertation, Harvard University, 1966.

167. Hamilton, Walton. "Price and Price Policies." President's Committee on Price Policy. Washington, D.C.: Government Printing Office, 1934.

168. Hickman, Bert G. "An Interpretation of Price Movements since the End of World War II." *The Relationship of Prices to Economic Stability and Growth.* Joint Economic Committee Compendium of Papers. Washington, D.C.: Government Printing Office, 1958.

169. Klein, L.R., and Popkin, J. "An Economic Analysis of the Postwar Relationship between Fluctuations and Change in Aggregate Economic Activ-

ity." *Inventory Fluctuations and Economic Stabilization, Part III*. Joint Economic Committee. Washington, D.C.: Government Printing Office, 1961.

170. Kuh, Edwin. "Profits, Profit Markups, and Productivity: An Examination of Corporate Behavior since 1947." Study Paper No. 15, Joint Economic Committee. Washington, D.C.: Government Printing Office, November, 1959.

171. Laden, Ben E. "A Monthly Model of Price-Wage Interaction." Presented at the Winter Meetings of the Econometric Society, New Orleans, La., December 28, 1971.

172. _____ . "Price Equations for U.S. Manufacturing." Presented at the Midwest Economics Association Meetings, Detroit, Mich., April 1970.

173. _____ . "Profit Maximization, Average Cost Pricing, and the Price Equation for United States Manufacturing, 1954-66." Ph.D. dissertation, Johns Hopkins University, 1969.

174. Laffer, Arthur B., and Ranson, R. David. "A Formal Model of the Economy." For the Office of Management and Budget. Washington, D.C.: Government Printing Office, February 1971.

175. Levinson, H.M. "Postwar Movement of Prices and Wages in Manufacturing Industries." *Study of Employment, Growth, & Price Levels*, Joint Economic Committee. Washington, D.C.: Government Printing Office, 1960.

176. Lucas, Robert E., Jr. "Econometric Testing of the Natural Rate Hypothesis." Presented at Federal Reserve Board Conference, Washington, D.C., October 1970.

177. Means, Gardiner C. "Industrial Prices and their Relative Inflexibility." Senate Document No. 13, Washington, D.C.: Government Printing Office, 1935.

178. Moore, Geoffrey H. "The Anatomy of Inflation." Report #373, U.S. Department of Labor, Bureau of Labor Statistics. Washington. D.C.: Government Printing Office, 1969.

179. Neal, A.C. "Industrial Concentration and Price Inflexibility." American Council on Public Affairs. Washington, D.C.: Government Printing Office, 1942.

180. Nordhaus, William D. "Recent Developments in Price Dynamics." Cowles Foundation Discussion Paper No. 296. Presented at Federal Reserve Board Conference, Washington, D.C., August, 1970, (preliminary version).

181. Nerlove, Marc. "On the Structure of Serial Dependence in some U.S. Price Series." Presented at Federal Reserve Board Conference, Washington, D.C., October 1970.

182. Phipps, A.J. "The Roles of Labor Productivity and Demand in the Pricing Process: An Interindustry Study using Time-Series Data." Bulletin of Oxford University, Institute of Economic Statistics. November 1969.

183. "Policies for Price Stability." Working Party No. 3 Report. Organization for Economic Co-operation and Development. Paris, February 1962.

184. "Productivity, Prices, and Incomes," Joint Economic Committee. Washington, D.C.: Government Printing Office, 1967.

185. Schultze, Charles L., and Tryon, Joseph L. "Prices and Costs in

Manufacturing Industries." Study Paper No. 17. Joint Economic Committee. Washington, D.C.: Government Printing Office., 1960.

186. "The Data Resources Econometric Forecasting System: A Preliminary Account." Data Resources, Inc. Lexington, Mass., November 1970, 103-47.

187. Wilson, Thomas A. "An Analysis of the Inflation in Machinery Prices." Study Paper No. 3. Joint Economic Committee. Washington, D.C.: Government Printing Office, 1959.

Index

hybrid, 18, 19, 23, 26, 35, 41, 50,
54, 57, 60, 62, 64, 83-98, 116,
117, 127, 168
Price models
multi-equation, 7, 25-27, 34, 41, 45
reduced form, 1, 3, 7, 9, 27, 35
single equation, 7, 35, 41, 45
stage of processing, 3, 40, 63, 67,
77, 111, 137, 139, 142-45, 151,
152, 155, 158, 159, 166, 169
structural, 1, 3, 7, 27, 35, 167, 171
Primary ferrous metals (SIC 331), 86,
93-96, 98, 99, 104, 113, 116, 117,
134, 137, 144, 149, 151, 153,
158, 160, 161, 168, 170
Primary nonferrous metals (SIC 333),
82, 84, 85, 90, 91, 97-99, 102,
103, 116, 122, 123, 128, 130,
131, 133, 168, 170
Product
durability, 102, 103, 117, 119, 120
type of, 67, 68, 103, 105, 117, 119-
21
Production to order, 106, 107, 109,
117, 119, 120, 125
Production to stock. *See* Production
to order

Regressor selection, 149-53
Rippe, Richard D., 19, 34, 35, 40, 41,
44
Rubber and plastic products (SIC 30),
86, 88-91, 94, 98, 99, 117, 122,
123, 127, 133, 168
Rule of thumb pricing, 11, 82, 130,
131, 134
Rushdy, F., 3, 19, 27, 45, 51, 53-55,
91, 92

Schultze, Charles L., 3, 7, 8, 14, 15,
18, 19, 34, 44, 45, 56-59, 61, 77,
94, 96, 97, 111, 112, 170
Shinkai, Y., 19, 25

Shoes, except rubber (SIC 3141), 100,
101, 107, 116, 127, 131
Simulation analysis, 3, 26, 34, 41, 137
equal percentage change, 149, 153-
59
ex post, 26, 77, 137, 145-49
industry specific, 149, 159-66
policy, 26, 77, 137, 149-52
Solow, Robert M., 19, 27, 33
Stage of processing. *See* Price models

Taubman, Paul, 11, 19, 34
Textile mill products (SIC 22), 80-91,
93, 94, 96-99, 116, 122-25, 130,
137, 139-42, 146, 149, 151, 152,
154, 161, 165, 166, 168
Tires and tubes (SIC 301), 86, 88, 90,
91, 98, 99, 117, 127, 133, 137,
139, 144, 146, 149, 151, 153,
154, 158, 160, 161, 166
Tobacco (SIC 21), 89, 94, 100, 101,
104, 105, 122-24, 168
Tryon, Joseph L., 3, 7, 14, 18, 19, 34,
44, 45, 56-59, 61, 77, 94, 96, 97,
111, 112, 170
Turning point analysis, 128, 137

Unions, 10, 25, 151, 169

Vanderkamp, John, 19, 21, 23, 25, 26
Vickery, W., 8

Wage-price spiral, 1
Walras, Léon, 17
Wharton econometric model, 7, 19,
26-28, 33
Wilson, T.A., 19, 35
Wyss, David, 3, 14, 17, 19, 35, 40, 44,
45, 59, 63-65, 80-85, 88, 96-98,
103, 105, 167-70

Yance, J.V., 19, 35, 40
Yordon, W.J., 19, 35, 40, 63

Zarnowitz, Victor, 18, 19, 35

About the Author

Paul H. Earl is an assistant professor of economics at Georgetown University in Washington, D.C. He received the B.A. from Bucknell University and the Ph.D. from Georgetown University. He has worked extensively in developing sectoral stage of processing price models as a consultant with the Bureau of Labor Statistics. Dr. Earl's primary fields are applied econometrics, microeconomic theory, and computer applications in economics.